BOYS, DOGS AND CHAOS

ESSAYS

STEPHANIE KEPKE

Cover Design by Michelle Fairbanks, Fresh Design
Proofreading by J.C. Wing

ISBN: 978-0-9976861-3-5

Breathe: Written by Ryan Star and Max Collins, Used with Permission
Copyright: The Scientists Canvas (BMI)/Okagar Music Publishing/Sony/ATV

Fake And Jaded Music (BMI) adm. by The Royalty Network, Inc./Emad Music (BMI)

ACKNOWLEDGMENTS

Thank you to my family: Jeff, Drew, Joshua and Aidan. You always inspire me. I know it's not easy when I'm working my butt off to get my words out into the world. Thank you to my mother and siblings, Beverly Kepke, Jodi, David and Shari. Thank you to all of my in-laws on both sides, as well. Thank you to J.C. Wing for proofreading this book—even after our publisher closed right in the middle of the process. Thank you to Michelle Fairbanks for my fabulous cover. You brought my vision to life. Thank you to Adam Bodendiek for rescuing my print layout. Thank you to Ryan Star for allowing me to use your amazing lyrics again. "Breathe" has gotten me through many of the stressful moments in these essays and this verse perfectly sums up the sentiment of this book—"Let the life that you live be all that you need." Thank you to Jill McCorkle—even twenty years later, your teachings (and friendship) continue to inspire me. Thank you to John Giannone—you play a big part in many of these essays, and rightfully so. My gratitude for everything you have done for my family is immeasurable. Thank you to Scott Syat for your sound legal advice (and of course you pop up in more than one of these essays...and always listen to me when the worst things happen). And to the women I've become friends with through these essays (you know who you are)—I will always be grateful to you for reaching out to me. There is nothing more rewarding than readers who become friends thanks to a connection—we are not alone. Thank you to my girlfriends who have supported me and encouraged me during every trying time in these pages (and perhaps even showed up at my door with my favorite "calming" face mask or sent me my favorite jelly beans or just listened to me rant, etc.)—

you all know who you are. I fear if I thank everyone individually, I may accidentally leave someone out. To every single friend who has read my work, who has encouraged me, who has shared some of these essays on Facebook—thank you. I wish I could list each one of you individually, but I'm blessed that there are too many to even list. Know that I cherish each one of you. I couldn't have ever gotten this book out without the love and support of my family and friends. Thank you all.

For My Boys:
Drew, Joshua and Aidan

AUTHOR'S NOTE

This is my heart book, and the book I didn't think would ever get out into the world. It has hit numerous obstacles along the way—the biggest being my publisher shutting down while it was in the proofreading stage. So when I should have been planning a book launch, I was instead left not knowing if it would ever see the light of day. I didn't have the patience, nor did I have the fortitude, to send this collection out. It took four years for me to find a home for my first novel, *Goddess of Suburbia*, and I know that essay collections are almost impossible to place, unless you're Tina Fey or Amy Schumer. My novellas were accepted much more quickly, and I love my other publisher, The Wild Rose Press—but, they don't publish non-fiction. I decided to take control of my career and launch my own imprint, Gold Coast Press. This is the third book I've published under this imprint. I hope to publish other authors soon.

I spent a lot of time thinking about which essays to include in this collection and how to organize them—by date, by subject? I settled on chronological order, because this collection is a journey, and that's the best way to read it. It opens with an essay about my struggle to forgive myself after my youngest son fell to the hospital floor at a day old when I fainted after nursing him. It closes with a letter I wrote soon after dropping my oldest son off at college. The letter is to young mothers exhorting them to enjoy the beautiful chaos of small children, before their homes are quiet. It goes by so fast. And in between those two essays is much of that beautiful chaos, that fullness of life with children. But also, there are essays about my love of hockey; parenting a child with mental illness; my health scares and what they taught me; growing older gracefully;

beauty secrets; giving up the idea of perfection in motherhood; eating disorders and so much more. I truly believe that there is something for everyone in these pages, and I so hope you, my beloved readers, agree with me. I would be nothing without you — my words would just float out into the air, disappearing as soon as they are typed, if no one reads them. So, from the bottom of my heart — thank you.

CONTENTS

Breathe, just breathe
Let the life that you live
Be all that you need
~ Breathe
By Ryan Star

FORGIVING MYSELF

~ October 21, 2007~

EVERY PREGNANCY HAS ITS ANXIETY NIGHTMARES. Every pregnancy has its moments of waking up at 3:00 am wild eyed, heart racing, rising to the surface of a horrific, baby in peril dream. Your hand goes instinctively to your stomach and there it is, hard as a drum, round as a basketball. Your precious baby safe inside. Now, imagine the nightmare is reversed. The horror, the unspeakable thing is there when you open your eyes. Closed, complete bliss. Open, you're hit with terror.

I spent the last few weeks of my third and last pregnancy worried. I fretted that I would have a repeat of my second labor and delivery — so much blood that the room looked like a CSI episode, so much blood I nearly needed a transfusion. I panicked when my labor stalled, but thanks to a mega dose of Pitocin, I sped from four to ten centimeters in twenty minutes and delivered my son, Aidan, after a mere fifteen minutes of pushing. Even with no epidural at the end, I was over the moon. Aidan Jacob was a ten fingered, ten toed, gorgeous platinum blonde with crystal blue eyes. The only thing I noticed amiss was a small blood spot in the corner of his left eye, but I knew that was common from the stress of delivery. I was left wondering, "Why do I worry so much? Why not enjoy the moment?" I vowed not to let the fear of what might happen rule my life ever again.

That resolve coursed through me as I held my beautiful boy, my Aidan, on my shoulder to burp him. He had just finished nursing, and that delicious weight of a new life sound asleep — solid, yet light as a feather, filled me with peace. I patted his back and breathed in his intoxicating scent. "He's here," I thought. "He's finally here."

That was the last moment I remember before hearing the screams, the newborn gut wrenching wails. It took me a second to understand that the sound was coming from Aidan. And, in that split second, I realized that he was no longer in my arms, but lying on the floor — the cold, hard, unforgiving hospital floor.

I opened my eyes to my worst nightmare, worse than any pregnancy anxiety visions. Worse than anything my hormone-addled brain could have conjured. I jumped out of bed screaming. As I scrambled to lift Aidan back into my arms, back to my heart, I pushed the leg of the bassinette into his stomach. I stumbled trying to get to him. In seconds a nurse was pushing me on the bed as I sobbed, while another nurse whisked Aidan away. I struggled against the monitor she hooked me up to. I struggled to follow my son.

I did not remember falling asleep. I did not remember a gentle slipping away. I was holding my baby and then I wasn't. I tried to stand up and fell back down on the bed. "We need to check your vitals," the nurse insisted. "You can't stand on your own."

My blood pressure (normally extremely low) and my heart rate (a bit high even when I'm calm) were through the roof. I didn't care. I wanted to see my baby. "I must have fallen asleep," I sobbed. "I don't remember." The fear and guilt that gripped me were a hurricane, a force, something that I'd never felt before.

"You didn't fall asleep," one of the nurses informed me. "You passed out. Your chart says you are extremely anemic and you refused treatment this afternoon." Her disdainful glance fell on me.

I didn't refuse treatment; I simply requested to see my blood levels before agreeing to take medication. My doctor hadn't informed me that I was anemic and the massive doses of iron I was given after my last delivery left my son with bloody diarrhea. I was nursing again and wanted to make sure the diagnosis wasn't a mistake. The nurses were overworked, and I knew there was always a chance the medication could have been meant for someone else. Sure, I had been dizzy, but I chalked it up to lack of sleep.

It wasn't a mistake, though. I was severely anemic going into labor, and the small blood loss depleted me more. My mind spun back to an appointment I had with a cardiologist for shortness of breath and rapid heart rate at seven months. He suggested I might be anemic, but I never got the blood work he prescribed done. My obstetrician did a finger stick test and assured me my iron levels were perfect. I assumed my shortness of breath was thanks to my huge belly on my tiny frame and my son crushing my diaphragm. I was getting biweekly blood tests for a platelet condition, idiopathic thrombocytopenia, and I just couldn't find the time to get yet another test while caring for two young children.

I berated myself for not taking the hour to get one extra blood test done. One dose of iron that afternoon probably wouldn't have made a difference, but two months' worth would have. Regardless of what I could have done to prevent it, the reality was that in my weakened state, I slipped out of consciousness and slipped into a fear so profound, I could not breathe.

I called my husband, Jeff, hands shaking, hot tears flowing. "I did something really bad," I whispered. "The baby, he fell." Rather than asking for a divorce immediately, my husband stayed calm and instructed me to call my mother to watch our older boys. My mother was not calm. My mother sobbed and vowed to come right to the hospital, leaving my father with the boys. Then she whispered, "How did this happen? What are we going to do with you?" Later, she would apologize. Later, she would agree with everyone that it wasn't my fault. She didn't mean harm. It was the same thing I would say to my six-year-old if he broke something precious, even if it was an accident. But, I took that statement in and held it.

As I hung up the phone, three doctors appeared at my bedside. The night neonatologist, flanked by two interns explained that one of three things could happen—nothing, no damage; a skull fracture; a skull fracture with bleeding. Aidan would be observed in the NICU (neonatal intensive care) overnight and they would decide on a CAT scan in the morning. It was only 9:45 pm. I honestly did not know how I could survive through the night without knowing my baby's fate. The only thing I knew was that if he had suffered permanent damage, I would never know joy again.

Finally, I was wheeled to the nursery where he was being examined before being transferred to the NICU. For the rest of my stay, I would not be allowed to walk to the NICU, to walk anywhere farther than my bathroom. I looked through the window. Aidan was pink faced and howling as he was poked and prodded. "He must be okay to be acting like that, right?" I whispered to the nurse. She just shrugged. "They'll let you know," she said softly, then wheeled me into a room behind the nursery.

Mere moments—and yet an eternity later—a nurse brought a still crying Aidan to me. "Can I please nurse him?" I begged her. She placed him in my arms and he latched on greedily, sucking with the same fervor he had displayed just an hour before. I softly stroked his downy blonde hair, stared at his china doll face. I saw no marks, no bruises, no swelling. The only thing I noticed was the blood spot in his left eye.

When I glanced up, the neonatologist stood in front of me, bouncing on the balls of his feet, his arms behind him. "He's nursing so great, he has to be okay, right? He wouldn't be able to nurse like this if he was badly injured, right?" I asked desperately. "I mean, he couldn't die now, could he? If anything terrible was going to happen, it would have happened, right?" If I wasn't holding Aidan, I swear I would have slid out of the wheelchair and dropped to my knees, begging him tell me what I wanted to hear.

The doctor continued bouncing. He answered in measured tones, "We need to observe him all night to get a definitive answer. Sometimes these things take a while to come out." In my mind I envisioned my child in a wheelchair, a child unable to feed himself or walk or play. A child imprisoned in his body because of me. Or, no child at all—I imagined coming home from the hospital with empty, aching arms. I shook my head to get the visions out.

As they wheeled me back to my room, I passed an orthodox Jewish family heading to the nursery. Their hats and suits black as night, their faces calm. "Pray for me," I wanted to whisper. "Pray my baby will be okay."

With sleep elusive, I cried all night, burying my face in the pillow so my husband and roommate could sleep. At 5:00 am the nurse came in to check my vital signs, and a few moments later my doctor came in. "Did you hear what happened?" I whispered. I could not imagine that he hadn't.

He shook his head. He didn't know and I desperately wanted to keep it that way. I wanted one person not to know, one person not to think, "How could you?" I had to tell him, though. I spoke slowly, hoping to stem the tears, which flowed as soon as I opened my mouth.

When I finished, his face was grave. "I didn't even see the anemia on your blood test," he admitted. "I was so busy looking for your platelets results. You were in labor and I needed to know if you could have an epidural. But, one iron pill wouldn't have made a difference. One iron pill couldn't have prevented it." One pill may not have made a difference, but it would have spared me the nurse's withering glance.

As soon as my doctor was done examining me, I asked to go to the NICU. The doctors insisted that I allow them to give Aidan a bottle during the night, so I could recoup my strength and I grudgingly agreed, but I was anxious to see him and nurse him again. I wanted my milk to come in at least, even if all else was failing.

When I got there Aidan was asleep, hooked up to monitors. His pulse rate and oxygen saturation flashed on the screen. The lines of his heartbeat dipped and climbed with regularity. He was so tiny in his isolette. I was certain the nurses were whispering about me, certain they were giving me dirty looks. I was the mother who put her child in the NICU. The only one who wasn't dealt an uncontrollable hand of fate—a premature birth, a genetic disorder, a complication during delivery. I was the only one who could have actually kept my son out of there—that's what I believed.

When my kids' pediatrician arrived, I glanced up at him. There was pity on his face as he took in my swollen eyes, messy ponytail and red nose. I pulled my robe tighter and glanced away. I felt the tears rising, hot in my eyes, and I couldn't bear to look at him. "Hey, he's blonde! You'll get in more trouble for that than dropping him," he joked, knowing that we are a family of brunettes. I tried to smile, but the tears spilled over, rolled down my cheeks. I was a breath away from full on sobbing.

"Look," he began softly, "You are not the first person to do this. You're just the first person today."

"Will he be okay?" I whispered. He couldn't answer me. No one could, yet. The neonatologist decided that Aidan did need a CAT scan and I spent the rest of the morning in an agonizing state of waiting for them to do the test. All I longed for was to hold Aidan, to nurse him, to sustain him. Yet, the nurses kept making me leave. Since I wasn't allowed to walk yet, getting back to the NICU was a battle.

I had to wait for both a wheelchair and someone to push me. I not only wanted to walk to the NICU, I wanted to run. When I finally got there, a nurse was giving Aidan a bottle. I was furious, but the nurse simply replied, "He was hungry."

"Please give him to me," I begged. "I want my milk to come in. I want something to go right." Again, I imagined that the nurses and even the other mothers were giving me dirty looks. They knew I was defective. They knew I couldn't even keep my newborn from slipping out of my grasp. I asked when he would have his CAT scan and was simply told, "Soon."

Back in my room, I stared at the ceiling, trying to quiet my mind. I didn't expect the results for a few hours, but Jeff returned quickly and sat down on the bed with me. In his silence, I heard everything. "He's not okay, is he?" I whispered.

He answered me slowly, as if speaking to a child. "The resident on duty spoke with me. He was very nice. He said Aidan has a small hairline fracture, but no bleeding. It should heal on its own." The words "skull fracture" — like a hammer, a fist, a lead ball — slammed into my chest. How could I ever forgive myself? I broke my baby's head. I sobbed silently, shoulders heaving. Jeff leaned his forehead against mine. "You know, Stef, they're more worried about you. That's what all of the doctors have said. Aidan will be okay. You really are not well right now. You're the one who passed out. You're extremely weak and your heart rate is still way too high. The nurses are coming in a few minutes to check your vitals."

After I was checked, I let Jeff guide me into the wheelchair and push me down the hall, but mentally I was gone. No matter how much anyone reassured me or insisted I was worse off than Aidan physically, I couldn't hear it. I hated myself and knew I did not deserve any kindness.

The resident's eyes were tired and his voice soft. I imagined all he must see. I knew that my baby wasn't as bad as most coming through the NICU, but that didn't matter. All those other babies were random events, out of the mother's control. None of those babies were betrayed by the one person who is supposed to protect them.

The thoughts crashing through my mind must have shadowed my face, because the only thing that resident said was, "Look, this happens." He then shared a story about a six week old in the hospital for a lifesaving heart procedure. His mother sat in the hospital issue rocking chair the night before his surgery, nursing him. The exhaustion of caring for and worrying about an ill newborn caught up with her, and as she rocked she fell asleep. She woke up when her son hit the floor.

That baby suffered a skull fracture, as well. But, he was able to have his surgery. He lived with a skull fracture and a heart problem. I wanted to call that mother and tell her it was okay. I wanted to find her and hug her. But, I couldn't extend that kindness to myself.

I was discharged late that evening, eight hours after I should have headed home. It was my health, not Aidan's that kept us in the hospital. My hemoglobin was dangerously low, and my doctor had to wait for the result of my last blood test to determine if it was safe for me to go home. With a hemoglobin of 8.1 (the normal range is from 12.1 to 15.1), I just made it. A bit lower and I may have needed a transfusion.

I begged the nurses to let me bring Aidan back to my room to dress him in his going home outfit, to take pictures, to pretend everything was normal. Generally, all babies are discharged directly from the NICU, but a supervisor took mercy on me and bent the rules. I was able to pose with Aidan and smile for the camera, pretending to be happy, pretending my thoughts weren't filled with gathering storm clouds.

At home I continued to pretend. I had two small boys reading my cues. If I was weepy and anxious, they would be too. So, I kept it in. Though, sometimes it escaped. When I called the pediatrician's office to schedule Aidan's first well visit, the receptionist asked me how he was. I was too raw. I opened my mouth to answer and only a strangled cry escaped. The receptionist was understanding, but I felt branded—not only did I drop my son, but I couldn't keep it together without crying.

Shortly after that my parents' friend from Florida called. I managed not to cry, but I could speak only in the shortest, sharpest sentences. "We're all fine. I need to go." I knew I was rude, but it was either that or tears.

At my son's preschool, everyone marveled at how thin I was. I wanted to yell, "I only lost the weight because I dropped my son and now I can't eat!" I couldn't tell them that I ate just enough to keep me upright and nursing, that the pleasure of eating was lost. The pleasure of anything was lost.

Shopping for party ware for Aidan's bris (the coming out party for Jewish baby boys), I confided in my mother that I felt no joy deciding between sherbet hued handprints and pale yellow ducky plates. I felt no joy picking out a centerpiece. I felt no joy, period.

"You're missing everything," my mother said. "This whole beginning – you're missing it. You can't get it back, either. This is it. You have to forgive yourself. You have to get back to living."

After I got home, I sat in the nursery and cried, just cried — great gasping sobs that racked my whole body. I rocked back and forth and back and forth. I tried to get my mind around what had happened and what I could do to forgive myself and enjoy Aidan's bris. I couldn't. I could not figure out a way to feel joy over the birth of my beautiful son.

The next day I called a friend who had fallen down the stairs two years earlier while carrying her six month old. Her daughter suffered a skull fracture. "How do you get over it?" I implored.

"Eventually you just do," she answered. "It's always there, but you just go on." I tried to see myself happy in the future. I tried to see beyond the torturous guilt. I knew only one thing would release me — Aidan's follow up CAT scan at three months. Finally, that CAT scan showed that the fracture had healed completely, that the danger was over. Aidan would be fine. I started to believe in happiness again. Slowly, I started to enjoy the small moments of motherhood — the toothless grin, the raspberries blown. I started to feel thankful for our tremendous luck in escaping tragedy.

Even as the guilt has started to retreat, the experience still colors my decisions, my feelings six months later. When Aidan violently protests being lowered into his crib, awake or asleep, I wonder if something inside him, some tiny nugget of remembrance startles him each time he leaves my arms. When I was sixteen years old, I fell off a boy's shoulders and shattered my ankle. For years after that, I could not do anything that recalled that feeling of falling — Ferris wheels, even a playground swing left my stomach churning. Could Aidan somehow relive the feeling of leaving my arms and hitting the cold hard floor each time he hits those cold sheets?

Logic tells me he can't remember what happened at one day old. Logic tells me his skull has completely healed. Logic tells me that lots of babies just want to be held. Logic tells me if I want to sleep soon, I should listen to my pediatrician's exhortations to "let him cry."

But, my heart says, "What if?" So, when he shrieks and wails ten seconds after I've placed him in the crib, I lift him to my heart. Even though I am exhausted and still owe thank you notes and have knee-deep piles of laundry in my basement, even though there are a gazillion other things I could and should be doing, I slide into the glider with Aidan in my arms. Even though he is six months old and not six weeks, even though his feet now almost reach my knees when his head is on my shoulder, I lay my cheek against his spun silk hair and let him tangle his tiny fingers in the curls that spill over my shoulders. Together, we rock into the night.

Epilogue: I am awakened this morning the same way I am every morning—two plump arms around my neck, a silken cheek against mine and "I give you a hug," whispered in my ear. I glance at the clock—7:06 am. I am sure this is not the first time Aidan has woken me up, I vaguely remember him crawling onto my bed in the predawn hours, but this is the first moment I am truly conscious. And, the first conscious thought I have is, "Three years since the worst day of my life."

As Aidan snuggles in closer, his chin resting on my shoulder, I reflect on what he has become since that day. He is, by anyone's standards, brilliant. At three years old, he can do simple math. (I learned this when I was helping my first grader with his homework and Aidan chimed in with the answers to one plus all the numbers through nine.) He can read simple words. At just over two years old, he began mixing all of his twenty-four piece puzzles together and then doing each one from the mixed up pile of five different puzzles. From the mishmash of pieces, he was able to extricate exactly the one he needed and complete all the puzzles in just a few minutes.

During a recent cognitive evaluation (part of a speech therapy evaluation) the psychologist said she had never seen a three-year-old perform the visual spatial tasks Aidan was performing. "I can't wait to score this," she gushed. "He is going to be through the roof." His score was indeed "through the roof"—above the 99.99%. When I shared this with my Ob/Gyn at my annual appointment, he said, "Maybe I should tell all my patients to drop their babies on their heads." Later when I told Jeff, he chastised me, "I bet you didn't even laugh."

"I cracked a smile," I protested. And this, I realize is what I am left with—the raw pain is gone. I am even able to crack a smile when someone jokes about what happened, but I will never laugh about it. I will never forget the profound fear. And, I will always appreciate the second chance I was given.

HALF FULL OR HALF EMPTY

~ December 27, 2009 ~

HALF EMPTY OR HALF FULL? I have always fancied myself a glass half full type of gal. I see the best in people and can sometimes even be, dare I say it, Pollyannaish. My husband, Jeff, vehemently disagrees with my view of myself. He is convinced that I spin everything out to the worst possible scenario—that I count myself out before the votes have even been tallied, that I am constantly holding my breath waiting for the other shoe to fall. Okay, he has a point, but he is generally the only one who notices that dark side of me. Maybe not the only one—my close friends and family know I am a champion worrier, but I try to throw the *upbeat, bubbly, everything will be okay Stef* out to the world at large. Whether I succeed or not is questionable. A few days ago, my son, Aidan's, ear nose and throat doctor shook his head, smiled ruefully and asked Jeff, "She's really a glass half empty type, isn't she?" Jeff answered quickly, "Absolutely. I'm so happy that someone else finally noticed it!"

I protested, explaining that I wasn't a glass half empty type, merely pragmatic. I liked to be prepared. We had just finished discussing the fact that Aidan's next strep infection would mean surgery, and I mentioned that three and a half years earlier when he told me that Aidan's next ear infection meant surgery, it was a mere week before I was ringing him. Aidan's tonsils are huge red golf balls stuck in his throat, making him sick constantly and leaving him with a Fozzie Bear voice. Perhaps I should have pretended that he won't need his tonsils out and chirp, "Great, you won't be hearing from me!" If I believed that, then the next time his cheeks turn pink, his eyes glaze over and the thermometer reads 104, I would be blindsided, completely unprepared. I don't want him to have surgery, but I know it's a strong possibility. Sensing I was upset, his doctor soothed me, "It's okay if you're half empty—that's just the way you are. It's fine to be prepared."

His words dogged me all day, though. For some reason I wanted to go back and insist that I was not a half empty person, that I was bright and cheery and optimistic, dammit! Truth be told, though—I was having a very hard time being cheery and optimistic. His assertion came on the heels of a very bad week. Okay—it was a terrible, horrible, no good, very bad week, much like Aidan's favorite book, *Alexander and the Terrible, Horrible, No Good Very Bad Day*. In the book, Alexander recites a laundry list of injustices he has suffered through the day—from waking up with gum in his hair in the morning to his Mickey Mouse nightlight burning out at night. While my week was at times merely annoying like Alexander's, it was also at times downright harrowing.

A bit of my Alexander-like laundry list: On Thursday, I noticed Aidan burning up, then the doctor proclaimed it looked like strep again—after being off meds for just three days. Then, in the wee hours of Friday morning, he woke up with a terrible case of croup. The barking cough and stridor (an abnormal high pitched sound, generally when breathing out) woke me up with a shock. Sitting on the toilet lid, with Aidan on my lap and steam filling the bathroom, I was sure it wasn't strep. That is, until the doctor called me at 8:00 am to say, "Yup, it's strep and it's only December—I think you have a lot more illness ahead of you." Thanks, doc.

I'll skip the multitude of merely annoying moments and the easily fixed, but scary moments (like my sixth grader, Drew, not finding Jeff in the parking lot at school pickup, while I was helpless, twenty minutes away—fixed it by sending him on the bus to a friend's house)—and go straight to the harrowing. On Tuesday I was lying on the table at the radiologist, feet in stirrups, while a grim faced doctor attempted to maneuver a giant ultrasound probe around my dainty bits. It was a follow up—just to make sure that a cyst that was getting bigger, but was still tiny, was just that, a cyst. Watching him stare at the screen, point something out to the tech and then click, click, click, my heart was in my throat. I stared at the water stained ceiling, counting the dots in the tiles, until I could no longer remain silent. "What is it?" I asked quietly.

"I'm not sure, it's on the other side—the one you came in for is just a simple cyst. This is definitely not a simple cyst—there's something solid. It's hanging off of your ovary. I can't believe your doctor didn't see this. It's..." Pause. Click. Click. Click. "It's 3.7 centimeters. They couldn't possibly have missed that. It's big and solid and just hanging off of your ovary."

Don't doctors need some sort of bedside manner training??? I wanted to scream. Instead, I asked slowly, "Does it look like cancer?"

"Umm, it's unlikely. But, I don't know what it is—a complex cyst probably." This statement really didn't assuage my fear, especially with that grim face delivering it. I should explain—my sister was the same exact age as I am—forty-one years old—when she was diagnosed with stage three ovarian cancer. My mother had uterine cancer, but it was an ovarian cancer gene. It was even the same time of year that both of them were diagnosed—my mother in early December, my sister in early January. I was right in between. I felt my eyes water and swallowed down the lump forming in my throat. The radiologist then asked a bit nervously, "Did you say your doctor is on vacation?" Fantastic.

"That was last week," I answered. "He should be back by now."

"We'll get the report to him tomorrow, and I'm sure he'll call you right away and discuss your options."

"What are my options?" I asked, almost afraid to find out.

"They'll probably want to watch it and see if it goes away. If it doesn't go away, they can remove it." That night I Googled "complex cyst." Big mistake. One site warned, "A complex cyst can be fatal, if left untreated." Another site was more positive, stating that 85% of complex cysts are benign. But, it led into that statement with the ominous, "In contrast to simple cysts, which are always benign, complex cysts are sometimes malignant." So, when I fretted about the flip side of the 85% of complex cysts that are benign—the 15% that aren't, was I embodying the glass half empty philosophy, or merely being pragmatic, bracing myself for all the possibilities?

My doctor, a glass half full type if ever there was one, did indeed want to simply watch it, for at least a cycle or "even better" two. "It's probably a hemorrhagic cyst. Nothing to worry about, but we need to follow you," he told me the next morning. The few friends I told urged me to get a second opinion and not just sit passively waiting for an answer. "Get a second opinion!!!!!" my friend, Cheryl, texted me. I compromised and am getting an ultrasound after one cycle, instead of two. If it's still there, then I'll get a second opinion. So, maybe I'm really a glass half full girl after all—thinking there is a chance that it may have gone away.

By Thursday though, my mind was completely off of my health and fixated firmly on my dog's health. On Wednesday I had noticed a lump on Sadie's hind leg. That turned out to be nothing—just a dried cyst, but there was a papilloma in her cheek that needed to be removed. The vet, not our regular one, said, "I don't know what it is, and I won't know until we get it back from cytology." Again, grim face. I felt like I was stuck in replay. And, again I struggled to be in glass half full mode—but, it was impossible. I had a nagging fear that it was worse than it seemed, that there was more going on than a simple papilloma. When we dropped Sadie off for her surgery, the day after Aidan's ominous appointment with his otolaryngologist, the vet tech assured us that papillomas are very common in shih tzus and that they are always benign—nothing to worry about. I went about my business all day, buying last minute gifts for all the people who touch my kids' lives, running, running until I got the call from the vet—the papilloma was actually a mass, much larger than originally anticipated, its fingers reaching down into Sadie's parotid gland. Dr. Bridget Brook, Sadie's regular veterinarian, had to remove much more than she thought she would have to and though she didn't think it was malignant, again, she wouldn't know until the biopsy came back.

Sadie and I both go back to the doctor for our follow-ups tomorrow. I to get back up on that sonogram table and see if my cyst—or whatever it is, the solid thing hanging off my ovary—has gotten bigger or, fingers crossed, has gone away. Sadie to see how her sutures are healing and maybe, just maybe, to find out if her growth is benign. The report may not be back for a few more days. But, see—I said to "see if her growth is benign," not to "see if her growth is malignant." Maybe, I'm learning to see the glass half full after all. Or maybe, I just can't contemplate the alternative...

THE GIFT OF HOPE

~ *January 24, 2010* ~

ON THE NIGHT BEFORE NEW YEAR'S EVE my husband, Jeff, sat down on the couch with a heavy sigh. His lips parted, about to speak, and then closed. He stared at me with such a look of anguish on his face that I dropped the holiday cards that I was addressing and whispered, "What? What is it?" The scene reeked of drama — reminded me of every woman wronged movie I'd ever seen. The husband sits down, unable to get out the words as his wife stares at him. Then, he breaks down crying and admits that he's having an affair, is in love with someone else or perhaps that he slept with someone just once and wants to repent. Jeff glanced sideways at me then back down at his lap. It was truly unlikely, but I couldn't help but wonder, *Was he about to come clean? Did he have a new year's resolution to be honest driving him to admit an indiscretion?* "Are you having an affair?" I asked accusingly.

He shook his head no, looked like he was about to cry. Then, it hit me — a punch in the gut. "It's Sadie, isn't it?" He nodded. Sadie, our beloved shih tzu whom we rescued almost three and a half years ago, had surgery a week earlier — as you may know; if you read my last post. "It's..." he paused ... "Well, it's not good. She has a very aggressive form of melanoma — it has a high rate of recurrence and metastasis."

I didn't say anything, just sucked in my breath. He continued, "The vet said we can set up a consult with a dog oncologist and talk about chemo and she can do a deeper resection to get the rest of the cancer cells. Or, we can do nothing and take care of new lesions as they pop up. But, she said that it's just not good."

I turned this over in my mind, attempted to process it. Of course, I couldn't. I burst into tears and blurted out the only thing that came into my mind, "No offence, but I would rather it be that you were having an affair." Not that I would trade my marriage for my dog, but if Jeff were having an affair, he would still be alive, because I probably wouldn't kill him. I'm sure I'd want to, but I am too law abiding to commit homicide. So, yes — it would have been less painful for him to admit he was having an affair, than for me to find out that I'm losing Sadie. And, the thought of her being in pain was just too much to bear. All I really could do was cry.

At about midnight I went upstairs and sat down next to Sadie, sleeping on my son, Joshua's, bed. (She starts her night in my son, Aidan's, bed, and then moves to Joshua's. Sometime after midnight, when she knows everyone is asleep and safe, she comes into our room and scratches on our bed until I kick Jeff to pick her up. I will never, ever be annoyed by her scratching again.) I kissed her on the forehead and she turned her tiny face to mine, covering me with kisses. She must have wondered why my face was suddenly salty — the tears were just streaming down.

This was not the first time I have dealt with a cancer diagnosis of a loved one (and yes, my dog is a loved one), but oddly I never cried when I found out my father had cancer, my sister had cancer and my mother had cancer. I don't think I even cried at first when I found out that my grandmother had cancer and had only days to live, her diagnosis was that late. I was stoic — dealing with it and trying to remain positive for everyone. I pointed this out to Jeff and asked, "What does that say about me — I didn't cry when I found out my family members had cancer, but I'm crying buckets about my dog?"

He simply answered, "You're her caretaker." I knew he was right. She is, unequivocally, my dog. From the moment we brought her home from the shelter, she has stuck to me like glue, following me everywhere. A montage of our first moments together danced before my eyes, like a cheesy Lifetime movie. It seemed like yesterday that my oldest son, Drew, my middle son, Joshua, and I went to the Town of Oyster Bay Shelter to drop off the donations that we had collected at Drew's eighth birthday party in August 2006. Drew had come home from school in June proudly clutching an essay in which he wrote,

"This summer my mom and dad are getting me a dog!" When Drew was four years old I told him we would get a dog when he turned eight years old. Almost four years later, he still remembered. In an effort to keep our word, we began visiting shelters as soon as school ended. By the time we brought those donations to the shelter though, we had given up our search—we needed a small, hypoallergenic dog—few and far between at shelters. But as we dropped the garbage bags full of the blankets, pillows and towels Drew's birthday guests contributed, there she was—just arrived that morning. Her name was Star and she cowered in her cage, crying. As soon as I knelt down though, she came right over, stuck her tiny snout through the bar and licked me. It was love at first sight, even though she was dirty and smelly—very, very smelly.

We were informed by the shelter that she was between seven and eight years old, but after we adopted her, two vets assured us that she was only between two and three years old. We were thrilled. Our bond was instant—she was a nursing mother (I had finished nursing my twenty-two month old less than a year before), her puppies cruelly ripped from her before they were weaned. We gave her a fleece puppy that first night, which she "nursed," squirting milk on it. She quickly became the boys' second mother—checking on them at night and even sitting in the bathroom with us during Aidan's frequent croup episodes. Steam filling the room, she sat at my feet waiting until Aidan's breathing returned to normal. She seemed to know when they were sick before we did—once she spent all night right next to Aidan before he woke up with strep the next day. She is an amazing, miraculous dog and even though we have a new dog now—Coco, a sweet one-year-old poodle mix rescued from a beach in Puerto Rico— Sadie is still unlike any other animal I have ever encountered. While Coco is a bundle of energy—jumping on everyone, chewing up toys and ripping into the garbage bag, Sadie is all zen calm, except when Coco plays with the boys—then she is right on top of Coco, growling—a mama making sure her babies are safe.

I kissed Sadie once more, checked on the boys and eventually fell into a restless sleep, awaking every couple of hours. Fresh tears fell as soon as I greeted the day and they didn't stop. Right after breakfast, the vet's receptionist faxed us Sadie's oncology report, which painted such a grim picture; Jeff tried to hide it from me. Sadie had only an 8% chance of surviving more than a few months. I was just so thankful that my kids are completely imperceptive of my emotional state. As long as their needs are met, they really don't notice how I am feeling—which, is exactly how it should be. None of them noticed that my eyes and nose were red, that I was uncharacteristically quiet. I did hide out in my bedroom for a bit, folding laundry, but for most of the day I took care of everyone and everything, while the tears rolled silently down my cheeks.

I did not want to go out for New Year's Eve. I did not want to see people—I just wanted to stay home and hold Sadie. But, knowing I couldn't force my kids to stay home, I pulled on blingy jeans and a sparkly silver sweater and bundled the boys up. We went to three different parties, but the veil of sadness remained. I knew that I had to cheer up quickly for my son's birthday the next day. I couldn't risk any of them realizing that I was so upset and why. I did manage to put on a cheerful facade at brunch on New Year's Day, but when my sister mentioned her friend who was depressed about the weather, I snapped, "At least she didn't get terrible news. She should be happy." Luckily, the kids were in the living room, completely oblivious to our conversation.

My mother chastised me, "You know, it's terrible, but she's not human. You have to remember that. Look at it this way," she continued. "God had to make a choice between you and her." She held her palms up, as if weighing the two options. "He chose you. She's your savior." Two days before I found out Sadie needed surgery, I had my own cancer scare. If you read my last blog post, you know how harrowing it was for me lying on the sonogram table and learning that there was something big and partially solid "hanging off of my ovary." You also know that as soon as I learned about Sadie, I pretty much stopped worrying about myself. Well, I went back for a follow up sonogram and had gotten a fantastic, reassuring call from my doctor on the same day that I found out that Sadie has cancer. Same day. The doctor informed me that the growth was indeed a hemorrhagic cyst and was shrinking. I simply needed to go for a follow up sonogram in three months. "You know they like to follow these things," the doctor explained, almost apologetically.

"It's fine," I assured him. "It's great. I'd rather make sure it's gone." I was so happy, so light. It seemed like everything would be okay. I called the vet a couple of hours later, looking for a sweep. Good news for Sadie too. The receptionist told me she would call the lab and call me back to let me know if the report was ready or not. I should have known when I didn't hear back—not even that it wasn't ready—that it was a call the receptionist couldn't make. I just wasn't expecting the vet to call at 9:30 at night, while I was putting the kids to bed. I didn't even hear the phone ring. That's why it was such a shock when Jeff told me. That's why I was blindsided, ripped apart. Would it have been easier if I was expecting it? Probably not, as much as I think that expecting the worst and hoping for the best is a practical way to live, in reality, nothing soothes the pain of learning that someone whom you love is so ill.

I know—I said, "someone," not "something." And yes, I know my mother's assertion that Sadie is not human and that I need to put it in perspective. Jeff felt the same way—he had hugged me close and said, "At least you got good news." I know it's tearing him up too; he's just the practical one in our union. I know no one can really understand, but to me Sadie may as well be human. She is my salve, my balm, my Prozac. With three bouncing off the wall boys, she is my calm in the storm, my oasis. I can't stick my nose in the impossibly soft fur on her neck, breathing in her doggy essence and not feel peaceful. When she covers my face with her tiny kisses, all is right with the world. No slobbery dog kisses. She kisses daintily, starting at the tip of my nose and working up and across my forehead. This is how I start my day, getting kisses and how I end it. She simply gives love—doesn't talk back, doesn't whine, doesn't complain.

I love my children more than anything on earth, but sometimes one just needs the unconditional love a dog gives. They are like infants—they love you, just because you are you. My husband, my kids—they love me as much as I love them, but they all have their moments when they don't like me very much. Those times when I've done something—I don't always even know what it is—to just tick them off. With dogs, they just love. This is why I am willing to do anything to save Sadie. I don't care if we run ourselves into debt; I just want to save her.

However, as I mentioned, I am married to an extremely practical man and wisely, I'm sure, he won't let us run ourselves into debt. "We can't spend $10,000 or $15,000 to save her," he informed me. "There's just no way." The only thing worse than Sadie's disease being too far gone for us to do anything, would be if we could do something to save her, but couldn't afford it.

This was my fear as we sat in the waiting room of the Veterinary Medical Center of Long Island in West Islip, NY, on pins and needles until Sadie emerged from her ultrasound. Dr. John Fondacaro had just examined her and offered us something no one else had—hope. He said that the oncology report really didn't mean anything—it just meant that 92% of dogs didn't make it, but 8% did and there was always that hope that she would be one of those 8%. "It would be unrealistic to expect a miracle, but you can always hope for one," he advised us. Sadie's liver levels were high and he feared the cancer had metastasized there. If that were the case, we really could only offer her palliative care and try to make her last few months as peaceful and happy as possible. If it hadn't metastasized yet, she was a candidate for a new vaccine that treats oral melanoma in dogs by injecting human DNA into the melanoma tumor site. Dogs given only months to live have been surviving at least two or more years cancer free after receiving the vaccine. With this treatment, Sadie could be one of the 8%. Better yet, if that was the only treatment Sadie required, the tally would be far below the $10,000 we feared.

Jeff and I held hands as we waited for Dr. Fondacaro to come through the swinging door and share Sadie's fate. Hope or no hope. "I think it's going to be bad," I whispered. "How are we going to tell the kids?" I so wanted to give my children the gift of hope.

Before Sadie's exam, a woman sitting next to us admired her. When I told her that Sadie has cancer, she replied sadly, "I have cancer too. Ovarian." I looked into her eyes and told her about my sister and my mother—their stories of survival. "My sister was diagnosed thirteen years ago with stage three ovarian cancer and she's just fine now," I offered. "My mother had uterine cancer, but an ovarian cancer cell and she is just fine too—almost four years out from chemo now."

"That's so good to hear," she said. "You don't hear that often. I'm stage three, had it now for two and a half years—been in chemo on and off since then. It's so hard. I didn't know if anyone with stage three could survive. Good to hear." She sat back in her seat, hands across her stomach and smiled, a small smile, but a smile. I thought about her as we waited to learn Sadie's fate. Had I given her the gift of hope, had I made her journey a bit easier, knowing that someone who had gone before survived, despite the odds? I squeezed Jeff's hand, just as the waiting room door swung open and Dr. Fondacaro greeted us with a big grin and a thumbs up. "Yes," I shouted, fists pumping. I didn't care how ridiculous I looked—we had hope and that, was a true gift.

*   *   *   *

Postscript: Four days later, Sadie saw Dr. Edwin Brodsky, a dog oncologist at The Center for Specialized Veterinary Care in Westbury, NY. He declared her cancer stage one. She received her first dose of oral melanoma vaccine that day. She received doses every other week—and then every six months. Through those vaccines and an additional surgery to remove her parotid gland, as well as a large section of her cheek, Sadie beat all the odds and lived for almost an another two years. One year and ten and a half months after her diagnosis I had to let her go. It was the hardest decision ever and I still miss her every day—four years later. But, she went peacefully in my arms—the vet administered a sedative, before euthanizing her. She was free from pain finally. She fought long and hard and I know we did everything we could for her. Still, I'm typing through tears. Two years sounded like a miracle when she was given four months to live. But it went far too fast…

BOYS WILL BE BOYS

~ *January 26, 2010* ~

I AM INSANELY JEALOUS OF MY HUSBAND, JEFF. I'm talking green with envy jealousy. I'm not jealous of the women he may talk to. He coaches two of our kids' teams every season—if I were jealous of all the moms he talked to, I wouldn't have the energy to watch the games. No, I may be jealous of the coach, but not the women. I'm jealous, because he gets to relive his youth every day with our three boys. He gets to bond with them and experience the joys of childhood. They build model rockets together and paint and glue intricately detailed model cars—Ferraris, Lamborghinis, Audis. They play catch and football.

When I asked if my boys wanted to play with my old Barbie dolls during a recent visit to my parents, what do you think the answer was? A resounding "NO!" of course. I gaze longingly at the doll aisle in Target, knowing I'll never need to shop there, except for birthday gifts (which, of course, I always look forward to buying). And yes, I tried to dispel stereotypes and bought my boys baby dolls and even the Barbie Happy Family Alan and Ryan set (a dad with a toddler in a stroller). The baby dolls languished in a dusty corner of my basement, until I passed them along to a neighbor, so at least her little girl would get joy out of them. The Alan doll suffered a much worse fate—he's now a gruesome headless figure used in battles, his preppy outfit and camera long gone, the stroller irreparably broken.

Don't get me wrong. I love having boys and I wouldn't trade any of them for a girl (at least not on most days). I've only threatened to sell them on eBay once and even then I really didn't mean it. I think. I wasn't even "trying for a girl" when I got pregnant the third time—an assumption an annoying amount of people jumped to. I knew I'd have another boy and that was just fine with me. Of course, I'll admit that if I did get pregnant with a girl now—a little sister to be doted on by her big brothers—I would be over the moon. Only one problem, though—I'd need to find a new husband first. No more babies in our house, girl or boy. I got Jeff to agree to adopt a second dog (another girl, of course) and even convinced him to allow our middle son to bring two frogs into the fold of our family, but another baby? It ain't happenin'. I just have to wait for daughters-in-law and grandchildren.

I've heard time and again that girls are harder to raise. I think that boys are harder until the teenage years, though. When boys are little, they are bundles of energy, using the couch as a trampoline and playing football in the hallway. Even my eleven-year-old does flips over the back of the couch and tosses passes in the living room. When they fight it pretty much always deteriorates into the physical. Like a clash of Roman gladiators in an ancient amphitheater, the fight's not over until someone is lying on the ground or I scream loudly enough to burst eardrums. They think bodily functions are hilarious and sneak in the word, "fart" whenever possible. They even put their own charming spin on songs—"Maybe, I can see your butt. Maybe, I can see you fart..." to the tune of Beyonce's lovely ballad, "Halo." I'm sure she didn't have those lyrics in mind when she and her writing partners penned the tune. But, they are also fiercely loyal and as one friend told me just after I gave birth to my first son, "Boys love their mamas."

And, they love hockey. This is very important, since it's my chance to truly bond with my boys. Sure, I read books to them and cuddle with them—that's all wonderful and warm. But, hockey has us jumping up and down and hugging each other and giving fist bumps and high fives. Jeff, a Boston native, gets them for baseball, basketball and football. I have no qualms that they love his Boston teams, even though we live in New York. I pass along all of the Knicks and Jets gear handed down from my nephew without a second thought—after all, Celtics and Patriots fans can't wear that. Raising Red Sox fans in Yankees country? I couldn't care less, but if any of them professed a love for the Boston Bruins—or god forbid the New York Islanders—I don't think I would ever recover.

I love that my boys get so excited, that they all pile up on me when our beloved New York Rangers score—all of them trying to hug me at once, before we do our fist bumps and high fives. I love that I can pass on that part of my childhood. I have been a Rangers fan since I was four years old and I have many happy memories of cheering them on with my older brother.

My bedroom wall was plastered with Rangers memorabilia and on my night table sat the puck my favorite player, Don Maloney, handed me during a public practice. My boys love hearing about those practices and how I sat in Section 314 at Madison Square Garden, whenever I was lucky enough to go to a game. When we watch hockey together, we get loud and I have to admit, it's so liberating not to feel like I need to shush them. As any mom of boys knows, loudness is their natural state of being and we quash it so often.

I would prefer them a bit quieter at other times, though. My boys are loud—plain and simple. When friends call, they often assume that I am in the middle of hosting a crowd. "No, no—those are just my boys," I explain. Add three boys, two dogs and daily drum practice together and you have the makings of hearing loss (or at least a nasty migraine) for mom. There are times that I just go into the bathroom, close the door, turn on the vent and the faucet and … Well, sometimes I'll just enjoy the moment and sometimes I'll hiss, "Shut the #&% up!!" half a dozen times and emerge ready to tackle the insanity anew.

Despite the overwhelming chaos though, I cherish all that boyishness—the mussed up hair, the sweaty cheeks, the constant motion and yes, even the loudness. Usually just when I've reached my breaking point, my little guy, Aidan, will come over and give me a hug, squeezing my waist with all his might. And, those are the moments when I realize how very lucky I am. Because, I do feel lucky—even when that hug is followed by Aidan informing me that for his 100 day project for kindergarten, he wants to use "one hundred pieces of poopies," instead of the dinosaur stickers we bought. Hey, boys will be boys.

KICKING SUPERWOMAN TO THE CURB

~ *February 2, 2010* ~

I'VE DECIDED TO KICK my inner Superwoman to the curb. I'm evicting her. Giving her the pink slip. Adios. See ya later. Don't let the door hit you on the way out. I've been thinking about severing ties with her for a while, but like any long term, codependent relationship, saying goodbye is hard to do. We've had a few trial separations, but I always let her back into my life—offering to bake two dozen cupcakes for the class Valentine's Day party last year, even though my mammogram was the same day; gluing together twenty-two pilgrim hats and rushing them to the school, even though my son was home sick. You get the picture.

I had my first inkling that Superwoman was no good for me when my oldest son, Drew, was just three months. I promised myself that I would go back to work as a creative services freelancer when he hit that three-month mark, but I didn't earn enough to pay for childcare—that left working at home as the only option. But, my inner Superwoman wouldn't let me work while Drew was awake. No, she said that when he was awake, I had to be entertaining and engaging him every moment. Oh, and I couldn't work while he was napping, because I had to do laundry or clean the bathroom during those precious hours. So, I stayed up all night proofreading massive corporate manuscripts before Fed Ex picked them up in the morning, taking a break only to breastfeed. I felt guilty when I was only able to keep up that pace for a few assignments—I was falling over with exhaustion, but that didn't make it any easier to stop working.

I should have told her to scram back then, over a decade ago. I probably would have been a lot happier in the ensuing years. I might

not have stayed up all night sewing a George Washington costume
by hand, after spending all day scouring craft stores for felt and
something (anything!) that could double as a white puffy wig. I
ended up winding curly white doll hair around the inside of a
triangle hat I had crafted out of stiff black felt, tying it with a ribbon
at the back. I slit the front of a black sweatshirt, sewing down
"lapels" and made a vest out of a red t-shirt. Sure, my kid looked
amazing and the teachers gushed, but would he have been any
worse off had I ordered a costume from the Internet? Of course not,
but that wouldn't have impressed anyone. Now, that costume is in a
crumpled heap at the bottom of his closet—never worn again.

How did Superwoman get such a grip on me? When did she
move in and decide to stay? I was always a perfectionist, never happy
until a project was perfect. This unfortunately also led me to be a
world-class procrastinator. Because being perfect is so overwhelming,
I would do anything to avoid class projects and later on writing
assignments for magazines. I always boasted that I did better on a
deadline—the adrenaline got my fingers flowing over the keyboard.
But, honestly was I really better off in my twenties staying up until
5:00 am the morning of my deadlines, faxing in all the pages of my
column as the sun kissed the sky? No of course not. But, I was the only
one who suffered. When I came down with a sinus infection and
bronchitis after one such deadline, I simply took to my bed and
emerged when I was feeling better. I can't do that with three children,
two dogs, two frogs and a fish to care for, not to mention a husband.

No, the stress that Superwoman imparts on my life has got to go.
I am constantly exhausted from trying to do it all and it makes me a
far worse parent than if I buy the baked goods once in a while, if I
say no to the PTA request, if I actually take a few moments to
exercise or even (gasp!) read a book. There are always going to be
moms more put together than I am, with neater houses and perfectly
behaved children. Instead of worrying that I'm underdressed in my
tank top, jeans and sneakers at the school book fair, I am going to
embrace my penchant for comfy clothes and feel sorry for the
woman teetering around in stiletto boots, no matter how good she
looks. I am not going to have a panic attack every time I drop my
kids off for a play date at a museum like home, wondering what the

mom will think when it's my turn to host. We live in a small house and it's—how shall I say this—lived in. And, I am going to just smile serenely as my children pounce on each other, rolling around on the floor—as long as there is no blood. I have to—there is no sense in trying for perfection in motherhood. You can't achieve it and if you think you have, you probably have some pharmaceutical help.

Back to that cupcake fiasco—I knew I had my mammogram appointment the same day, yet Superwoman compelled me to offer to bake and decorate two dozen cupcakes for my son, Joshua's, Valentine's Day party. I figured it was no problem, because I could simply bake them the night before. Only the moment I pulled the eggs out of the fridge, the mixing bowl out from the cabinet and the oil out of the cupboard, the electricity went out. Gone, nothing—no lights, no heat, definitely no oven. I had no choice but to pack up my kids, the dog (at that point we had only one), some toiletries, pjs and all the frozen food I could carry and haul everything and everyone to my parents' house across town. Of course my husband, Jeff, was away on business. At 11:00 pm as I climbed into the pull out couch bed at my parents', I realized that I never baked the cupcakes.

In an amazing fit of misguided optimism, I felt certain that I could have my mammogram, bake the cupcakes, decorate them and get them to the school in time for the celebration. When I was still sitting in the radiologist's waiting room an hour and a half before the party, I called Jeff in a panic. He had returned from his trip in the wee hours of the morning and was napping, but still offered to bake for me. All I had to do was get home within the hour to frost the cupcakes and sprinkle them with tiny sugar hearts. Forty-five minutes later, still waiting to be called, I felt so guilty thinking about those damn cupcakes, that I left the office without even getting my mammogram. I rescheduled it for the next day, ruining my Saturday morning. I could have had Jeff frost and decorate the cupcakes, but then I would feel like a failure. So, I rushed like a lunatic to frost, decorate and transport the cupcakes to school in record time, only to be late anyway. Joshua's teacher looked at me and said, a bit nastily, "Why didn't you just buy the cupcakes?" Why, indeed?

I could have easily kicked Superwoman to the curb that day—I had more than enough reason, but she was like that bad boy boyfriend whom you break up with, because you know he's just no good for you, but then you let him back in, because sometimes he is really good for you. Okay, I have to admit—I ended up marrying that bad boy boyfriend, after breaking up with him every few months for the first year we were together. And, he did end up being good for me in the long run. Sometimes, Superwoman can be good for you too. Like the way that my inner Superwoman lets me believe that I can really make a difference as Community Services chairperson at not one, but two schools. Or the way that she spurs me on to collect hundreds of dollars for Haitian children, because, well what other choice do I have? I have to help, plain and simple. Those are the times that Superwoman is a great motivator. But, too many times most of us are just spinning our wheels, trying to do everything, but succeeding at very little, or so it seems.

If I had a dollar for every one of my mom friends who has admitted to me that she often feels like a failure, I would be a rich woman. If I had a dollar for every time I've felt like a failure, I would be a multi-millionaire. Why do we doubt ourselves so? Do dads stay awake at night ruminating over all of the mistakes (real or imagined) they made during the day? Do they wonder if they've shortchanged their children, their spouses, their co-workers? I suspect they don't. I suspect that most men are like my husband—anything that happens during the day is forgotten as soon as the sun sets, or at least as soon as the kids are in bed. He's a great dad; he just doesn't wallow in self-doubt, as I am prone to do. The kids were fed, dressed and warm during the day? No bones were broken? Great, then we've done our job well. When I lie down at night, I relive the screaming matches, the hurt feelings, the book I didn't get to read or the board game I didn't get to play. What a waste of time. Superwoman roars up in the waning hours of the day—reminding me of everything I didn't accomplish and chasing away sleep. That is why she's getting evicted.

Repeat after me, ladies—"If my kids are fed, dressed, loved and happy, then I am doing my job, even if they say that they hate me." I know, it's easier said than done. But, believe me—even if you didn't prepare a gourmet meal with all of the food groups (they're probably happier with mac and cheese anyway) or you didn't read even one developmentally appropriate book, or even if you

BOYS, DOGS AND CHAOS

screamed your head off for some small transgression, your kids will survive and they will still love you. Just relax and know that kissing them goodnight and tucking them in (and in the case of my five-year-old, curling up in his bed with him until he drifts off to sleep) makes you Superwoman in their eyes. Now, if I could only take my own advice...

WHAT IF?

~ February 15, 2010 ~

"WHAT IF?" The most insidious phrase in all of the English language has been popping up in my brain with annoying regularity over the past week and a half. Like some sort of whack-a-mole game, every time it pops up, I try to bash it down, but more often than not, I miss. It pops up at the times I least want it there—when I am putting my five-year-old to sleep, his plump little arms wrapped around my neck, a wet kiss planted on my cheek, or when I am resting my head on my husband's chest—the kids finally asleep, a moment for us to just breathe, instead of running man to man defense on three constant motion boys. It doesn't pop up when I am running around, doing a million things, it pops up at those moments I treasure the most—the moments when I realize how much I really have to lose.

By now, you know that I had a cancer scare two months ago and that my dog, Sadie, has been battling cancer for those same two months. She is doing amazingly well and is now in remission, thankfully. I didn't mention in my previous blogs that while I was waiting to hear about Sadie's second biopsy, I was waiting to hear about my biopsy, too—a second cancer scare, just weeks after the first. Both results were great—Sadie's cancer was gone and my biopsy was benign—the problem was decidedly non-life threatening. I was so happy to put that chapter behind us—that awful stretch of cold, dark winter when I really didn't know what the spring would hold. Burying our dog, illness for me—I just didn't know.

Of course, as soon as you are sure things are looking up; life often throws you a new curve ball. Getting into pajamas after a long day, tired as could be, my breast suddenly hurt, really hurt—in just one spot. I never do breast self-exams, but I felt the area, pressing slightly, and there it was—a discernible lump. Pea size, solid, immovable. Definitely tender. That's a good thing, I told myself and proceeded to do what anyone in the Internet age does when faced with a health concern—I Googled "Does breast cancer hurt?" Apparently, breast cancer can hurt—in its advanced stages. I told myself that with regular mammograms, the chances that I had advanced breast cancer were slim. (Of course in my head, my grandmother's voice admonished, "Don't give yourself a kinehora*!") I also found though, that inflammatory breast cancer does hurt, and progresses at an alarming rate. I was stressed and exhausted and spinning things out to the worst possible scenario, a terrible habit of mine. I was going to just snap my laptop shut at that point. Googling was not providing reassurance, as I had hoped, but was simply fanning the flames of my anxiety.

Google won, though and I visited one more site—a blog written by a woman who had the same experience: breast pain, felt a lump, needed to have a mammo and sono and then, well I couldn't find the follow up. Maybe she had cancer and just couldn't deal with it, so she never wrote the follow up, or maybe it was nothing and she just didn't bother to bring it up again. Either way, reading it convinced me that I should share this experience, that I wasn't being a melodramatic crybaby to find this whole thing unsettling. If someone else thought it was a blogworthy subject ... that was good enough for me. It's an important tool to warn women to take breast pain seriously. Plus, I think most of the women reading this will have either gone through a biopsy or will know someone who has.

I didn't put the symbolic pen to paper for quite a while, though. After booking my mammogram and sonogram for the following week, I really forgot all about the lump. I was doing what needed to be done and worrying wasn't going to change anything. As an extra measure, I made an appointment for a Halo test—my doctor had been pushing me to get one for two years. It's like a pap smear for your boobs. After making and canceling an appointment a few months before, I decided it was time.

Let me tell you—the sweater puppies had a tough two days. The Halo test sounds all gentle and benign—invoking images of angels and Beyoncé. It is more like something on loan from Guantanamo Bay. I will spare you the details, but if they have breast pumps in hell, they will be similar to this machine. But, and this is a big but—I am glad I did it. And I urge other women to do it, as well. It ferrets out abnormal cells that a mammo and sono might miss. It doesn't replace those tests though, so the next day I found myself being pancaked by those cold, hard plates. But honestly, compared to the Halo, it was a walk in the park. The mammo looked normal, so off I went confidently into the sono room. If the mammo didn't find anything, how bad could the sono be?

The radiologist did the sonogram himself and when he squinted at the screen and asked the technician, "Have we biopsied her yet?" it was a bit disconcerting. I answered for her, "No, you haven't. I was told about three years ago that I might need a biopsy, but then I received a letter stating that everything looked benign and I should just come back in six months." My mind reeled with the possibility that the letter was sent to me in error, that I should have had a biopsy then and that, however improbable, every test that I'd had since then missed the original problem, which now was three years more advanced than it would have been.

A check of my records indicated that it was a new lump—the one I had felt a week earlier. Ironically, when I tried to find the lump right before my mammogram, so the technician could place a sticker on it, I really couldn't. I put the sticker where I thought it was and told the tech that maybe it was just a cyclical thing. It wasn't. It was a 9 mm "complex mass." 9 mm sounds so ominous. Like there's a locked and loaded weapon residing in my breast. The doctor assured me that it wasn't overly large—only pea sized, but even a pea sized mass is disconcerting, especially when the doctor says you need a biopsy (and others, well-meaning as they are, say things like, "That's big!" and "That's not tiny! My lump was smaller than that.").

The "what-ifs" started on the car ride home. What if it's cancer? What if I have to tell the kids I have cancer? I don't even like to take antibiotics, what if I need chemo? I had to get it all out before walking in the house. I have to admit, there was even a shallow "what if" or two. Like most women, I have had a love/hate relationship with my breasts. When I was an "early bloomer," I hated the attention they brought me. My nickname was Dolly Parton and I walked around with hunched over shoulders. In my twenties, they seemed just right for my frame and by my thirties, they disappointed me. After three pregnancies and three years of breastfeeding, they were somewhat deflated. Then, a miraculous thing happened—after years of being underweight, I gained five pounds as I entered my forties and they perked right back up again. My formerly comfy B cup bras left me sore, with angry red imprints. A few weeks ago I went to Target and bought an armload of 34Cs. (I know it's not Victoria's Secret, but I bought five at Target for the amount I would have spent on one at VS. And they really are quite nice.) I am kind of ashamed about that completely shallow "what if". What if I lose my breasts when I'm finally filling out C cups? Come on. So many women lose their breasts and end up with better ones, end up alive—the most important thing. Look at Christina Applegate—she maintains that she'll have the "best boobs in the nursing home." And you know what, she's right.

That shallow "what if" is, arguably, the easiest one to contemplate. I'd miss my C cups, but I can certainly live without them. The others (radiation, chemo or worse)—not so easy. I tried to put everything out of my mind, but it was hard. Understandably, my mother and sisters were worried and called, giving me support and advice—which forced me to face facts and take action, when I would have preferred to just forget about it until my appointment. Of course, this was a good thing—I ended up switching to a much better radiologist, one specializing in women. If I kept my head in the sand, I would have stayed with the radiologist that had a receptionist explain the test to me (in five minutes), instead of switching to one that had a nurse speak with me about the test for forty minutes. (More importantly, this new radiologist is doing a core biopsy—more invasive—but also more accurate than the fine needle biopsy my old doctor planned to try first and she noticed a second spot she wants to check.) Unfortunately, my family is full of cancer experts. My mother, sister, father, grandmother and aunts all had cancer. All but my grandmother beat it and my grandmother's cancer was so advanced, that she only had a week to live when the doctor discovered it. We are a family of survivors, to be sure, but worriers as well. I have at times felt like a ticking time bomb thanks to my family history.

Even with all this weighing on me, I was still fairly calm, despite the "what-ifs?" Most of the time, I was too busy to think about it. But then I discovered that due to a communication mishap, I was actually six months late for my mammogram. I had booked my appointment this year, assuming that I was right on time. When I picked up my films from last year to bring to my new radiologist, I glanced at the report sent to my doctor. I felt physically sick, reading the closing line, "Continued clinical and mammographic vigilance is advised, including bilateral mammogram studies in 8/09." The only letter I had received advised me to get my annual mammogram.

The "what-ifs" came crashing back down. What if the 9 mm mass was just 3 or 6 mm last summer? What if it is something terrible? At first I was furious, blaming the radiologist, my doctor, swearing a lawsuit, but my righteous indignation crumpled when I learned that I had screwed up. Last year's check was only partial—my full mammogram was in September 2008 and I was due back in August. I really should have known that. I know I am my own worst enemy— over thinking everything and blaming myself. As the biopsy draws closer though, I am really trying to just forget about it. There isn't anything I can do—no amount of magical thinking will change the verdict. In a way it's not all bad—the fear has taught me to appreciate what I have—from my boobs to my family. I feel like shaking my fist, yelling, "Lesson learned. Good enough. I get it. Appreciate what I have."

And I do appreciate what I have. Really. While I was writing this, Aidan came over to me, wrapped those little arms around my neck, kissed me on the cheek and said, "You're the best mom. You will be my mom forever and ever and ever, right?" I answered, "Yes, of course, I'll be your mom forever and ever."

"And ever," he finished for me. Then, he added, "Even when I'm forty-nine, you'll still be my mom—right?" I hugged him close and overwhelmed by my love for him, said, "Yes, even when you are forty-nine, I will still be your mom." Kinehora*. Knock on wood. Fingers crossed and all those other things that chase away the evil eye. He hugged me again and I tried my best to chase away the "what-ifs," as well.

*Kinehora n : A curse in reverse. A colleague says with best intentions; "Looks like you're going to get a promotion, Jack." Kinehora! You quickly cover his mouth, for to utter such a thing is to ensure it will never happen—source: the Yiddish dictionary.

THE DINOSAUR

~ February 26, 2010 ~

I AM A DINOSAUR. A relic from the dark ages—the dark ages of pre-internet life. I have published at least thirty-five to forty articles, but there is no evidence in cyber space that I ever earned my keep as a journalist. Maybe earned my keep is a bit too strong—barely covered the rent and was really lucky to find a guy who would spot me a few on the first of each month, is more like it. But, I had a by-line. A regular one, until I quit my job as a calendar editor, as much as I loved it. I even loved lugging home the giant bags of mail—yes, that's right—actual snail mail. I couldn't wait to slice open the envelopes I received, pulling out glossy head shots and CDs, checking out the free tickets and media passes. I discovered some of my favorite musicians through those PR packages. When I slipped Edwin McCain's CD out of the envelope and into my boom box, it didn't come back out for months. I had to quit, though. I had no choice—the rent seemed to come pretty regularly and I really needed to find a way to pay it, without borrowing from my future husband, Jeff. When I left that job, I dipped my toes into the public relations pool, hoping for a bit more of a cushion with each pay check. I only lasted two weeks, though. I hated being on the other side of the fax machine (remember, this was the nineties), trying to get journalists to pay attention to my client. I wanted to be the one who was wooed.

Eventually, I found my niche as a music writer and I loved it—really, really loved it. Even in my earliest journalism jobs—writing for gift industry and art gallery magazines in college—interviewing gave me the biggest rush. I saw my subject as a puzzle that I had to unlock, by asking the right questions. Plus, I got to meet some really cool people—denizens of the underground Boston music scene and even some eighties and nineties era musical icons. I morphed into a fourteen-year-old when I met Howard Jones, stumbling over my words and gushing about how much I loved him in high school and college.

I almost had to pinch myself as I sat in the back room of a bar on Lansdowne Street in Boston interviewing Mike Peters of The Alarm. The local musicians were my favorites, though—feeling like I was right there at the start of something big. I was working on an article chronicling the struggle to make it in the Boston music scene—had pages and pages of notes in my ever present journalist's flip pad—when I split the muscles in my stomach coughing. I was eight months pregnant and my doctor warned me that it would just get worse if I sat at my desk, working on my computer. Most women get this split—diastasis—but, it affects only the bottom of the stomach—mine was on the bottom and top. I called T. Max, the editor at The Noise, and informed him that I would have to finish the article after giving birth.

I never finished it. Having a newborn didn't exactly mix with frequenting bars, hanging out with musicians. I was lucky if I was able to secure a willing relative to watch my baby, Drew, while I escaped to see Jeff's band, Tiring Sky, play. While Jeff's presence in the Boston music scene deepened, mine slipped away. His band released a CD to rave reviews—the magazines and newspaper I wrote for were the same ones that gushed over Tiring Sky's music. I however, was never published again. I still wrote. In fact, when Drew was a year old I took part in the most amazing, private, invitation only fiction workshop. Taught by Jill McCorkle and Elizabeth (Betsy) Cox, we gathered in a beautiful converted barn on Betsy's property in the Massachusetts countryside. I drove an hour each way and felt like I escaped from my life as a stay-at-home mom, falling back into my pre-baby writer's existence for a few hours each week. The women in the class all had MFAs and most were in the process of being published, if they weren't already. When Jill invited me (I had studied fiction with her at the New England Writers' Workshop for the previous three years), she told me that it would be "peaceful" for me and make me a happier mom. She was so wise. It did exactly that. It was short lived, though—as the other members went on to publish novels and short story collections, I just fell back into stay-at-home mom mode after the workshop ended. The following year, when I was six months pregnant with Joshua, we left Boston for Long Island and I lost my opportunity to attend another workshop. An entire decade passed—two more children, two dogs, the house, the van—without a workshop, without a byline, without a writing mentor.

When my youngest entered pre-school I started writing again—in bits and pieces. Sitting in my car while Aidan slept, the proverbial light bulb went off—an idea for a novel. I started writing it on a scrap of paper. One scrap became two, then moved into a notebook, then finally onto my computer. I started a writing workshop of my own at the library. I sent an excerpt of the novel off to an editor whom I knew. Only, she had left her publishing house the year before. But, she really liked the excerpt and told me that if she were still buying, she would want to see the whole manuscript. She advised me to get an agent. That novel is now eight chapters long, five of which still need to be rewritten. It's been a year since I swore I would get an agent, two years since I started the novel and still it languishes on my laptop, waiting to see the light of day. I gave myself until June to finish it or to at least reignite my writing career with freelance work. My deadline is looming and I haven't gotten paid for one written word. Worse yet—I don't know how to claw my way back in, especially since, according to the Internet, I never published a word.

This truly hit home when I attempted to set up a journalist's account on Typepad. Setting up an account required that I provide a link to published articles. I Googled myself in an attempt to find something, anything, that I had published lurking in some dusty corner of cyber space. All I could find was a mention of my name in an artist's bibliography. I had written about her in *The Improper Bostonian* in 1996. I searched *The Improper Bostonian*'s web site, hoping to find article archives. Nothing. *Northeast Performer*—nothing. *The Patriot Ledger*—nothing. Some publications I wrote for have gone belly up and the rest certainly don't have links to articles written in a different millennium. All of my work is contained in a Rubbermaid bin in the corner of my basement. I have been thinking about hauling it out, scanning all of it and setting up my own archives—a web site with all of my published writing—just to prove that I was once who I claim to be.

I am sure that I'm not the only one struggling to reclaim my career once a youngest child hits kindergarten—this scenario is being played out in home offices from Long Island to Laguna Beach. It is the age old dilemma (especially if your child attended nursery school for only a few brief hours, as all of mine did): After years of spending all day taking care of children, how do I reinvent myself now that I have a stretch of morning all the way into afternoon free? That question is even more complicated when our rapidly changing world makes ten years out of the workforce seem like a lifetime. And, many days I don't even have that stretch free—there are errands and laundry and volunteering for a myriad of things, but there are some days that I can get a chunk of work done. I really don't have the answers on how best to utilize those free moments, on how to use them to jump back into my livelihood.

In the meantime, I'm going to dust off my copy of *The Girlfriend's Guide to Getting Your Groove Back*, by Vicki Iovine. My mother gave it to me as a gift when my middle son, Joshua, was a toddler. I only read a few pages, before taking Iovine's advice not to even bother, since I still had a child in diapers. It might help me now, though—if I could just find it. The opportunity to "get my groove back" seemed so far off back then, that I packed the book away. Even before I was pregnant a third time, I hoped that when Joshua emerged from toddlerhood and made his way out into the big world of kindergarten, I would have another toddler waiting in the wings to take up my days. Well, now that toddler is riding a bus to school every day and doesn't return for six and a half hours. I can only hope that's plenty of time for this dinosaur to find a way to drag my career out of extinction...

A CORVETTE? AN AFFAIR?
UM, NO...

~ March 15, 2010 ~

REMEMBER GETTING EXCITED FOR BIRTHDAYS? Counting down the days until your party, dreaming about presents and cake? Of course those feelings of true birthday rapture are generally reserved for the pint sized set. But, even into my twenties, I looked forward to birthdays. The first time I truly dreaded a birthday was the year I turned twenty-four. I had recently broken up with my boyfriend of two and a half years and was facing my first birthday uncoupled since I turned twenty-one. (Of course turning twenty-one is amazing, coupled or not—I celebrated by jetting off to Jamaica for spring break.) The year I turned twenty-four was not quite like luxuriating on the beach in Jamaica. I was stuck in a cold, dreary suburb of Boston—living in an apartment building crawling with drug dealers. I had spent the better part of the previous month lying in bed eating Little Debbie Snack Cakes and feeling sorry for myself. I dragged myself to work that day and there on my desk was a gorgeous bouquet of flowers—sent to me by a girlfriend who knew I really needed it. (Thanks, Tina!) And, just like that, my birthday mood went from self-pity to gratitude for my great girlfriends.

Over the years my birthdays have swung the pendulum, as well. Twenty-six was hopeful—I had long since realized that awful breakup was really for the best and my on-again off-again relationship of almost a year was back on. My boyfriend took me out for a nice dinner and he gave me a gift certificate to my favorite bookstore. I knew we had something special and a gift that "really got me" confirmed it.

Twenty-seven was a tough one. Same boyfriend, but this time I expected something momentous for my birthday, something sparkly that slipped onto my left ring finger. He got me a keyboard—very thoughtful, considering that I told him I wanted to learn, but after almost two years together, well ... I just thought the logical next step wasn't something featuring ninety-nine different sounds. Twenty-nine the pendulum was back up—two surprise parties planned by that same dragging-his-heels boyfriend, only now he was my husband and helped me celebrate the last year of my twenties in both Boston and my native New York. Same thing for thirty—two more surprise parties—but, the most magical moment of turning thirty was feeling my baby move for the first time. There was no better way to celebrate a new decade than by growing a new life. I was pregnant for my thirty-sixth birthday, as well—but this time I celebrated with my first bout of morning sickness. Still special in its own way. Forty brought another surprise party (I don't know if I should worry that I married someone so adept at keeping a secret) and the excitement of a new decade, ripe with possibilities.

Forty-two is starting off quite nicely with Facebook wishes and a surprise package of my favorite candy arriving in the mail (thanks, Meri!), plus a new laptop, courtesy of my son's creative fingers (he made me a "banana computer," his take on the Apple Mac, featuring a complete keyboard drawn in painstaking detail). But, I can't shake this feeling that I am staring down the freight train of middle age and there really is no way off of the tracks. It will either flatten me or I can try to jump on and enjoy the ride. Is this the feeling that drives men to have affairs and buy shiny speed machines? Am I facing a mid-life crisis of my own? I can't afford a Corvette and I am really way too lousy of a liar to have an affair. (Unlike my husband who can pull off not one, but five surprise parties—I have managed to plan and execute only one—fourteen years ago for his twenty-ninth birthday.) And— besides the obvious fact that I love the man I have—after spending almost seventeen years learning the ins and outs of one guy, would I really want to start over with someone new? Um, no.

So, what other tonics are there for a mid-life crisis? Travel the world? No vacations for us right now, at least not more than a weekend and certainly not a vacation that would satiate a mid-life crisis—sans kids at an exotic locale. Start a new career? I finally managed to jumpstart my old one—publishing an essay in a local parenting magazine. I don't have the energy, nor do I have the desire, to branch out into something new. Another baby? I passed my self-imposed deadline to add to my family two years ago, but still haven't brought myself to give away the blue bin of baby clothes tucked under my basement stairs or the bin of maternity clothes right below it. But, a pregnancy is about as likely as an exotic vacation—as I mentioned in one of my previous essays, I'd need another husband, and as I mentioned in the paragraph above, I'm far too lazy to find one.

What's a forty-something girl to do? I already volunteer as much as my overstuffed life can possibly allow. I just finished collecting roughly 300 pairs of shoes for Haiti that I still need to pack up and send and I am already planning my next charity drive. Finish the novel languishing on my laptop? A great solution, if I could just get myself to do it. Maybe it's fear of failure holding me back. While it's still merely a file, I can hang onto the dream that it will eventually be on bookshelves. If I send it out and it gets rejected, well there's not much to look forward to other than social security and grandchildren with the thrill of teenagers (yikes) wedged in between.

Okay, that's not completely true—there's plenty to look forward to, but I just always assumed I would be a novelist, from my first creative writing class my freshman year of college. My teacher wrote on my final project, "To be a writer is to be ostracized and rejected, but when success comes and it will, it will be sweet." I believed her and I believed my junior year creative writing professor when he told me I would "make the big time." I just didn't think that over twenty years later, that "big time" would still seem as far away, if not farther, than it did when I was twenty-one. I know that's my own doing. I don't have a stack of rejection letters. In fact, a former editor at a major publishing house read an excerpt and suggested that I get an agent. Maybe a bit of a mid-life crisis is good—the impetus I need to take stock and do the one thing that I really can't put off anymore. I'm facing down that freight train and waiting for my moment to swing up and hitch a ride.

FAREWELL MY FRIEND

~ March 28, 2010 ~

AT TIMES HE IS CHEEKY, AT TIMES WISE, but always hardworking and very useful. He helped me take showers or just take a breather. He is a good friend—really a family member—who will be so hard to say goodbye to. But, say goodbye we must. I thought our relationship could hold out at least another six months or perhaps, dare I say it, a year. But alas, Thomas has left the building. Figuratively of course—we still have probably thousands of dollars-worth of the little blue engine and his friends, plus tracks, buildings, engine washes and even a pig that oinks residing in my basement. The train box is barricaded behind hockey nets and Legos—the detritus of three boys, but I really thought that when I offered to pull it out and build a track with my five-year-old, Aidan, the other day, he would jump at the chance. "I hate Thomas!!" he exclaimed in response, breaking my heart right then and there.

"But Aidan, we have so many cool trains—so many tracks and buildings. We could make a great track," I reasoned.

Aidan looked at me with the seriousness of a five-year-old determined to keep up with his two older brothers and their more worldly pursuits and offered, "Just have another baby and he can play with it." If only it were that easy. I am not giving the trains away, that much I know. Even if Aidan never casts an eye on them again, I will keep them for my grandchildren, no matter how much my husband begs me to clear out the space in our basement.

It's more than the money spent that gnaws away at me whenever I think of those poor abandoned engines, just gathering dust after being the objects of affection for so long. It seems as if saying goodbye to Thomas equals saying goodbye to early childhood. Yes, there is still plenty of adolescence left to go around my house. Nerf guns and footballs litter the living room, board games reside in the TV stand, but early childhood—that chubby fist maneuvering a train around the track while mouthing "Peep, peep"—well, that's just about gone.

My oldest son, Drew, loved Thomas with a passion. He never cried harder than when he was told he couldn't bring a Gordon train home with him from the toddler playgroup he had attended for the first time. It was his first venture out on his own, he had become a big brother a month earlier and it was all just too much for an almost two-and-a-half-year-old to take. But, there was Gordon, big and blue and strong and he made Drew feel so much safer that first day. He clung to that train like a lifeline. Of course he wanted to bring it home—he felt it was his payment for enduring two hours away from Mommy. The teacher let him that first time, provided that he return it two days later at his next playgroup. But that next time, he cried even harder when he needed to leave it, despite our assurances that it would be there for him to play with it when he returned. He lasted only a few more sessions—every time he had to leave that train, he would wail, even though I bought him his very own Gordon—it just wasn't worth the pain, his and mine.

Thomas even helped Drew potty train in record time six months after the Gordon debacle—cost me a pretty penny, but it was worth every dime, especially when Drew returned home with a new train and "introduced" him to all the old trains. I so miss those little moments, especially now that if Drew's not playing basketball or baseball or doing homework, he spends most of his precious free time on his iPod Touch, tuned out from the world.

We were sure Drew's baby brother, Joshua, would follow in Drew's footsteps and be a Thomas aficionado. But, by the time Joshua was old enough to emulate his big brother, Drew was a preschooler, already becoming enamored of Power Rangers and Super Heroes, much to my dismay. His Thomas back pack gave way to the Justice League one he just had to have for kindergarten. He still loved Thomas, though—enough that when he graduated kindergarten, his gift was a Thomas video.

Joshua was into Thomas for a brief time, but he truly loved those Power Rangers (which I despised—I was thrilled the day we sold most of them as a lot on eBay and donated the rest) and, thankfully, Rescue Heroes. The wholesome message of Rescue Heroes balanced out all of the nasty fighting in Power Rangers. In fact, far from selling our huge lot of Rescue Heroes on eBay, I've tried valiantly to get Aidan to play with them. No go. But, as much as he shunned Rescue Heroes, he embraced my beloved Thomas trains. He has rarely watched our vast library of Thomas videos and DVDs, but then again, he has never really watched TV—I can't take the credit for that, it is more a product of his sensory integration disorder. Television is just too much overload. Instead, he built tracks and begged for new trains and told stories about the Island of Sodor and sat in my lap every night while I regaled him with the tales featured in his giant Thomas anthology.

Then, we moved the Thomas trains into our basement in an effort to convert our overstuffed playroom into a less chaotic den. Yes, my den is now a den and not a catchall for every toy in the house (okay, that may be exaggerating just a bit—it's still a catchall, just marginally neater)—but, we lost Thomas and all his very useful friends in the process. Did I not realize that out of sight meant out of mind? Did I think Aidan would love Thomas right up until elementary school, even if he hardly played with his trains?

You may be wondering why putting Thomas in the basement seems tantamount to sending him to Siberia. My kids just don't play in my basement, even though it is finished (completely overhauled just six years ago, with nice comfy carpet and bright high hats), even though it looks like Toys 'R' Us mated with Sam Ash (the music emporium) and they had a love child. For one thing, it's cold in the winter—the heating vent is just below the ceiling, quite possibly one of the worst design flaws ever. For another, they just won't go down alone—whatever the reason, apparently the boogie man resides down there—and getting a sibling or parent to accompany one is often, I imagine, more trouble than it is worth. Drew is the exception—he goes down to play the drums, but he's not playing with Thomas and friends. And, if all the boys are down there, especially if my husband joins them, the only things being played are instruments. Thomas can't hold a candle to a family jam session, even to a five-year-old.

Instruments are one of the few things in our basement that actually hold Aidan's attention, at least for a bit. He didn't slide from little kid toys to medium kid pastimes, no superheroes or Bakugan for him. No, he enjoys more cerebral pursuits. Like multiplication and division and cube roots and converting Celsius degrees to Fahrenheit. He is, as his school's education specialist phrased it, a "math phenom". He was "off the bell curve" for cognitive math skills, scoring an astounding "above the 99.9 percentile" when he was evaluated for hearing services last month (which of course he didn't get, because the school just cannot believe that a child scoring in the very superior level on some things and low average to average on others could possibly need services, but that's another blog post). If I want to know the weather forecast, no need to check—I just have to ask Aidan and he can spout off the ten day forecast, complete with highs and lows and precipitation. I was wrong when I said he doesn't watch television. He watches channel 61 traffic and weather and will tell you it's, "Only on Cablevision, never on Fios, never on satellite. Know before you go." The exact tagline.

While other kids are playing superheroes, Aidan is doing negative number problems on his calculator (all he wanted for Valentine's Day was a calculator with negative number capability— he was extremely disappointed in the Hot Wheels pack and sticker book I bought him). All he wanted for Chanukah was a working otoscope, because he wants to be a pediatric otolaryngologist (an ear nose and throat doc) when he grows up. He looked at my tonsils with that otoscope and declared them a "plus three." You know what, he was right. He is amazing and unique and I love him just the way he is, but I sometimes worry that he may be missing out on something—that perhaps he's simply not playing enough. That's why I am mourning the loss of Thomas, that's why I am so hesitant to let him and his cheeky friends go. It has always been Aidan's connection to the magic of childhood.

Just seven months ago, we took Aidan and his brothers to Thomas' Day Out. His brothers didn't even want to go on the train ride, but Aidan jumped right on, clutching his conductor's certificate and staring around in awe. I'm afraid to contemplate what he would say now if we went, probably "No thanks, Mom — it's just a train." Recently, I called Aidan, "My baby." He looked at me and said, "Mom, you know you only call me your baby because I am your youngest. I'm not really a baby." Nope, I guess he's not.

TWICE EXCEPTIONAL

~ April 7, 2010 ~

IF YOU'VE READ SOME OF MY PREVIOUS BLOG POSTS, you know that I had a tough winter. My dog had cancer. I had three cancer scares. My son had strep so often, he nearly needed his tonsils out. Those cases of strep were right on the heels of swine flu, which was right on the heels of another son suffering from excruciatingly painful inflamed lymph nodes in his stomach. Yes, it was a tough winter. But, there was one thing that I didn't write about—something that was tougher than everything else—watching my son Joshua battle his demons. Joshua has OCD—obsessive compulsive disorder. OCD is a formidable enemy who can suck the joy out of parenting. Its fingers wrap around every facet of our lives, strangling all of us. It hurts my other children, as much as it hurts me and my husband. One son told us that he loves hanging out at a friend's house, "because at least everyone in his house is normal." Ouch.

Although, OCD is "more prevalent than many other childhood disorders or illnesses" (source: kidshealth.org), it is rarely mentioned in parenting magazines or even talked about. That's why I've decided to share my experience. The first time I read a description of OCD, a wave of relief washed over me—I had a name for the menace that transformed my son from a happy kid to one tormented by routines, unable to even get out of bed in the morning without an elaborate ritual of tapping and bouncing that left him exhausted before the day even began. With knowledge, I knew I could begin to help him heal.

OCD is usually diagnosed between the ages of seven and twelve years, however since children are often masters at hiding OCD rituals, a child may have been suffering for months or years before a diagnosis. (One study found that it took OCD sufferers, on average, a heart-breaking nine years to receive the correct diagnosis.) OCD often masquerades as other disorders—last year my son's teacher was convinced that he had ADHD and this is not uncommon. The obsessions and constant rituals make it difficult, if not impossible, for a child to concentrate. We were lucky, after six months and five therapists, we found one whom we love. She diagnosed Joshua with OCD right away. Looking back, it's amazing to me that the other therapists missed it. This underscores the fact that OCD is so easily overlooked, especially when children might not engage in noticeable repetitive behavior, such as hand washing.

Scientists believe that OCD tightens its grip on a child when either the flow of serotonin in the brain is blocked or, surprisingly, a child is exposed to a strep infection (25% of cases). It often occurs in conjunction with other disorders, such as ADHD, learning disorders and trichotillomania (defined by Wikipedia as "hair loss from a patient's repetitive self-pulling of hair"—a habit we are, unfortunately, all too familiar with, but which, mercifully, has seemed to have subsided). Similarly, OCD often goes hand in hand with giftedness—children with both are referred to as "twice exceptional" (as is every child with the yin and yang of any type of disability coexisting with giftedness).

Discovering the term "twice exceptional"—and the description that goes along with it—brought tears to my eyes. It was so familiar (actually resonating with me for two out of my three children, but that's another blog), that I felt as if I was reading about my own child. My son is gifted—this is objective, he is in the gifted program in his school—yet, last year he was barely completing his work. He has been in therapy since last spring and truly has made progress, but sometimes it seems as if we take one step forward, only to take three steps back. A cliché, I know, but never truer than in the case of OCD. When one ritual is tackled, another often springs up in its place. That getting out of bed routine I mentioned earlier—gone, thankfully—but of course there were others just waiting to take its place.

Last month, on the first warm day after a punishing winter, I knelt in my tiny garden and pruned away the dead branches and withered leaves that were crowding out the brave bits of green trying to push up through the hard ground. Within weeks, verdant leaves had filled in all the sparse spots. By trimming the dead excess away, I allowed new life to emerge in its place. Unfortunately, OCD is the same—but, it's not lovely foliage springing up, it's debilitating new routines. Prune away some old ones and new ones quickly fill in the open spot. It is frustrating and depressing and downright scary. When Joshua told me he wanted to "kill the OCD with a machete," my heart gripped in fear that he really wanted to use that machete on himself, even though he insisted that was not the case. And yes, I know that he can't get his hands on a machete, nor can he secure anything else to do much damage, but he is still a child. What if we don't conquer OCD before he is a teenager or an adult?

I really can't contemplate that now, because I will become so mired in my own fears, that I won't be able to be strong for Joshua. I need to just encourage him to put one foot in front of the other every day and keep moving forward. When anxiety has him in its white knuckled grip, I tell him to imagine the future—his life as a grown up. He tells me that he wants to be an orthopedist and have four children—two boys and two girls. He will drive a Mustang (though this changes—it was a Prius, then a Ferrari, then a hybrid crossover, the name of which I can't recall). He will also be a master chef and cook for his family every night. Most importantly, he will move up the street from our house, because he "loves our neighborhood." When Joshua dreams like this—big dreams for a bright future, I believe him. I truly believe that one day all those routines will seem far away, like they happened to another person. But, right now it is so hard to watch such a brilliant, vibrant boy crushed by fear, doubt and a prison of rituals.

LOVE STORY

~ April 26, 2010 ~

I'VE RECENTLY SPENT A HUGE CHUNK OF TIME working on an essay for a contest sponsored by *Redbook Magazine* and *A Cup of Comfort* books entitled, *Your Love Story*. I used to devour *Redbook* every month when I was in my twenties, sometimes reading the whole issue in one sitting. Once I had kids, I let my subscription slide in favor of *Baby Talk, American Baby, Parents, Parenting, Family Fun*... You name it, if there was a mag on raising children; it arrived at my doorstep each month.

Eventually, I let all but my *Parents* subscription expire—my kids were getting bigger and I didn't need the handholding of those glossy, comforting pages. With only one magazine coming in (which was near its end, as well), I treated myself to a *Redbook* subscription. It was only $5 for a whole year and I couldn't resist the bargain and the chance to get reacquainted with an old friend. When my first issue arrived, I couldn't believe it—right there below the editor's letter was the call for essays. It was kismet—for years I read the magazine only once or twice a year as a treat and the first issue of my subscription arrived with this opportunity staring me in the face. That was in late January and it provided a bit of optimism during the dark days of winter. The deadline was April 20th and of course, I worked on it until April 20th. It just didn't seem done, though—something rang false and again a stroke of kismet—the deadline was extended five days.

I am a text book procrastinator—I really can't get going on a project until a deadline is looming, when my adrenaline is flowing and my fingers finally fly over the keyboard. So, it was really no surprise that I kept revising until the eleventh hour. But, it did surprise me how much I enjoyed the process—okay, maybe not at the very end when I was nibbling on my nails and rubbing my eyes and swearing that if I had to read that stupid essay one more time, I was going to pull my hair out. But, I did enjoy the process of writing my love story, our love story. I remembered the night I ran into my husband, Jeff, on the street. I could see what he was wearing, could remember the flip of my stomach when I turned around and saw him. I remembered what it felt like when he stood behind me as we ordered a late night pizza—the charge between us. I reminisced about what he was like as a bad boy rocker, before the responsible disaster recovery specialist took over. The day he proposed was like yesterday in my mind—a fallen log at Walden Pond, a song written just for me, beginning with, "You're the sugar for my sweet tooth. You're the keeper of my private truth," and ending with, "Stephanie, will you marry me." The moment we returned to Walden Pond two years later and decided that we were ready to start a family came flowing back, as well.

Writing the essay also forced me to revisit tough times—breaking up with Jeff every three months for a year, because he was incapable of committing, our difficult first year of marriage, when my sister was battling cancer and I felt constantly ill from survivor's guilt; not to mention an ongoing inner ear infection; a small, but steady gas leak in our apartment; and bottoming out hypoglycemia. I chose not to mention the gas leak—I just didn't have enough space. I also left out the fact that on the first night we ran into each other, in a fit of vanity I took off my glasses and placed them in my jacket pocket. They promptly fell out and I spent a good chunk of the night on my hands and knees on the sticky floor of a bar peering under tables, hoping to spot them. I never did find them and, ironically, they were a replacement for the same exact pair I had lost while on a date seven months before. Those fell out of my pocket into the ocean and floated away as my date and I stood on the beach and watched helplessly. Remembering that nugget of information reminded me of how vain I was in my twenties, never letting a guy I was interested in see me wearing my glasses. That was the unexpected benefit of telling this story—remembering who I was before I had children (good or bad), before wife and mother came first in my description of myself. It was also interesting to find what I left out and what made it in—2,000 words really isn't a whole heck of a lot of space in which to tell a story spanning seventeen years.

Of course, the essay had to spin into the present day, into where our love story took us, not just where it started. One of the themes of the contest was how something that could have torn you apart has made you stronger. I had to admit that Jeff and I have been on the brink of disaster many times parenting a child for whom just getting through the day is sometimes a seemingly insurmountable task (see the previous essay *Twice Exceptional*). But, in writing about it, I was able to appreciate the fact that after many battles and rounds of blame, we are finally working together as a team in trying to help our child.

I know that the chances of my essay winning are pretty slim — I'm sure there are thousands of entries in which couples have emerged from the darkness of more earth shattering road blocks — but, win or lose, I've gained something precious. How often does one really take the time to reflect upon the origin of one's union, to really get down the narrative of one's own love story? Not too often, I would imagine, in our running around lives ... Here's an excerpt from that contest entry, the opening ...

We met on a night when spring turned into the anticipation of summer and even though a chill hung in the air, I knew warmth was just a breath away. I was twenty-five years old and treading the murky waters between adolescence and true adulthood. Yes, I was living on my own—doing laundry, paying bills—but, I had only myself and my own little world to worry about. No children, no significant other. I had sworn off men sixth months earlier. A year of therapy had helped me get over a devastating (at the time) breakup. I was working out regularly and felt stronger than ever—happy on my own.

Walking down Boylston Street in Boston, I heard my name drift out from the doorway of one of the trendy, packed bars. Turning, I saw a guy whom I had a crush on years earlier in college. I was a senior in high school visiting the University of Massachusetts, Amherst the first time I laid eyes on my future husband, Jeff. He was a freshman at UMass working in the school store. My friend grabbed my arm and whispered, "I have such a crush on that guy." I glanced over and there he was—leaning into the beverage case, unloading bottles. His muscular arms extended into the refrigerator case, sinewy and framed by a soft blue sweatshirt, the sleeves cut off to expose perfect biceps. Faded Levi's hugged his undeniably cute butt. Even his glossy, chestnut mullet, fringing over the collar of his sweatshirt was sexy (this was 1986, after all). I sucked in my breath. "Do they all look like that here?" I asked.

I attended the University of Massachusetts the following September and although I did see Jeff around—I was in the audience many times as he pounded the drums for one of the hottest bands on campus—we never dated (though, we did meet once through friends). I was dating my high school sweetheart my whole freshman year and Jeff left school at the end of my sophomore year to live in Boston with his band. I fell into another serious relationship that continued beyond college—that breakup I mentioned. By the time I was twenty-five, I hadn't thought about Jeff in ages.

But, on that night—that spring night whispering with possibilities—all the giddiness of a schoolgirl crush rushed back. Jeff wasn't the one who called my name—that was our mutual friend—but, he was the one I saw first and my heart somersaulted into my throat. The pushed up sleeves of his cream shirt set off his still sinewy arms. His long chestnut hair still fringed over his collar and, face to face for the first time, I noticed his striking eyes—amber, circled by green. We talked the whole night—he even admitted that he had asked our mutual friend about me two years earlier, but was told that I had a boyfriend. I felt the charge between us and wished that I had known earlier that I had piqued his interest too. It would have made that terrible break-up much easier to bear, had I known the hot drummer who caught my eye years earlier was interested in me...

THE MELTDOWN

~ May 4, 2010 ~

"GET OUT OF MY BED!!! I WANT DADDY!!!" Aidan, my 5½-year-old, screamed this, while alternately pushing me off his bed and hitting me. I have lain on top of his covers next to him, while he cuddles underneath, almost every night for six months—since he moved into a big boy bed and suddenly couldn't fall asleep on his own. He's my youngest, so I know all too well how fleeting those falling asleep moments are. I'm more than willing to comfort him as he drifts off. How could I not? Aidan still smells like a baby as he's falling asleep, damp hair scented with Johnson and Johnson's Baby Wash. For a few moments I can believe that I still have a little one, rather than a constantly evolving school age child. But, my sweet, little one had suddenly morphed into a very small, very pissed off teenager. It was my fault—one tiny mistake that I made, one sleep dazed slip of the tongue—and I paid dearly.

Aidan was finishing his book report next to me on the couch. It was already 9:00 and he should have been sleeping. In the after school frenzy of snacks and baseball practice, I forgot to have him do his homework. I thought it would be better if he stayed up a few minutes late to finish it, rather than doing it in the morning. I, however, could not stay up for even a few more minutes and found myself dozing off. In my dream state—I truly do not know what I was thinking—I told Aidan he "needed to take pride" in his work. Seriously, he's in kindergarten—I think I dreamed that I was scolding my sixth grader or maybe even my third grader whose goal in homework is to finish it as quickly as possible. Aidan on the other hand is meticulous—he has fine motor delays and works so hard on every assignment, because it is so difficult for him. Had I been awake, I would have never in a million years uttered those words. As soon as Aidan started wailing, "What's wrong with my picture?" my eyes snapped open and I gushed, "Great drawing! That's a bear at a table, right?"

Too late. Aidan was inconsolable—he said that I hated him and that I thought his work was terrible. He asked me to "white it out and make a copy," so he could make a new picture. After I managed to get him to his room, he climbed under his covers gripping the book report in his fist, then threw it in the Sesame Street garbage can next to his bed. He cried and cried and then I cried too. I was helpless—he's my baby and I made him miserable. He sobbed that he couldn't bring it into school the next day, because then he'd have to tell his teacher that I thought his work was terrible. No matter what I said, I could not convince him that I loved the picture and that I was proud of him. His brother even explained to him that by saying, "Take pride in your work," I meant that he should be proud of it, because it was so good. Aidan was quiet for a moment, contemplating, and I thought the problem was solved, until he started wailing again, "You hate me. You think my work is terrible. I can't bring it in!"

My husband, Jeff, switched with me and convinced Aidan to give me a hug. But when I tried to hug him, Aidan simply pushed me away and started crying again. I curled up next to him, and did the only thing I could—cried too—but, that just made him even more agitated. Jeff told me to just go downstairs and leave Aidan alone. "I can't," I protested. "That would be admitting defeat."

"Grow up," he admonished. "You don't always have to have the last word." But, he didn't get it, I didn't want to beat Aidan at some game, I didn't want to get in the last word—by defeat I meant that I would have to admit that I couldn't make him feel better. That was the crux of the whole matter and why I was so determined to make him realize that I loved that picture, that I've loved every picture that he's ever drawn—from scribbles to faces. I couldn't bear the thought of my baby being so sad and it being my fault. As a mom, I'm used to soothing bruised feelings from the slings and arrows of others' words, not my own—we all are. My self-worth is tied up pretty tightly with my children's happiness. It's like the old saying, "You are only as happy as your saddest child." Or, more simply put—if your kids aren't happy, neither are you.

I know that an awful lot of my stress and tears over Aidan's anguish stemmed from circumstances that had nothing to do with him. I had passed the twenty-four-hour mark on a nasty migraine and was beyond exhausted, having spent the whole day cleaning the house, despite the pain. Plus, I knew that Jeff was heading out of town after the kids fell asleep and that I would need to put out any lingering fires in the morning on my own. I just wanted to know that Aidan was happy as he fell asleep and that he would wake up happy in the morning, knowing that Mommy is his biggest fan.

Before Jeff left, he confided that he couldn't understand why I "needed everything solved before going to bed." It was true—I did want everything solved before going to bed. My mantra in marriage is "Never go to bed angry." Why would it be any different in parenting? Part of me also wanted it solved, because seeing Aidan that devastated made me panic that perhaps he's pathologically sensitive. Having one child with emotional struggles puts you on high alert for your other children, as well. But, of course I couldn't solve it before bed. I shouldn't have even tried. Aidan fell asleep as I lay next to him, just like he does every night, but I knew he fell asleep hurt and angry and that broke my heart. Wouldn't you know it, though—when he came into my room at the crack of dawn; he was happy as could be. He crawled into bed next to me, threw his plump little arm around my neck and whispered, "I love you, Mommy! So much!"

A's dark mood had dissipated in the thin light of morning, like fog being burned off by the sun. Jeff was right—he told me that there was no point in trying to match wits with an overtired five-year-old. No amount of words could have made Aidan feel better—sleep was the only tincture. I had braced myself for a continuation of the previous night's meltdown that morning—but, when I asked Aidan what the picture was about, so I could write a caption for him, he simply smiled and answered, "A bear at the table. The bear doesn't have manners, so he is thinking about them." I wrote the caption as relief washed over me, then told him again how much I loved the picture.

My migraine was still going strong that morning, even after I knew that Aidan was just fine. It would last through most of the day, before suddenly lifting—pain, then no pain. There really wasn't much I could do to hurry it along—it simply had to run its course. I'll try to remember that when dealing with my kids—sometimes you have to just let them be sad or hurt or angry, let the feelings run their course without trying to fix everything. I was afraid that Aidan's hurt and anger would linger for days; that perhaps he would never trust me with his creations again after that one comment, for fear that I would strike them down—of course that was ridiculous and my own tired brain talking. So, the next time a meltdown bubbles up, I will resist the urge to fix it right away. Okay, I will try really, really hard to resist the urge to fix it right away, even if my tears flow as freely as the kids'.

A BITTERSWEET PLACE

~ *May 13, 2010* ~

"SO, HAVE YOU BOOKED A PLACE YET?" I dread those words, yet I am hearing them with more and more frequency as sixth grade draws to a close for my son and seventh grade—replete with bar mitzvahs every weekend—looms on the horizon. I know that each party will outshine the last, that nubile young dancers will entice both kids and adults onto the floor—a practice I find creepy at best. (Sorry if that offends anyone—but, come on—lycra-clad, cleavage bearing young women dancing with barely pubescent boys?) I know that flash will rule and the centerpieces will likely be breathtaking. That is not me, nor is it my son—I think. But, when he starts reveling at party after party, will he be disappointed in a more down to earth celebration?

A bar mitzvah on Long Island can easily run upwards of $40,000 to $50,000—all that glitz doesn't come cheap. But, when I do the math in my head, I realize that if I shell out that kind of cash to host three bar mitzvahs—with a grand total likely well over $120,000—I will blow my opportunity to move my family into a bigger home or perhaps to send my children to college without loans—that's if I even manage to scrape together that serious a chunk of change. If not, if I steal from Peter to pay Paul—running up credit card debt—well, I don't think we'd ever escape from that kind of financial hole. So, I've been doing the only thing I can—not thinking about it and hoping I win the lottery.

When I asked Drew what he wants, his response was actually, "No party." He wants to go to Israel. This shocked me—I expected him to want the whole shebang—or at least a lower key whole shebang. Unfortunately, right now Israel is not an option, but perhaps someday—maybe when my youngest becomes a bar mitzvah. I would imagine it is far easier to travel to Israel with three teenagers, than with a thirteen-year-old, an eleven-year-old and a seven-year-old. My kids are restless on a drive from Long Island to Boston. We practically have to bring an entire refrigerator in the car with us. Traveling halfway around the world? Not going to be ready for that in a year and a half.

So, with Israel off the table, Drew wants a "sports party." He would be happy as a pig in poop with a bar mitzvah in which sports was the only thing on the menu. Okay—food, yes—but, no dresses and monkey suits, no dance floor, no overactive MC. So, that leaves me with the decision—do I rent a sports facility—maybe the Y—and have a party that Drew and the kids love, but the grown-ups could pass on? Or do I go for the sedate luncheon—with a DJ, of course? Good food, hopefully good conversation and lots to celebrate with friends and family. Do I follow in my family's tradition and go for the whole shebang? Well, $40,000 for a party is out of the question, but I could cut out the photo booth and the air brush stand and the dancers and—I guess I'd have to cut a lot. Drew only wants a chocolate fountain—we can do that. Not at the Y, though.

This all seemed to come about so quickly. I got his date almost two and a half years ago and it seemed so far away—almost four years. Way too long to even think about it, but now it's creeping up. I still have a year and five months to plan. I planned a wedding in a year; I think I can plan a bar mitzvah in that time. Maybe my hesitancy has more to do with my inability to even digest the notion that I will have a teenager—a man according to Jewish law—in such a short time. When did this happen? How did this happen? It truly seems like I was just pregnant for the first time—the most magical pregnancy of all three. Everything seemed like a miracle—everything was a miracle. I even felt movement for the first time on my thirtieth birthday—what a gift. My mother told me, "Enjoy the first one—there's nothing like it." Boy was she right.

You know, after I wrote the paragraph above, I got seriously choked up—tears spilling onto my cheeks. And, I realized that this blog post is actually about something far different than I thought it was about. I was musing about the craziness, the "Keeping Up with the Steins" aspect of planning a bar mitzvah and how I just want to avoid it, how I just want to stick my head under a pillow every time I think about catering halls and DJs and menus. But, now I see that it's really about my reluctance to face the fact that my first baby is growing up—that before I know it, he will be a man. It dawned on me a few weeks ago that I am as close to having my first child leave the nest for college as I am to my last pregnancy. I am halfway between the early stages of an empty nest and childbearing. It is a bittersweet place to be. I am proud of the young man Drew is well on his way to becoming, but sometimes I yearn to go back to the small child he was.

It seems like yesterday that I was planning Drew's third birthday party—not thirteenth. I pulled out all the stops—it was the first birthday party we hosted in our very own backyard—not the shared square of grass outside of our apartment. I spent days painting three cardboard boxes blue, red and green, then painstakingly drawing on faces, transforming the boxes into Thomas, James and Percy. I printed out railroad tickets and spread out a lavish brunch. (At least lavish by three-year-old party standards—mini quiches and assorted pasta salads didn't show up on most toddler party menus.) If the last nine years went by that fast, how quickly will the next nine go?

When I hug Drew now, he is solid. He is only a fraction shorter than I am and his shoes are far bigger than mine on the boot tray. But, I hold onto the fact that I am still a pretty important person in his life, at least for now. For Mother's Day, he wrote me a song. As he sang and strummed his guitar, my eyes filled with tears. He crooned, "I love you, Mom. I always will. When my heart's empty, you make it full." I can only hope he feels that way even when he's grown into a man...

THE RUSH

~ May 22, 2010 ~

LIKE AN ACTION HERO racing to defuse a bomb before it detonates, I kept one eye on the clock as the moments ticked away — 12:48, 12:49. I had two minutes to reach my destination. I screeched to a halt in front of the building, cradling my precious delivery as I jumped out of the car. I sped down the hall, dodging obstacles. The fate of the world depended on my getting the delivery into the right hands by 12:50 PM. Huffing and puffing from the exertion (this action hero forgot to take her inhaler); I made it with only seconds to spare. "Aidan needs this right now," I gasped. The sour gate keeper looked me up and down disdainfully, as she silently took the *Clifford* book from me.

She glared at me as she spoke into the phone, "Send Aidan down. His mother just brought his library book." She may as well have said, "Send Aidan down. His mother is here to sell him on the black market," her tone was so disgusted. I beat a hasty retreat to the hallway and waited for Aidan to come down. I knew my lingering was frowned upon, but I just had to make sure he got the book on time and I wanted to see that smiling face. I was handsomely rewarded for my efforts — I received a smile, a hug and a "Thanks, Mommy!" Mission accomplished.

Okay, I didn't screech to a halt in front of the building — it is a school, after all. And, I did pause for a moment to turn on my hazard lights, lest anyone think that I was planning on leaving my car smack dab in front of the entrance. The objects I was dodging were kindergarteners on their way back from recess, not bullets. And, of course the fate of the world didn't depend on my delivering a *Clifford* book to school before my kindergartener went to library. But, the happiness of a five-year-old did and—let's be honest—the self-esteem of a mom did too. Aidan told me before school that he needed his library book, because apparently he is way more organized at five, than I am at forty-two. He actually remembers which day it is in the six-day cycle and what special he is attending that day. I am usually stumbling about, trying to get everyone dressed and out the door and can't remember anything.

In a panic, I realized that his library book was not in the basket by the front door (in which I corral backpacks, library books, musical instruments, etc. in an effort to combat my natural tendency to lose all things the day they are needed for school). I sent Aidan to school and promised him that I would deliver the book before he had library. I spent the morning out at my son, Joshua's, field day, completely forgetting my promise until half an hour before the book needed to be there. I frantically looked under the couches—the most likely spot for a *Clifford* book to hide. Not there, nor was it under Aidan's bed; between the couch cushions; under the kitchen table; in the storage ottoman; on the office desk; in the newspaper bin or any of the other gazillion places I checked.

I sat down on the couch, head in my hands. It was 12:44—I had six minutes to get it to him and couldn't find it anywhere. Of course, he has forgotten his book before, and it was just fine—he brings it back the next day and goes without a book that week. Losing books was nothing new either—I paid the public library for *Tuck Everlasting*, then found it a few weeks later sitting on the book shelf, camouflaged among all the other paperbacks—never even read. But, for some reason this time I felt like not being able to find that damn library book just hammered home my inability to keep track of the avalanche of things my children bring into our home every day. Trip permission slips, reading logs, you name it—when something is due back in school; I spend way too much time scrambling to find it. Eyeing my den, I was overcome with frustration and a touch of despair. I felt like a disorganized failure. Why couldn't I get my act together and just get everything cleaned up and organized? I actually asked one of my kid's therapists if one is a hoarder if all one hoards are school papers and toys. Thankfully, the answer was "no." But, that didn't make me feel that much better.

My head still in my hands, I stared at the floor. A corner of yellow caught my eye. Turning, I noticed a large picture book. I had glanced at it as I looked under the couch, but didn't think to look under it. It was big enough to cover a *Clifford* chapter book. I slowly lifted one corner and sure enough, there it was—*The Stormy Day Rescue*. I was filled with joy. That's the good thing about disorganization—when you finally find what you are looking for, it is exhilarating, even if your blood pressure is sky rocketing at that point. I glanced at the clock—12:46. I had four minutes to get the book to school. That's the other thing about disorganization—it certainly keeps life interesting, with the adrenaline pumping rush to get something where it needs to be at the very last minute. Oh wait, that's not interesting, that's just really stressful. I truly plan on getting more organized, before I'm forced into another white knuckle race to the school. Fine, I'll admit the chances of that happening are slim to none, but a girl can always hope...

BEWARE THIS TOUCH

~ June 14, 2010 ~

I HATE THE IPOD TOUCH—hate it with a passion. Hatred of this intensity is generally reserved for cheating lovers, dirty politicians and rival sports teams, not palm-sized inanimate objects. But, nothing raises my ire like that hand-held spawn of the devil. It wrecks my mornings, makes homework time a nightmare and renders dinner table conversation non-existent. Yes, I know it is in my control to not allow it at these times—but, it finds its way in, even after I have taken it away. Both of my older boys, Drew and Joshua, have one and I often threaten, as I snatch it out of their hands, to not return it until their respective 18th birthdays. I also know that I should just hide it, but Drew is merely a fraction of an inch shorter than I; there really isn't anywhere I can hide it that he can't reach. And, even though Joshua is more diminutive, he is a little monkey and climbs on counters and desks peering into spaces far above his head. This of course sends my heart rate soaring and my blood pressure spiraling ever upward—one more reason to hate the iPod, since that is usually what he is searching for.

The only way I can truly control it, is execution style—a hammer to its sleek touch screen. The touch screen isn't so sleek on Joshua's iPod anymore—decorated as it is with fingerprint smears and scratches. Every time I see it, I wonder about the logic in giving a child still in the single digits a $200 toy. Drew's is relatively pristine—sure, it has fingerprints, it is a touch screen after all, but he keeps it in a case. When he's not playing with it (which is far more often than Joshua is not playing with it—Drew spends a good chunk of his free time shooting hoops), he stores it somewhere safe. Joshua can never find his, and when he does, it is often under the couch, getting even more scuffed up. It's really not Joshua's fault—it's mine for expecting a nine-year- old to take care of something so delicate. A child on the cusp of the teen years is much better suited to that job.

I am far from alone in bestowing such a responsibility on my child. According to Joshua, "Everyone in the third grade has an iPod Touch." That's hardly true, plenty of parents stand firm or simply can't afford one. Believe me, I couldn't afford to buy him one either. He saved up his money and hoarded gift cards he received for his birthday to purchase it. I was truly on the fence in deciding whether or not to allow him to buy it, so of course I turned to the biggest body of parenting experts I know—my Facebook friends. The consensus seemed to be that the iPod was worth the extra money and allowed for a richer gaming experience than the DSi (though, of course there were dissenters). They actually weren't far apart price wise. And, considering that the games for the iPod are often free and generally not more than $5, while DSi games run at least $15—$30 a pop (and come with plastic packaging), it seemed like a greener, more economical choice. But, I think the DSi would have caused me less stress. It's meant to be a toy, not a tech gadget, and it snaps shut, protecting the screen. But, Joshua wanted the Touch and nothing but the Touch.

I didn't hate it at first—it seemed like a wonderful way to calm Joshua down and even taught him a bit about responsibility. If he didn't feed his virtual fish, it would die. I guess the animosity settled in when I realized that Joshua was taking great care of his virtual pets and neglecting his real pets. Time playing with our dogs gave way to time playing Tap Fish. Feeding his fish and harvesting zombies on Tap Farm distracted him from the only real world pet responsibility he has—feeding his frogs, Lily and Swampy, every Monday and Thursday. Oh they got fed on those days, but only because I nagged him.

It has reminded me a bit, but only a bit, of the Tamigotchi. Remember those? How many hours did I spend making sure those stupid eggs hatched and the "pet" was given his snack, so my kids would be spared the agony of watching the little angel float up and off the screen? Too many. But really, the only thing the Tamogotchi and the iPod have in common is the time wasting factor. The iPod touch is like the Tamigotchi's older, more sophisticated, racy cousin—you know, the one who gets caught smoking in the school bathroom, and gets a back tat and a belly button ring before graduation.

The iPod was supposed to be innocent fun, but unfortunately, it's sometimes anything but. I nearly had a coronary when I checked Joshua's history and saw that he had been viewing an f-bomb laced YouTube video—the Fred is Dead parody – among other things. Internet access was supposed to be disabled on his iPod, and I still haven't figured out how he got it back up and running. Knowing the Internet, in all its sordid glory, was at his fingertips, left me feeling faint. I'm sure there must be some way to install parental controls, but I haven't figured it out yet. I simply disabled Internet again and I make sure I am hovering over him at all times.

Instead of bringing people closer and making the world smaller, in the case of children, the Internet creates a chasm in families—tech instead of talk—and thrusts our babies into uncharted waters, best navigated by a person at least old enough to legally down a beer while surfing. So, the other day when Joshua begged me for a netbook, because his friend has one, my answer was a firm, "No." I don't care how many gift cards he amasses or how much cash he has stashed in his wallet. Plus, if anyone in this family gets a netbook, it's going to be me.

THE DREAM

~ *August 3, 2010* ~

I HAD A DREAM THE OTHER NIGHT that I was talking to an ex-boyfriend. I told him that I was lost in my twenties (the decade during which we dated), my thirties were a haze of sleep deprivation and anxiety, and in my forties I had finally grown into myself. I hadn't spoken to or even thought about this person in ages, yet he showed up in my dream—a symbol of my past. Waking up, I had the oddest sensation of an epiphany. Shaking the sleep off, I suddenly remembered the dream and wondered if my slumbering self was trying to tell me something. Had I discovered a nugget of truth during my sleep? Was I really more content at forty-two years old than I was at twenty-five years old?

Turning forty had filled me with an awful foreboding—if my life were a movie, somber music would play and dark clouds would roll across the screen every time I thought about it. But, even though two years past that milestone birthday I am not even close to where I thought I would be at this point (which you know, if you read an earlier essay—*The Dinosaur*), maybe I am more content. I was sure that I would be a published novelist, or at least have a regular column in a magazine by forty years old. I was sure I would be living in a big, neat house, perhaps with a cleaning woman to tidy up after the kids. I am not quite at the coasting stage yet, though. I am still at the establishing myself stage. Whether that's necessarily a bad thing—well, I haven't quite figured that out.

Obviously, I would love to be a success at this point in my life, instead of still struggling, but maybe the struggle itself keeps you young—keeps you on your toes. Plus, the older you are when you succeed, the sweeter it is. My first writing teacher penned a message in my notebook at the end of the semester. I memorized it almost before her pen left the paper, it resonated so: "To be a writer is a truly honorable thing. You will be ostracized and rejected, but when success comes—and it will—it will be sweet." When I read that (over and over again), I felt sure that success was maybe ten years away, not over twenty and counting. But, the message still stands all these years later—success, whenever it comes, will always be sweet. But, what if it doesn't—how do you reinvent yourself then?

These questions that we ask ourselves are part of the beauty of growing older. When you're young, the questions don't revolve around the big picture. At least they didn't for me. In my teens, they revolved around school, friends, teenage love. In my twenties, they revolved around college and then work, yes, but mostly the questions revolved around love still—my brain was consumed with my relationships. I took writing classes, I worked as a journalist, but mostly I mourned the end of one relationship, obsessed over the beginning and progress of another, with a few relationships sprinkled in between. I planned my wedding and got pregnant right before saying, "goodbye" to my twenties—married at twenty-eight years old, pregnant at twenty-nine years old.

My thirties obsession was motherhood. New motherhood, especially. I had my first baby at thirty years old and pretty much spent the entire decade either pregnant, nursing or chasing a toddler. My youngest child exited the toddler years the same year I exited my thirties. At times I feel that decade is a blur of diapers, vomit and spit out peas. And sometimes, I'll see a young mother with a toddler and a baby and think, *Did I appreciate it when I was there? Did I stare at that rosebud mouth? Did I gaze in wonder at the impossibly long eyelashes fringing over porcelain skin?* I don't really know the answer and it kills me. Yes, I do remember moments of pure baby bliss, of simply realizing how lucky I was. But, just as often I can only recall running on fumes, completely frazzled and sleep deprived. I saw one such young mother at the pediatrician's office yesterday. Her daughters were about the same age difference as my two oldest boys. I told her to enjoy her two-and-a-half-year-old and five month old. "Enjoy them before they talk back to you," I advised her. And this is where I believe becoming a parent in your late thirties or early forties trumps younger entry into the ranks of motherhood—just like success, it's sweeter. Waiting for anything makes one appreciate it more and with age, comes wisdom and the ability to truly feel blessed, rather than overwhelmed.

Of course, ruminating over the past isn't going to do anything to help me appreciate the present. Soon enough, I'll be looking at parents of twelve year olds and saying, "Appreciate them before they are driving, before they leave your home." I realized this morning that I am exactly the same distance from my last pregnancy as I am from my first child leaving for college—six years. Quite frankly, I'm a bit scared of the teenage years. My oldest son, Drew, and I were walking home from a street fair behind a group of teenagers—two boys and two girls. Their conversation was peppered with f-bombs. One of the girls actually joked about being raped. "Oh, I only liked to be raped on Tuesdays!" she squealed. I wanted to grab her by the shoulders, shake her and say "Do you even realize how horrible it is to be raped? Do you even realize that your life is destroyed?" Instead I whispered to Drew, "The dumbing down of our youth. The Snookification of America. It's sad." Mercifully, though he is a voracious consumer of pop culture, he did not know who Snooki is. He simply said, "Mom, can we walk around the corner, please?" I asked if he was worried that they'd hear me talking about them. He answered simply, "I just really don't want to hear them talking anymore. Who knows what they'll say next." I was incredibly relieved. I was horrified that he had to listen to them, but when I voiced my concern at that first f-bomb, he told me he'd heard worse. Yikes.

We took the long way home, glancing into houses lit up in the soft summer night. Drew tried to cup a firefly in his hands, jumping up to reach it—a glimpse of the small child he used to be. I put my arm around his shoulder, which is the same height as my shoulder now, and told him that I know he will move into his teenage years as a thoughtful, articulate young man. Did I breathe in everything about that moment—the balmy August night, the firefly dancing above us, just the two of us on a walk? Of course I did. Being on the other side of forty has taught me something, you know. And, that is the nugget of truth my slumbering self was trying to tell me.

TIME MACHINE

~ *October 25, 2010* ~

I STUMBLED INTO A TIME MACHINE RECENTLY—no, it wasn't a magical hot tub, nor was it something out of HG Wells. It wasn't even a fourth dimension wormhole. My time machine was a red folder, the color softened with age, the edges frayed. It was stuffed with pages and pages of my past—short stories, novel excerpts, personal essays and tiny scraps of paper, scribbled notes from which I hoped fully formed work would spring. The folder had been sitting in a tote bag in the cubby of my desk, ignored since my mother had handed it to me a few months earlier when cleaning out her basement. I knew that once I started looking through it, I would be tempted to linger for hours, probing for treasure, so I set it aside and quite frankly forgot about it.

When I found it again, I decided to just take a quick glance—but, it sucked me in. Page after page illustrated that I was (as my friend, Scott, put it after I sent him an excerpt of the novel I was writing in college) "a funny chick." In my last blog post, I wrote that I was lost in my twenties, but most of these pages (written between the ages of twenty-one years and twenty-five years) proved that I was anything but. Finding them seemed like a gift—a chance to travel back in time and relive the passion, the dreams, the innocence and even the self-knowledge that it would all end soon enough, that I was on the cusp of adulthood and I better enjoy my free youth while I could.

This is an excerpt of that novel (but not the funny one, that's too R rated for this book)—this scene takes place on the last night before graduation:

"... As I float off, I let my mind wander through the last four years, a journey seen through the haze of impending sleep, but with the startling clarity of thoughts poised on the brink of a new beginning.

What have I learned? What do I leave this whole experience with? With Jake breathing softly next to me and the perfume of a May night swirling through the room, filling my sleepy senses, I realize that we make our own lighthouses, those small moments when you can see the whole world around you and you realize right then that you are exactly where you want to be."

Yes, melodramatic—I was twenty-two years old, after all. But although it was fiction, my protagonist, Sam, felt what I felt. Lighthouses were a big theme—here's another excerpt, same theme:

"As I sit here by myself, listening to the rain beat down on the roof, I realize that I've taken that leap across the shimmering water to the lighthouse in my mind. I've reached it and I'll reach it again. As long as there are crisp cellophane wrapped roses to open and breath in with sweet cards attached, as long as there are babies to hold, smelling of Desitin and baby lotion, as long as Jake loves me, whether from far away or close by, as long as I do what I want and love with my heart and soul, as long as I let the everyday occurrences warm me and the special moments surprise and enchant me, I'll keep reaching that place. Because we make our own lighthouses, those small moments when you can see the whole world around you and you realize right then, you are exactly where you want to be."

That boasts perhaps the longest run on sentence around, but you get the point. I think this was an alternate ending—one I wrote a year or two after the first. It surprised me, because I didn't remember being that hopeful. I remembered feeling adrift, missing my boyfriend and feeling caught between youth and adulthood, trying to decide if I should move out of my parents' house or not. It was so very odd revisiting this moment—yes, it's fiction, but it was inspired by a moment in my life when I was twenty-three years old.

Traveling back to the eighties, even if just in my mind, seemed particularly ironic (and bittersweet) just a few days later, when my father suffered a stroke and lost a chunk of his memory. His brain spun back and planted him firmly in his life twenty-five years earlier. At one point, he got out of bed in the hospital, tubes and all, because he had to "get to work at the place." The place, as he called work, was a girls' clothing factory, of which he was the general manager. It closed in the mid-eighties. But, that's where he landed — a work morning decades earlier—and I started to think, if I had to relive any moment in my life, which would it be? Yes, the stroke was horrible and scary and you never, ever want it to happen, but he didn't seem unhappy at first, just confused, even though the rest of us were torn apart and devastated. Thankfully, though his short term memory is still iffy, he is back in 2010 with us and will hopefully continue to improve. But, I can't help but wonder what sparked landing there? Was that a happy time and in order to cope with the trauma, his brain let him relive it?

Sometimes, I wish I could hop in a time machine and travel back to when my kids were babies—I know in my previous essay, I mentioned how completely crazy and stressed I was as a new mom, but the more I thought about it, the more I realized that there were moments of great joy, as well. Moments of pure bliss. My boys didn't talk back to me. They loved me no matter what—I couldn't screw up. Now, "I hate you," is a really close second to "I love you." I know it's just part of growing up—asserting independence—and more often than not I get a heartfelt apology. But, it still stings.

Other times I think that if I could relive anything, it would be college—a moment in time when anything was possible and the future stretched out in front of me. A time when my personality was untouched by work stress, then parenting, then just the daily grind of keeping a household up and running—I was a combination of badass and sweet (a description that I found in a creased and faded love letter to me). I don't know if it's possible to be that combination on the other side of forty, or even thirty, or if I'd even want to be. It's one thing to be a badass when you have no one relying on you, except perhaps a boyfriend, quite another when you have three children, two dogs and a husband. If I ever do find a way to fit into a wormhole or if I stumble upon a magical hot tub, it's very likely that I'd decide to just stay put. As tempting as it is to imagine flying free, I think I'd be content with just visiting my past lives on the papers stuffed in that faded red folder.

I'M A SCREAMER

~ December 14, 2010 ~

IF MY SHAMELESS ATTEMPT to a get a few extra clicks beyond my regular readers (you know I love you) worked and you are expecting a bit of erotica, sorry—this is a classic horror story of the spinning head and split pea soup variety. Okay, so I'm not quite as bad as Linda Blair, but I do act possessed far too much for my liking. Enough that sometimes I scream at my kids so loudly, I hurt my own ears and feel like my head is exploding. Far worse though than the burgeoning headache and sore throat that follow my losing it, is the shame, not to mention shame's cousin—guilt.

The other day my fourth grader, Joshua, was just dawdling—dawdling and causing my blood pressure to spike. When I told him he needed to hurry it up, he responded, "Why are you so mad? It's just school, it's not like you're going to get arrested if I'm late!"

The reason for my anger—his teacher asked me to get him to school early, but despite my best efforts, I can't get him there more than two minutes before the door closes. And, when he gets there just in the nick of time, his younger brother (whose teacher also wants him there early) gets there just in the nick of time, as well. So, when Joshua started playing with the dog, instead of getting his shoes on and then decided to put away a Wii game lying on the floor, my blood was boiling. I thought, Really? The moment we need to leave for school, he decides to clean up—not the gazillion times he was asked to before... and the demon voice reared its ugly head. "GET YOUR JACKET ON NOOOOWWWW!!!"

Joshua looked at me with such shock and sadness, it killed me. "That just proves that you don't love me," he said quietly. "You would be happier if I lived on the street. I just know it." Now, of course I know he was playing me, but I do think he was upset and hurt. I am always dumfounded when my kids say, "Why did you yell at me? You could have just asked," after I've asked nicely for something about a dozen times to no avail. I have to scream, because I am not heard when I speak softly. Even simply yelling doesn't do the trick—only a true scream gets their attention. But, that doesn't mean that it's not psychologically damaging—to both of us.

On the ride to school after my tirade I watched Joshua in the rearview mirror staring out the window. I swallowed—my throat was sore from screaming so loudly—and asked if he was okay. He didn't answer. When he got out, he gave me a kiss, but still looked haunted. There was a line of cars in front dropping off and a few cars pulling up behind me. The boys weren't late, but they weren't early either. Did any of the other parents feel as stressed as I did? I wondered. Or were they just happy to get their kids there before the door was locked. Was my making Joshua feel so bad worth it? Did he truly believe that I would be happier without him?

I knew that Joshua would be seeing the school social worker that day (he sees her to help ease his anxiety), and as I pulled out of the parking lot, I panicked that he would tell her that I screamed at him and that he didn't think I loved him. When I shared this with my husband, Jeff, he looked at me like I had three heads. "Do you really think she would worry about you? You're always concerned about Joshua. You always talk to her—you always care. Don't you think she sees parents who truly don't care? Who truly don't act like they love their children? It's completely ridiculous for you to worry."

Intellectually, I knew it was ridiculous, but still I saw the hurt in his eyes and felt like the worst parent in the world. The week before when I admitted to the social worker, an amazingly calm woman, that I sometimes used Joshua's participation in the gifted program as a bargaining chip to get him to do his homework, she counseled me to never do that and to simply tell him that I am proud of him. My screaming, if he reported it, cast me in an even worse light. What parent of a child with anxiety would make them feel as crappy as I made my bundle of nerves, Joshua, feel? Didn't I realize that the dawdling was because he was anxious to go to school and therefore was putting it off? I hung my jacket and scarf on a hook, then sat down on the landing and pulled off one boot, then the other. I felt weary and beaten down. I hung my head as the tears just spilled over and rolled down my cheeks, leaving tiny wet blossoms on the knees of my jeans.

I couldn't figure out why that morning had gotten to me. I yell at my kids on a pretty regular basis. It's a terrible habit and I hate it, but I hope that they understand that I only do it because, as I mentioned, I am often not heard. But, that morning I literally felt so furious that the scream was almost menacing. Jeff doesn't yell at the kids often, but when he does, they sit up and listen. His voice is, of course, much louder and deeper than mine and since he doesn't do it as often, it's not just white noise to them—they take notice. Perhaps that was the difference for Joshua—usually my yelling goes in one ear and out the other, because the boys are immune to it. It holds no weight. But, this time I screamed with every inch of my being and that shocked Joshua. It worked, of course—he put on his jacket and we left, but at what price?

I actually didn't get to see Joshua until almost 9:00 that night—I had a doctor's appointment before he got home from school. When I returned Jeff had already dropped Joshua off at a play date. Jeff picked him and his friend up before dinner and they headed directly to a birthday party. By the time Joshua returned at bedtime, he was tired out from rounds of Play Station at his buddy's house and an evening of laser tag. He hadn't eaten dinner at the party, because he never does, and between his exhaustion and hunger, he was cranky, but he did not mention the morning at all. I decided not to bring it up, even though I desperately wanted to know if he got over it and how quickly. Was he upset until recess or did the sadness evaporate by the time he sat down at his desk? I suppose it really didn't matter. There was not a damn thing I could do to change that morning, except say, "Sorry," which I already had. What's done is done. A cliché, yes, but still it made me feel a bit better.

We had a whole weekend to not rush—okay, not true, we had to rush to basketball on Saturday and Hebrew school on Sunday. Both times were agonizingly stressful, but I didn't scream. I also didn't scream today when the clock was ticking and shoes and jackets weren't on. Of course, we got to school at 9:18—three minutes after the door closed. But, when I walked the boys into school to sign them in, the woman at the front desk waved me away with, "They're fine. They can just go to their classes." I could only hope that their teachers were fine with it too. I suppose my children's perpetual last minuteness and lateness are poetic justice—payback, if you will. Yes, that's right—I was late far more often than I was early as a kid. (Full disclosure – as an adult, I'm still late far more often than I am early, but that's a whole other blog.) So, for all those missed buses in the seventies and eighties, for all those mad dashes into school, I guess there's only one thing to say, "Sorry, Mom! Now I know how you felt."

RESOLUTION

~ February 2, 2011 ~

EVERY YEAR ON NEW YEAR'S EVE, I sit down with a pretty piece of paper and a smooth flowing pen and record my resolutions for the year. Then, I promptly break them. I may just be setting myself up for failure, though. I think that the time to reflect upon resolutions should not be when the champagne bubbles (or in my case, sparkling cider) are still tickling your lips, but in the dreary days that follow. In the dark hollows of late January and February, it is so easy to lose the optimism and energy that spawn those declarations of bettering oneself. Do you really feel like hauling your tired ass to the gym, when it involves bundling up and slogging through the snow and slush? Curling up in front of a fire place (or even a space heater) sounds oh so much more inviting.

When it's bitterly cold, my butt wants to stay put, preferably with a bowl of something hot and a trashy magazine (mac and cheese and *Us* is a good combo—though one I hardly ever get to indulge in). Now that we are in the dead of winter, I wonder how many resolutions have already been broken. Even Target seems to have given up its aggressively optimistic flyers—last week's balance balls, free weights and sports bras have given way to chips, cookies and soda in this week's flyer. Yes, as we head toward the biggest couch potato event of the year—the Super Bowl—even mega chains realize they shouldn't bother pushing workout gear, since even the "desperate to keep that resolution" crowd has probably given up by this point of the deep freeze.

I'm not talking about those who already own equipment that they use every day or those who actually make use of their gym membership, hardening their muscles and whittling their waists on a regular basis (I count some of you as my friends, but I don't hold it against you). I'm talking about those of us who swore that this year would be different and are already back to using the recumbent bike in our bedroom as an extra dresser (guilty!). My resolution was to ride that bike more, okay—can't really say more if I never rode it before. My resolution was to start riding it. The bike is in my bedroom, with a place to rest a book, so I can read and exercise at the same time. I don't even have to step foot in the bitter wind. I can read a book while I exercise, for god sakes. Why can't I keep that ridiculously easy resolution? Well, life gets in the way. Laundry, cleaning, packing lunches and making dinner (even if it's in the microwave) just take up so much damn real estate in my life. Add in running errands, breaking up fights and of course Facebook and, well, there's just no time for taking care of myself. And yes, Facebook is in there too—if I completely cut out Facebook, I could certainly ride the bike for fifteen minutes here and there.

Does it make it any better that I use Facebook for good, to help save homeless dogs and cats? Maybe, but I'd be lying if I said that I never clicked on pictures or commented on a status here or there. But, the biggest chunk of my time is spent posting dogs and cats to my rescue page and commenting on death row dogs' pictures. So, maybe I should just change my resolution to, "Save more animals this year." Perhaps that would be the best way to guarantee that one keeps resolutions—observe what you are doing, what's important to you and make that your resolution—to simply keep doing it. Is it reading to your child every night or at least most nights? Done! Is it donating to charities? Done again. Or maybe cooking more often (okay, can't claim that I do that, but I'm sure a lot of you out there do it already). Another easy resolution.

One of my favorite tricks to make myself feel productive is to put tasks I've already accomplished on my to-do list. I know it's cheating, but if I wrote a to-do list the night before, making beds and throwing in a load of laundry would be on it—so why not put it on, so I can have the gratification of checking it off? At least I know that at the end of the day, I won't be looking at a list of everything I haven't accomplished. Silly, I know. But, it's the same thing with making a resolution to just do more of the good stuff you are doing—you're practically guaranteed to succeed.

There are only three times that I recall actually keeping a resolution. Those three resolutions were the same: "get pregnant." It was incredibly optimistic or perhaps incredibly misguided for me to think that just by writing, "get pregnant" on my resolution list, I would. So many things could have upended my plan—infertility, health issues, economic issues—there are a myriad of reasons people can't have the family they want, when they want it. But, I was extraordinarily lucky to get pregnant each of those years I listed it as a resolution. And you know what, looking back at the end of the year, even though I had broken every other resolution to work out more, I felt like I had accomplished something great.

So, make some February resolutions instead of New Year's resolutions. Think about all of the good stuff you do now—even if it doesn't include working out and eating more fruits and vegetables—and put that on a list with the promise to simply keep doing whatever it may be. My list includes, "Reading to my son each night. Telling my kids I love them every day, even if it seems like I'm constantly yelling at them. Helping save homeless animals. Contributing to charity. Doing community service work." You get the idea. What it doesn't include is riding that damn bike. (Though, I do plan on starting to do it anyway, so hopefully it will make it onto next year's February resolutions, because it will be part of my routine by then. Hey, a girl can hope …)

THE NOTE

THERE HAS BEEN A LOT OF TALK LATELY in the news about bullying—its devastating effects; how to stop it; how to prevent it from happening at all. Unless you are living under a rock, you know that bullying is a crisis in our country that needs to be stopped—a completely preventable cause of death in healthy adolescents. The recent spate of bullying related suicides surely can make any parent shake in his or her shoes. Every time I read about a child who has killed himself or herself thanks to merciless taunting and physical aggression, I find myself extremely grateful that my older boys, ten and twelve years old, are neither bullied nor bullies. I really didn't think that I had to worry about my six-year-old son, at least not yet.

Boy was I wrong. My son, Aidan, a first grader came home from school in tears a few days ago—a boy who has teased him before had pushed him down during gym and put his hands around his neck (but didn't choke him, as my son sweetly pointed out—well, that makes it much better), then he spit on him. Aidan drew several pictures of the incident and was distraught enough that he was still talking about it at bedtime. The next morning, I wrote a note to his teacher, explaining what happened—not accusatory, just to give her a "heads up," since I knew Aidan didn't tell her.

I'm happy to say that I got a call from the gym teacher that afternoon, saying that the situation was taken care of and the offender had suffered consequences—a removal of privileges. I felt guilty—as nasty as his actions were, he is, after all, only six years old. Plus, she explained that while he admitted to doing it, it may have been out of excitement during a game. My guilt, however, dissipated when I received a second phone call at the end of the day. "There was an incident at recess," the gym teacher reported. The same boy had approached Aidan, who was drawing quietly in the corner, snatched the drawing out of Aidan's hand, then tore it in half. "Aidan was devastated," reported his teacher. "He was really bawling. But, I had the boy write a note to him apologizing."

Knowing Aidan had to endure having his picture ripped apart in front of him (a picture that he no doubt worked very hard on) was like a knife in my heart. "He just wants to draw during recess," I said quietly. "He draws all seven continents, the equator and the prime meridian." Aidan loves geography and he prefers drawing maps of the world to playing superheroes or tag with the other boys. I know this is unusual—Aidan is, quite frankly, brilliant (this is objective—he scored above the 99.99th percentile for cognitive skills when he was evaluated in kindergarten). He is also unique (his favorite thing to watch on television is the weather and he knows exactly where Kazakhstan—and pretty much everywhere else on the globe—is) and this combination, more than ever, makes me terrified that he will be a target as he gets older. I just didn't think that it would happen so soon. But let's face it, kids hone in on anyone who is different.

Aidan's gym teacher warned me that he would probably still be distraught when he arrived home. To my surprise, he was happy when he walked in the door. I asked him what happened and if he was still upset. He told me to look in his folder. In it I found the apology note his teacher mentioned. I took it out and Aidan asked me to read it to him. (It was written in a typical first grader's scrawling hand, with phonetically spelled words, so it was difficult for him to read.) A smile spread over his face as I read the note and he pointed out where the boy signed it with a heart. He carried that note around for the rest of the day and asked me to reread it often. I'm proud that Aidan was able to forgive easily, that he was able to drink in that note and let it fill him with peace.

I truly hope that the note is sincere and Aidan won't be tormented again during recess and gym. I truly hope that he won't become one of the bullied. I'm optimistic, after all six year olds are malleable. They can be taught compassion much more easily than teenagers can—when habits of nastiness are entrenched and not easily melted away. I'm sure this boy is sweet most of the time and I'm sure that his mom was not happy when she got the call either. Both of us are in a stressful spot—two sides of the same coin. I don't know her—if I did I would call and tell her that they'll probably be friends someday. I hope that this is the case and I wish that bullying in the middle schools and high schools could fixed with as simple a salve as a note. Who knows, maybe if Phoebe Prince (the teen from Ireland living in Massachusetts, a victim of brutal bullying, committed suicide just over a year ago) had received a note from her tormentors offering a sincere apology, she would have thought twice before taking her own life. I know it's not likely, but one never knows what just a bit of compassion can do. Too many young people have followed in her footsteps. It is the school's responsibility to make the bullies reach out to their victims, to make them look them in the eye and say, "I'm sorry" and truly mean it. Punishment alone is not enough—forging a path to forgiveness, as well is the only solution—even if it's forced at first.

I'm grateful that my son's school has a zero tolerance policy and took action as soon as the transgression was reported. I'm also thankful that my son felt comfortable enough to tell his gym teacher the second time he was victimized. But, more than anything I'm happy that he seems to have emerged unscathed (so far), thanks to that simple note. High schools and middle schools where bullying is rampant could learn a thing or two from these first graders.

VALENTINE'S DAY

~ February 22, 2011 ~

I USED TO HATE VALENTINE'S DAY. If there was a "bah humbug" term for February 14th, I would have uttered it all through my early to mid-twenties. In my early twenties, I was simply disappointed—either I wasn't dating anyone, or my boyfriend just didn't measure up. But, there were some lean years when Valentine's Day wasn't just disappointing—it was the darkest day of the year. Even when I started dating my future husband, I just felt it was a lot of pressure to be perfect, when life is often anything but.

The Valentine's Day I remember most clearly from the days I was dating my husband, Jeff, was a disaster. It was a snowy weeknight and by the time we both got home from work and he fought the traffic from his apartment just south of Boston to my apartment just west of Boston, every romantic restaurant was jam packed with couples more organized than we were. Why hadn't we thought to make a reservation? Why didn't I just meet him in Boston, so we could get an earlier start? Who knows what we were thinking? We drove around the snowy streets looking for someplace, any place, with a romantic vibe. Finally, we settled for our usual—a neighborhood pub with a mostly young, single crowd—and ate our chicken sandwiches while trying to hear each other over the din of come-ons and desperation.

That night simply didn't live up to expectations, though I'm sure I was fairly happy just being with Jeff. A year earlier my Valentine's Day was something out of a clichéd single girl sitcom. My roommate and I decided to treat ourselves to dinner, since neither of us had a valentine. I planned on ordering salmon, mashed potatoes and a decadent dessert. I was going to enjoy the meal and the conversation. That is, until I walked into the lobby of the restaurant and saw my ex-boyfriend (who was my Valentine the three previous years) on a Valentine's Day date. Not only was it awkward for me, he was clearly flustered, since he introduced my roommate, whom he had known for years, by the wrong name. It was so bad it was funny—well, maybe not right away. Let's just say I imbibed a good deal of white wine with dinner that night.

The year before was almost as bad—it was the beginning of the end for me and that ex. Sitting across from each other at our romantic dinner, I gazed at him as he pulled out a small black velvet box. I sucked in my breath—I had been waiting for this moment for months. We talked about getting married all the time and I couldn't believe he was finally asking me. My heart raced, tears sprang to my eyes. He opened his mouth to speak as I rolled the "yes" around my tongue, practicing in my head how I would respond—loudly, so the whole restaurant cheered or a whisper, so the moment stayed between us. He placed the box in my hands, as I listened for the words I had been waiting to hear, the "yes" ready to burst forth ... Only, I never heard them. Instead of saying, "Yes," I found myself asking, "What??"

My ex repeated himself, "It's not an engagement ring." I downed my vodka and cranberry and motioned to the waitress for another. Then I slowly opened the box. That lovely black velvet box, that "just the right size" box contained a pair of earrings. Beautiful earrings to be sure—amethysts surrounded by gold swirls dusted with diamonds—but still, just earrings. I couldn't hide my disappointment. I was dumbfounded. We had talked about getting married for over a year and when I saw that box, well I just jumped to the nearest logical conclusion.

Of course now that I am a grown up, I realize that it would have been a huge mistake. I was a month shy of twenty-four years old. My boyfriend was just a couple of weeks shy of twenty-three years old. We were kids. His reason for not giving me a ring was perfectly valid—he wanted me to gain weight and he dangled that ring in front of me like a carrot. As a parent who has dangled plenty of fancy carrots in front of a child who just won't eat, I see the irony. And I could spend an entire blog post exploring my past and how my son's refusal to eat feels like the worst possible karma, but that is for another time. I also completely understand it. Simply put—if we had stayed together long enough to get married; we probably would have been divorced by now. We were just too young. He was just twenty and I was twenty-one when we started dating. So, of course it was for the best, but when we broke up two days later, it felt like my world came crashing down. After that year and the restaurant debacle of the next, I was ready to swear off of Valentine's Day. I wanted to wear all black and a frown as my only accessory on February 14th.

But, a funny thing happens when you hate a holiday for no good reason at all—it's hard to stay hating it. Life changes and suddenly you may find yourself not only over your hatred of Valentine's Day, but actually looking forward to it. That turning point for me was my first Valentine's Day as an expectant mom at twenty-nine. I was almost three months pregnant and blissfully soaking in every joyous moment of first time pregnancy. I loved everything about it. But, I was not happy that Jeff was working Valentine's Day night as a DJ. I really didn't want to be alone—every moment being pregnant was special and that night should have been special too. When he told me he would be working, it just confirmed my belief that Valentine's Day was simply a big disappointment—too much pressure and it's never perfect.

Perhaps knowing how much it meant to me (and having to balance that with the need to bring in some extra cash as our family grew), Jeff proposed a solution. We would celebrate Valentine's morning, instead of Valentine's night. Since I was exhausted by 7:00 pm after a day of creating life, I jumped at the chance to celebrate when I was actually alert and upright. We went to our favorite breakfast haunt—a charming little restaurant that served the best banana walnut pancakes. Much better than a fancy dinner, those banana walnut pancakes satisfied my cravings like nothing else. After breakfast we wandered into the gift boutique next door. While I sniffed candles and inspected picture frames, Jeff surreptitiously bought me my Valentine's Day gift—*The Pregnancy Journal* (Chronicle Books). It was so special—exactly what I wanted, with a place to record all of my thoughts, dreams and pregnancy minutia. We didn't have the night, but the morning was great and thirteen years later, I still remember every moment like it was yesterday.

The following year cemented Valentine's Day as one of my favorite holidays—back in my good graces again. Before I hated V-Day, I loved it—when I was a little girl my father always brought me gifts. Some years it was fancy chocolates, some years stuffed animals—one year I even remember getting pearl earrings. In high school I had a sweet boyfriend who made Valentine's Day special and even sent me candy hearts all through college. The year I was thirty was better than all of those combined. I had the perfect Valentine—one with whom I could cuddle, one who loved me unconditionally and always made me smile—my baby. Drew was five and a half months on Valentine's Day and I made sure he had a special present—his first drum. It had miniature plastic drumsticks attached, so he could bang on it and when he pressed a large button, it played an electronic drum track worthy of an eighties pop song. Last year I was going through baby toys to give away and Drew grabbed that drum. He brought it up to his room and kept it. He's an amazingly talented percussionist now, playing in both the school band and on occasion the symphonic orchestra. Yes, his dad is an amazing drummer too, but who knows—maybe that first drum set him on a musical path.

I know it set me on a path—to relishing Valentine's Day. I have three boys now and every year I buy each of them a small, but special present, candy and a card. Even more importantly, my two younger boys still make me cards. And I know that even though that little baby who reminded me how wonderful Valentine's Day can be is now a big boy in seventh grade, he still appreciates my Valentine's Day gifts. When he saw that his brothers got die cast cars for Valentine's Day this year, along with candy, while he had only candy, he was disappointed. That is until I told him to look in his card, where he found a pile of scratch tickets. A grin spread across his face—he wasn't too old to get a Valentine's Day present from his mom. I know I need to enjoy celebrating Valentine's Day with my kids now. In a few years, Drew will be in his mid- teens and probably have his own Valentine. But for now, Valentine's Day is really more about the kids.

Of course, celebrating with one's children leaves less time for celebrating with one's spouse. This year Jeff and I ate lunch at Cosi surrounded by moms with preschoolers and business people on lunch break. Then, we did a grocery run at Trader Joe's next door. Not exactly the height of romance, but at least we were together and really, is Valentine's Day about the roses, candy and jewelry, or is it about showing love in little ways? A fancy dinner at a stuffy restaurant or holding hands and locking eyes over pizza and a salad—even if it's at a restaurant where you order at the counter? I vote for the pizza and salad. And, I vote for looking for true love—the true Valentine's Day spirit—in places where you least expect it.

My favorite Valentine's Day moment this year? Watching my six-year-old, Aidan, read a Valentine's Day card to our dogs. He spotted the card when we were Valentine shopping and insisted I buy it. (Yes, they make Valentine's Day cards for dogs.) I explained to him that we didn't need to buy it, because the dogs can't read.

"But, we can just read it to them," he reasoned. I couldn't argue with his logic, so I bought the card and he carefully wrote it out. I'm glad I did. Watching him read the card to my dogs one at a time was by far the sweetest, purest, most full of love Valentine's Day moment I've ever witnessed. And that is the perfect reason to cherish Valentine's Day—now and for years to come.

TEACHING TOLERANCE

~ April 15, 2011 ~

CLEANING UP THE KITCHEN THE OTHER NIGHT, I found a purple Post-It note stuck to the floor. I picked it up and squinted at the scrawled writing. "Who is ..." I paused and looked closer at the paper, "Gerald McGaybutt?" Hysterical laughter from my two older boys ensued. They thought it was great that I walked into their trap. I, however, wanted to cry. I have tried so hard to increase their compassion and open-mindedness. My kids would never, ever utter a racist comment, but it seems like prejudice against gay people is the last frontier. It infuriates me when I hear them toss out, "That's so gay."

I drill into them that all people are equal and whom a person loves is simply whom a person loves—no more, no less. Who are we to judge? The most important thing is being capable of love, not whom the object of desire is—man or woman. I tell them that I couldn't care less if they grow up to be gay—I just want them to be happy. I remind them about the kids they know with two moms. I tell them I have gay friends. I tell them that they have gay friends; they just don't realize it yet. I promise them that by the time they are in high school at least one or more of their friends will be gay—it's a statistical probability. I tell them that gay teens who are bullied may even kill themselves. I am turning myself inside out, trying to teach them tolerance.

What kills me even more is the possibility that others will think they learned their attitudes from me and my husband, Jeff. Nothing could be further from the truth. I worked in magazines and was an arts reporter, if I didn't feel comfortable with those different from me, I'd be in trouble. One of the reasons I fell for Jeff, was because he had zero homophobia. He had a gay friend who had a crush on him. This friend would sing little songs about how he wished Jeff was gay. Jeff didn't run away screaming. He laughed and was flattered. When we got engaged, this friend came over to me and said, "You won, bitch." I have to say, *I* was really flattered then. Jeff didn't care that the gay men I worked with asked me if he was available. He took it as a compliment.

I have been hit on by lesbians and I saw it as the highest praise. At a show Jeff's band played at the Hard Rock Café not long after I had given birth to my first child, a woman asked me to dance and told me I was beautiful. You know what, I was so appreciative—I thanked her (and yes, I danced with her, after telling her that my husband was on the drums, only so I didn't lead her on). I wasn't feeling very beautiful with the lack of sleep and she changed that. I feel like my kids should have inherited the compassion and openness gene.

There are glimmers of hope. They love watching Nate Berkus, the openly gay talk show host. (I love him too.) They watch HGTV and love *Color Splash* with David Bromstad, another openly gay host. My son will be on the art track next year and in high school, allowing him to build a portfolio and work toward a career in art even before college. He wants to go into sneaker design. Surely he will have gay friends. But, here's the thing—I don't think that my boys are homophobic. I don't think that they are hateful in their comments. I think if they found out that one of their good friends was gay, they would be just fine with it, supportive. I think that in middle school especially, "That's so gay" and other slurs are part of the vernacular. It's part of the way that kids speak and that needs to change. There needs to be some sort of tolerance program in school, specifically dealing with accepting others' sexual orientation. Because no matter how many *It Gets Better* videos a teen watches, no matter how many grown-ups tell him/her to be comfortable in who he/she is (and you would hope grown-ups will be the ones to tell a gay teen this), no matter how wonderful role models like Chris Colfer and Darren Criss in *Glee* are, if peers aren't accepting, it's a rocky road. And that is a damn shame.

THINGS LEFT UNSAID

~ May 17, 2011 ~

"THERE ARE ALWAYS THINGS LEFT UNFINISHED," the rabbi said as he turned from my father's body. We had been sitting in the hospital for hours and none of us could bear to leave, even though there was nothing left to do, nothing left to say. My father had been sent home the day before with, while not a clean bill of health, certainly an optimistic outlook that the episodes of chest discomfort, dizziness and fainting were behind him and a healthier tomorrow beckoned. The last thing that he had said to me when I left his house the night before was, "I feel good! I guess the stent fixed everything." Did he know that was the last time we would speak? I certainly didn't, so I merely answered, "Great! I'll see you tomorrow," and with a wave up the stairs to the room he was sitting in, I left.

I told the rabbi that I was devastated that I didn't say, "I love you," that I didn't climb the five stairs to lean over his chair and give him a hug. I just gave a short wave and said, "I'll see you tomorrow." Because, I did believe that we had tomorrow. I believed that there was plenty of time for hugs and plenty of time for "I love you." In the hospital during the previous week, I blew kisses (I had a sore throat and didn't want to bestow my germs) and said, "I love you," before leaving, because I didn't know what would happen. But that night my kids were waiting, and I was tired. And I really thought everything would be fine. Everything was fixed. I wasn't thinking that the next time I told my father I loved him his forehead would be ice cold when I kissed it; his face graying; his hands waxy and yellow. But really, unless someone has died from a long drawn out illness, whoever thinks it will be the last time? Whoever says everything they need to say?

I sometimes think it's easier for the living to have a loved one die after a long illness, because you have said all you need to say, you have prepared yourself and you know that person is finally at peace. Although, I would imagine the anticipation and knowledge that you are going to lose a loved one is equally painful, not to mention the pain of watching that person suffer. Quite frankly, it all sucks — whether you've said I love you at every opportunity and anticipate a quiet slipping away, or you've treated the moments before death as any other moment crowded into a lifetime of days. It sucks for the living. It sucks for the dying — but, I am glad that it was over quickly for my dad. I'm glad he didn't suffer and I'm glad he didn't know. Or did he?

Just before he passed away, he told my mother, "I love you. You know I love you." And he asked for a kiss. So, did he know? Was he sick of the hospitals and just didn't want to fight any more? That is my son's theory and increasingly mine, as well. Not that he wanted to die, but that he didn't want to live his life in and out of hospitals. He wanted to live vibrantly and fully, the way he did before a stroke robbed him of his short term memory eight months earlier. Before the stroke he went to the gym every day and walked miles. He looked much younger than his years and acted that way too, even after the stroke. But in the two months prior to his death, he was in three different hospitals four times. Who knows if he just decided, I'm not going back to the hospital and that's it? He said what he wanted to and I think he passed away knowing he was deeply loved.

Now, it's up to us, the living, to make peace with his passing, as well. It's not easy. And it's especially difficult during the season of rebirth. The flowers bloom. The sun shines. And still we grieve. It seems like it should be gray and rainy to match our moods, but even when that weather arrives, it doesn't do anything, except make us more depressed. My kids tell me that they can't stop thinking about their grandfather. They worry that no one will ever make them chocolate chip pancakes like he did. You know what? They are probably right. There are a lot of things that will never be the same.

It is the new normal, something I said often after his stroke. It's a new normal that will take months, even years to get used to. Someone told me recently that even decades after his father passed away, he still dreams about him. He still sees him and hears his voice. I still dream about my childhood pet that has been gone for almost twenty years, why should my father be any different? And, that's good. I want him to show up in my dreams and I want my kids to keep thinking about him, to keep hearing his voice and seeing his face as they did in the days following his death. We all did and he was telling each of us that it would be okay. My ten-year-old heard him say, "I love you" not once, but three times.

If my father were alive, he would tell me to stop worrying about the things I didn't say and just be glad about the things I did. A few days after he died, I confided in my husband that I just couldn't get over the fact that I didn't say, "I love you" the last time my father and I spoke. He answered, "I'll let you talk like that for a couple of more days and then I'm going to tell you to stop, because there's no point in beating yourself up over it." I knew he was right, but I bristled. "There are only two words you need to say," I informed him. "And one thing you need to do."

He was quiet for a moment and then offered, "I'm sorry?" "That's one," I answered. "And hug you?" he asked, hooking me close to him. "That's the other," I said quietly. I wasn't ready to forgive myself then, but I know I have to eventually. Beating one's self up is not the way to honor the dead. It was sudden. We didn't expect to have to say goodbye. There were things left unsaid. That's life. And death. But, perhaps the best way to move forward is to simply say, "I love you" often to those who remain, so the pain of things left unsaid at least has a purpose—to teach us to embrace the moments we have and to tell those around us how much they mean to us while we can.

CARPE DIEM

~ August 28, 2011 ~

Carpe Diem #1
Her pale blue eyes cloud over
As she speaks of him
The other one she could have loved
A wrinkle forms between light eyebrows
As she thinks of him
It could have been
She says
Out of sync
He was in a war
She got divorced
He got married
If I had just gone to see him
She says
I love my husband,
But I loved him too
It could have been
I think hard on this
He is dark
With eyes made of light
We are out of sync
He says
We can't be
Not now
Timing off
We can make the timing

I say
Because in twenty years
I don't want pale eyes that cloud over
And a wrinkle on my brow
Carpe Diem #2
I used to sit underneath the big oak tree
In my backyard
Drinking sticky, sweet lemonade
Reading romance novels
I believed the heroes and heroines lived up there
Ensconced in that cool green world
I knew at fifteen
That if I just stared long enough
At that lush canopy of thick green leaves
I would find all the answers
I would just know
Now, as I sit on my deck years later
The leaves seem achingly green,
But the sky is growing darker
And the clouds hang low
The heat stirs up in a breeze
That brushes my skin
Someone once told me
He always feels closer to God
During a storm
I sit back
Close my eyes
And wait for it to rain

I WENT INTO MY 4TH GRADE SON'S CLASSROOM to talk about my "writing life" a few months ago and the kids all asked me if I write poetry. They had just finished their poetry unit and would be holding a poet's celebration the following week. I told them, "No." I said that poetry made me a bit nervous and that I wasn't very good at it. I truly didn't remember ever writing poetry. And then, last night as I was moving pages and pages of writing from a cardboard box in the basement to a plastic bin in anticipation of Hurricane

Irene, I found the two poems above. I wrote both of them for a college creative writing class. Titled "Carpe Diem #1" and "Carpe Diem #2", I'm guessing that the assignment was to write two poems with the theme of carpe diem—seize the day.

I don't think I wrote much poetry after that—I focused on fiction and journalism, so finding these two poems was something of a gift. I don't know if they are even any good, but for some reason they speak to me. And even though I had forgotten writing them, as soon as I read them I remembered the emotion and experiences. I remember the woman with the star crossed love—I believe I interviewed her for a magazine I wrote for the summer before my senior year. I do remember that she seemed quite old, yet I wrote that I didn't want to be like her in just twenty years. Twenty-two years have passed. I don't feel old though, I feel in some ways as if I could still "seize the day." But, in some ways—it seems as if centuries have passed, as if I will never have another carpe diem moment again.

I have been thinking about the concept of carpe diem often lately, even before finding the poems. I went to a funeral for someone way too young to die and every single person in that overflowing chapel knew that this woman lived the motto of carpe diem from the moment of her terminal illness diagnosis until her last breath. She likely lived that way before (I unfortunately did not know her as well as I would have liked to—so I can't say for sure), but she caught the attention of everyone who crossed her path with the joyful spirit with which she embraced the days she had left. Although we had gone to high school together and lived in the same town as adults, it was really on Facebook that our friendship resided. But, based on our Facebook interactions alone, I felt we were friends. We exchanged messages and she left insightful and amusing comments on my posts. She always had a kind word to say and a mega-watt smile in every picture. I could tell from those pictures that she lived more authentically than most people in her short life.

So many of us just go through our days on autopilot—I know I do. Feed and clothe children; break up fights; run errands; wash and fold laundry; pick up toys; walk dogs and the list goes on. How many times do you stop and appreciate all that you have? How many times do you say, "Yes" to something that matters and "No" to everything else? I know for myself, the answer is rarely. There are nights that I lie in my bed and think, "What did I do today?" There are days that 10:00 pm rolls around and I couldn't tell you one thing that I accomplished that actually meant something more than getting the laundry off the couch or keeping my kids from killing each other. I have been working on a novel for so long and I finally had an opportunity to get it into the right hands — an amazing agent, but the days spin away from me and I still have not finished it. I feel as if that opportunity has just slipped right through my fingers — I did not seize the day. At least not yet.

There are so many lessons to be learned when someone lives his or her life so fully and authentically, no matter how short. This woman made more memories for her children than most parents do in a lifetime that is not cut tragically short. The rabbi at her funeral service talked about her bucket list. She tackled that bucket list and then some. She was an inspiration to everyone around her and a lesson in how to carpe diem.

Our younger selves didn't need a bucket list or a diagnosis or the death of a friend to know that coasting through our days is no way to live life. But, with children, work, laundry and countless obligations that's far too often what happens. Finding these poems when the notion of seizing the day is so fresh in my mind seems to me a sign. A sign that perhaps I should remember what that energy felt like, what that sense of possibility felt like. And that it's wise for all of us to seize the day while we can.

CRIME AND PUNISHMENT

~ *January 6, 2012* ~

THE PUNISHMENT SHOULD FIT THE CRIME. One would think that a school, of all places would follow this edict and my son's school generally does, but not this past week. If you have read the previous essay, *Twice Exceptional* , then you know that my son, Joshua, has been battling Obsessive Compulsive Disorder (OCD) for years. That blog post was written two years ago and while some things have gotten better, some have gotten far worse. His therapist warned us that entering middle school might cause a flare up of his symptoms. She couldn't have been more on target; he entered middle school and everything seemed to fall apart. He was even pulled out of the gifted program for doing poorly in his regular classes. This did nothing really, except make him feel hopeless.

A psychologist who tested him for a childhood OCD study at a major psychiatric hospital told me that he shouldn't be punished for his disability, because that is really what's interfering with his ability to function in school. "He is gifted," she reasoned, "And, he should be in a gifted program to challenge and engage him." Regardless of this being true, I knew that I couldn't protest his being pulled out of the program, because there is a district-wide policy that any child who receives a "C" in a class can't remain in this program. But, there was something that I could protest, something that left me shaking and furious when I happened to stop at the school office for another matter.

As I walked down the hall, I saw Joshua coming out of the main office, his lunch box in hand, a dejected look on his face. When I asked what was wrong, he told me that he had to eat his lunch while sitting in the main office, because a detention that he was to serve during recess actually included lunch, as well. The horrible crime that he was being punished for? He went to see his guidance counselor during class, because he was being bullied and felt distraught. He did not tell his teacher he was going, which is the crux of her complaint. Her first punishment was even harsher—she gave him a zero on the quiz he missed when he left. This brought his overall grade to an F, a grade that he had worked tirelessly to bring up. She decided that he should have known that they were having a quiz and should have told her that he was leaving, so therefore, he did not deserve a second chance—fail and that's final.

She told me this in a note, a long derisive note. I wrote a note back, explaining that he was being bullied (two other students were calling him "stupid" and "ugly," teasing him for a poor test grade and an eczema rash on his face) and at the moment he did not realize that he had a quiz, he simply wanted to feel safe. He did what grown-ups have always told him to do if he's bullied; he went to a trusted adult and told her what was happening. He told his teacher first and she told him it would be taken care of, but he needed to feel safe at that moment and not wait until it was "taken care of."

Because of his OCD and the distraction that it brews up in him, we requested that his teachers check his agenda and make sure that everything is in it and then sign the page. That spelling quiz was not in his agenda, so chances are that he didn't even know he had a quiz even before the kids teased him, even before he walked out the classroom door and down the hall to his guidance counselor.

I mentioned all of this in my note and I requested that his teacher show him compassion, that she allow him to take the quiz. I requested that the punishment fit the crime. I did not receive a note back and I found that F for the class, thanks to the zero, on his "in-progress report" on the school website. The Friday before winter break—a full four days after I wrote to her—I called the school and requested to speak with the principal. I was told that I needed to speak with the guidance counselor first. She called me back and informed me that she, the principal, the teacher and the school social worker decided that I was indeed right and that the punishment did not fit the crime. He would have a chance to take the test over again,

BOYS, DOGS AND CHAOS 111

but his teacher felt very strongly that he should suffer a consequence for what he did and that he would have to serve detention.

I was under the impression that the detention would be served during recess, because he already stays every ninth period for either band or extra help. This made sense to me and seemed a reasonable consequence for not telling his teacher he was leaving. All through the vacation, Joshua asked me if he would have to eat lunch during his detention, or if it would only be during recess. I assured him again and again that he could eat in the lunchroom and would only be punished during recess. "Why wouldn't they let you eat?" I asked him. "That's not right—I'm sure it's just during the fun part, recess."

Which brings me back to finding him leaving the office, lunch box in hand, a look of despair on his face—he did in fact have to eat his lunch in the main office, like a pariah, like he was ostracized. I was livid. I knew he didn't eat—OCD has affected his eating more than any other activity and it is hard enough for him to eat around friends in the lunch room. He has routines that he tries to hide, but when he can't, he just throws his lunch away. I am sure his hunger is why he has an even harder time in his afternoon classes than his morning classes. I knew when I saw him, that there was no way that he would have eaten a bite with a roomful of adults around him, especially adults whom he doesn't know.

I went into the office and confronted the poor secretary, asking her, "Is this acceptable—to have a child eat lunch in the office, all by himself?" But, of course she knew nothing and sent me to speak to the school psychologist. The psychologist admitted that she was "surprised" when she saw Joshua in the office, eating his lunch. She said that she felt bad for him, so she brought him some tests that he needed to complete. You see, Joshua is in the middle of the evaluation process, which hopefully will secure him an Individualized Education Plan (IEP), which truly makes this whole debacle even more unfathomable. Why would a teacher punish a child, one who has a documented mental health disability, so harshly?

I was fuming at this point, so I told the psychologist that I wanted my child switched into a different class; that he's a square peg who doesn't fit into the teacher's view of an ideal student and he'll never get a fair shake. She told me she couldn't help me, and that I should speak to the vice principal. Off I went to the vice principal's office.

Halfway through explaining the situation to the vice principal (who was very sympathetic), Joshua's guidance counselor walked in and asked to join us. She explained that it was she who decided that Joshua should serve his detention during the entire lunch period, rather than just recess, not his teacher. She explained that it is common practice when a child receives a lunch detention that it is for the duration of the lunch period and that they need to eat wherever they are serving their punishment. She apologized profusely that I didn't realize that his punishment would encompass lunch. She said, "No one can understand how difficult it is for you on a daily basis." She said that she felt terrible that I was so upset.

I appreciated her apology and her sympathy, I really did, but had I realized that his detention encompassed lunch, I would never in a million years have agreed to it as a punishment. When I initially spoke with his guidance counselor about Joshua's punishment, I was at Target and perhaps it was hard to hear or perhaps it was just unfathomable to me that a child with such severe anxiety surrounding food—an anxiety that the school has been made well aware of—would be made to eat his lunch in an unfamiliar setting amidst a room full of adults. I am a people pleaser by nature. I don't like confrontation. If I had known the guidance counselor, a very nice woman who does seem to care about Joshua, had determined the punishment, I may not have been as vocal about my displeasure, especially since we were face to face.

I'm glad I didn't know, because having already said something, there was really no point in hiding my dismay. "I think there should have been more sensitivity shown in doling out his punishment," I maintained. "I think you all should have taken into account his anxiety surrounding food and whether it is common practice or not to make a child eat his lunch in the main office, you should have adapted the punishment to fit not just the crime, but the child, as well."

To be honest, Joshua's teacher seems like a lovely woman as well, just completely clueless about OCD—she told us when we met her that she has OCD, because she likes everything in her classroom in order, a sure sign of a lack of understanding of the true disease.

She also told me at conference that she feels Joshua is lazy and she "doesn't really see any evidence of OCD interfering with his academics." That's because he expends a tremendous amount of mental energy hiding his "routines" and presenting a façade of normalcy. But, even with all of this, had she been in the room, I probably would have softened my reaction, because as I said I don't harbor ill will against her as a person, just her methods. Instead of demanding that Joshua be switched out of her class, I may have simply stated that I wish she had shown him more compassion.

In fact, when the vice principal suggested that I sit down with Joshua's teacher to talk to her about how I feel Joshua is being treated, I bristled. I really don't want to make her feel bad, even if my son feels bad. I realized as I was sitting with them in that office that this really isn't about blame, about who did what to whom — it's about guaranteeing that my son gets a fair shake and that stereotypes (kids with OCD are simply neat freak germophobes who need everything a certain way and are always washing their hands) are blasted away, because even if it's not malicious, which I'm sure it's not, misconceptions about OCD hurt my son and to use an even broader stroke, all children with mental illness.

I agreed to have the school social worker speak to Joshua's teacher and try to educate her, rather than speak to her myself. This absolves me of the need to be confrontational and at the same time removes any subjectivity from the equation — this is not a mother speaking about her child, it is a professional speaking to another professional about the best way to handle a classroom situation, a situation which I hope and pray will never again result with my son in so much pain. I hope that armed with newfound knowledge, Joshua's teacher will see my son for who he is (a gifted child, eager to do well, but imprisoned by mental illness) and not for what he does. When asked by the school psychologist during the IEP evaluation process what he will never do, my son answered, "Realize my dreams." I am hoping that Joshua's teacher will step up and show him that nothing could be further from the truth.

Postscript: My son's IEP was approved and he now receives the services he needs in order to achieve the greatness that I know resides within him.

THE BYSTANDER EFFECT

~ February 29, 2012 ~

THERE'S NOT MUCH THAT I REMEMBER from those basic college classes outside of my English major—sociology, history, etc. But, one thing that I do remember very clearly is the case of Kitty Genovese. Supposedly dozens of people (thirty-eight to be exact) witnessed her murder, but not one person intervened. Later on, that report was debunked. A more accurate account of the night stated that a dozen people heard some sort of disturbance, but that the majority did not realize that a woman was being attacked. Most thought it was a group of drunk friends or perhaps a bar brawl. The two that did hear the screams more clearly called the police. Despite the discrepancy between later accounts and the initial account, in college we were taught about the case to illustrate the "Bystander Effect" or the "Genovese Syndrome"—the tendency of people, when witnessing a grisly crime, to simply do nothing, for fear of getting involved (or simply because of apathy to the human condition).

That case always chilled me to the bone, especially after a friend of mine was murdered at the mall close to our university and her body sat in her car for two days, before anyone even thought to call the police. A man confessed to the crime—said that he was sitting in his car about to kill himself when he saw her and decided in a deadly instant to kill her instead. The case of Kitty Genovese fresh in my mind, I often wondered if anyone saw anything or heard anything and just ignored her. She wasn't a close friend, but we did have plans to go for a drink together the week that she was murdered. And her death hit me hard (especially since I had had my own brush with violence, but that is a story for another blog post)—I was afraid to walk around campus and town at night that winter, only going out with my very imposing boyfriend and our equally imposing friend. I called them my Twin Towers. One was 6'1" and one 6'5" — they made me feel safe during that long, dark winter. By spring, I was brave again, but I never forgot my friend or the case of Kitty Genovese. And to be honest, I still don't like being in parking lots alone at night.

Both of those tragic young women haunted me again recently as I stood on my porch watching my middle-school-aged son walk from his corner bus stop to our house. A woman's scream of, "Oh my god!" was quickly followed by more blood curdling, pulse quickening screams. I saw my son jump a bit and then turn around, searching for the source of the screams, a frightened look crossing his face. I had thought at first that I had imagined the severity of the screams; that perhaps it was just children playing, but his reaction told me otherwise. I motioned him to hurry up to the house and as the screams echoed down the street, he rushed in.

"Mom," he sputtered, "It sounds like someone is being ripped apart with a knife out there."

"Where did it sound like it was coming from?" I asked him quickly, hoping to figure out where to send the police, if I called.

"The next block, I think," he answered.

I wasn't sure—it sounded like it was coming from our block, three or four houses down. But, that was exactly where he was walking and he would have known if it was coming from a house that he was passing. "Are you sure?" I asked.

"I'm pretty sure." Then a stricken look passed his face, "Do you think the girls are okay?" He was worried about two sisters at his stop who live on the next block.

"It sounded like it was coming from inside of a house. I'm sure they're fine." I answered. "Maybe we should call the police, though. But, I don't know where to send them. You sure it was the next block?"

"I don't know," he shook his head sadly. I didn't want to make him feel worse—he was already shaken up, as was I.

Our exchange took merely a few minutes, but we both realized that the screams had stopped. "I guess she's dead," my son said with a sigh.

There was nothing I could do. I felt completely helpless. I couldn't call the police and tell them to knock on each door on my street checking for a possible crime scene. For the next hour or so, I listened for sirens or any further evidence of unrest in our suburban neighborhood. There was nothing—silence, except for the occasional passing car or barking dog. No sirens, no police. Nothing. I didn't stop thinking about those screams though and sent a message to the mom of the other girls at the bus stop. I asked her if her girls were all right and if they heard any screams. They were fine and didn't hear a thing, convincing me that the screams must have come from one of my neighbors' homes. I only know a few of my neighbors well, because many old timers have passed away, with new young families moving in. Could one of those young mothers be the victim of abuse? I wondered. What was going on behind closed doors—hidden from neighborhood eyes, but not ears?

It's been two weeks, and I still don't have any answers as to what transpired that afternoon. I checked the online community police log. I asked the neighbors that I am close with if they heard anything. No one else heard anything, but I know that the fear, desperation and horror I heard in those screams was not a product of my imagination—it was real—my son heard it too. Was my not calling the police right away an act of complacency—an example of the "Bystander Effect?" Was someone seriously harmed or even killed, but no one, other than the perpetrator, even knows? Would the police have even come in time—before the screams died down—so, they could locate the source? The only question I can even attempt to answer is the last—probably not. Whatever happened—perhaps just a mother finding that her child had spilled grape juice all over a white couch or more likely something far more nefarious—I'll never have an answer, but that won't stop me from remembering the chilling sound, which still, even weeks later, haunts my dreams.

Postscript (2016): I did eventually find out that the mother of two young boys a few houses down was being abused. Another neighbor saw her husband drag her out of the house in a chokehold. The police came more than once in the ensuing months and probably years. Eventually, I believe the couple divorced—or perhaps the father landed in jail. The mother and boys moved out and the small run-down cape-style house was gutted to the studs, a fancy colonial twice the size springing up in its place. I think about that young mother often. She was sweet, quiet and beautiful. Her boys were the same age difference as mine and reminded me much of my boys when they were toddlers. I sometimes gave them items my boys had outgrown—a perfect condition Bob the Builder backpack, pumpkin themed treat sacks on Halloween. The new colonial was just sold, no vestige of that small white cape remains, but the memory of those screams and that family still haunt me. I hope that young mother started her life over somewhere far away—far out of the reach of the monster masquerading as a husband and father ...

THE EMPTY SETTING

~ April 6, 2012 ~

IT'S ALWAYS HARD CELEBRATING A HOLIDAY for the first time after a loved one passes away, but if that holiday is also the anniversary of when your loved one either died or fell ill, it's doubly hard. So, how do you keep the holidays joyful when there is a thread of sadness weaving its way through the festivities? I have to say that I honestly don't know, but hopefully by tomorrow night, I will have an answer for how I tackled that dilemma.

Passover starts at sundown tonight and brings with it not only matzo, wine and of course the Seders, but a memory of last year when my father's health took a turn for the worse, leading to his death a week later. Just a few weeks before, he was, while not perfect, better than anyone could have expected seven and a half months after suffering a stroke. He had good color and looked fit and healthy, even if his mind was still somewhat cloudy. But, on the night of the first Seder what he assumed was heartburn from all of the greasy, oily (though still delicious) food was actually a heart attack.

My father had always been a stubborn man when it came to his health, toughing out more things than he should have and refusing to go to the hospital until he was more than once literally on the floor. And, that night was no different. Added to his headstrong belief that he was okay, even when he wasn't, was his compromised cognitive state—a disastrous combination that led him to just go to sleep, instead of going to the hospital when chest pains struck.

It took almost a week and a fainting spell until he went to the hospital; almost a week until that heart attack was diagnosed, giving it plenty of time to damage the heart muscles. The doctors tried to fix him up with stents, but the day after he left the hospital six days after he entered, he told my mother that he loved her, dropped his coffee cup and was gone. So, now Passover is laced with sadness and memories of sitting in the dingy hospital room in the waning days of the holiday eating macaroons and matzo sandwiches, waiting for news. It's laced with the memories of that night at the Seder, thinking that he just didn't look right.

Of course, Passover is always laced with sadness—the bitter herbs evoke the bitterness of enslavement and the salt water evokes the tears of the slaves. We are reminded that our ancestors were not as lucky as we are. But, it is also a time of celebration—a time of rebirth; the rebirth of spring and of ourselves. It celebrates the journey from slavery to freedom. It even has a lesser known name: Z'man Cheiruteinu, meaning "The Time of Liberation." I learned that on the "Passover for Dummies" website. Even a secular website like that—probably meant for people new to the holiday, perhaps celebrating for the first time with a Jewish friend—mentions the combination of sadness and happiness. It says that Passover is celebrated with "a groan."

So, with all this juxtaposition of sadness and happiness, how is the holiday different for my family than it is for others not mourning a loss? Well, for one thing the sadness is personal. It's kind of hard to get truly broken up about the tragedies that befell our ancestors thousands of years ago, but a tragedy as fresh as eleven months ago—that's easy to feel bereft about. Last night as my mother walked around with two of my kids searching for the hametz (bread) with a candle and a feather, my son, Joshua, put his head on my shoulder and asked for a hug.

"Are you sad about Papa?" I whispered.

He shook his head yes. "It's okay. I am too," I assured him. I don't think it made him feel better, but at least he knew that he's not alone.

My father always sat at the head of the table at the Seder—it will be odd without him in that seat. He also presided over the search for the afikomen and doled out $5 bills to all of the grandchildren—even the grown ones—with a smile. I'm sure my son is wondering who will preside over the search this year; who will take his place. Well, the answer is: no one can. But, that's okay. The whole message of Passover is that life is a journey—we suffer setbacks, tragedies even, but as long as you keep moving forward, you'll survive. There's sadness, to be sure, but there's also rebirth. No matter what has happened during the dark winter, come spring the flowers will bloom again, the grass will grow green and lush and the trees will shade us with their canopies of leaves. Passover reminds us of this— the egg on the Seder plate represents rebirth. It's there to remind us that life goes on.

And, life does go on—it always does. Perhaps it's fitting that the anniversary of my father's death is just weeks away. It's is a good time to liberate ourselves from the shackles of grief and simply remember the good times of Seders past with a smile. I'm sure my father would have wanted it that way.

ICE DREAMS

~ *May 11, 2012* ~

MY HUSBAND AND I HAD A LITTLE DISAGREEMENT the other night. It's a disagreement that we've had many, many times over the course of our nineteen years together. "It's boxing on ice," he declared, referring to my beloved sport of hockey. "It's kill the guy with the puck."

"It is not boxing on ice," I countered vehemently. "There's finesse to it. It's poetry in motion."

"They count hits. What kind of sport is that?" he shot back. "Why are there even hits?"

"There are hits because a clean hit gets the man off of the puck, allowing you to grab it and head back up ice. Clean hits are a part of the game—always have been, always will be," I answered as calmly as I could manage.

My husband is a baseball and basketball guy. In fact, he coaches our kids in both. He loves everything about baseball and I still don't know if he's gotten over my convincing him to leave his beloved Red Sox and move to New York—to Yankees territory, no less—twelve years ago. I'll be honest, unless my kids are playing; watching baseball is about as exciting to me as watching paint dry. The World Series is an exception, but for the most part, I find baseball mind-numbingly dull.

Basketball is more exciting, of course, with the back and forth action, but it's not the same as hockey. With hockey, you get two for the price of one. They're not just running—anyone can do that—they're skating with a speed that often defies the laws of physics. If you've never skated in a fast moving hockey game or even taken a "hockey skating" class, both of which I've had the pleasure of doing, you don't know how completely exhilarating, adrenaline producing and hard it is.

Skating was my sport from middle school on and I spent every possible minute at the ice rink. I was even a volunteer at the rink, which was also the New York Islanders' practice facility, teaching very young children to skate. I might not have gotten paid in money, but the greatest payment was ice time on an empty rink. Sometimes the Islanders would be skating at the same time and they'd tease me for my Rangers jerseys and t-shirts. A few times they pretended to check me into the boards. I used to follow Billy Smith—their goalie at the time—around and taunt him. Now that I look back, I guess they could have been really offended and done some damage to me, but they laughed me off. I was seventy-five pounds soaking wet, skating with the big boys. But, as much as I enjoyed that, I loved nothing more than taking to the ice when it was empty and just zipping around as fast as I could. I even took early morning hockey classes in college and relished lacing my skates up while my roommates were still slumbering.

I still have dreams that I'm stepping onto a clean sheet of ice and just taking off. I can feel that slight breeze on my face as my hair flies behind me. My thighs burn as I go faster and faster and then I abruptly spin and head in the other direction. Those dreams break my heart, because I haven't skated in almost two decades. In my early twenties, my time on the ice started leaving me with excruciating pain in my feet and hands. I couldn't even unlace my skates; my fingers just didn't work. I was diagnosed with Raynaud's Phenomenon, as well as small vessel disease in my feet—both circulatory diseases made worse by cold. Raynaud's is not serious—really the best treatment is avoiding cold, especially sudden cold, such as entering a skating rink.

I really tried to keep skating, but eventually I couldn't walk for hours after pulling off my skates, thanks to the one two punch of both circulatory diseases, so I had to give it up. It was a cruel joke, because my apartment was on the same street as an ice rink (one of the things that sold me on it just months earlier)—and I could skate every night, only I couldn't. My love of hockey never faltered, though. It was the one constant in my life. A few years earlier in college, I had been the only female referee for men's intramural ice hockey. Some of the guys would try to pull me over the boards if they didn't like a call, but I didn't care. I loved pulling on the stripes, even if I did wear them over spandex skating pants. I loved being right in the middle of the action. My brother sent me his hockey helmet and pads because, as he pointed out, at five feet I was the exact height most intramural players carry their sticks.

Hockey made me feel free and powerful. I was never a fast runner, but in a pick-up game with a bunch of guys, I could skate circles around them and score. That was another bonus, being a hockey nut meant that I was never uncomfortable in the company of guys in high school and college. In fact, I was often more comfortable in their presence, because I could talk hockey — something I never tired of. One male friend in college declared that I was a "guy with boobs." I took that as a huge compliment. It pretty much summed up my personality — I could scream, "Hit him!" as loudly as anyone when we'd watch games at a bar. Something I still do, much to my kids' amusement.

But, that conversation with my husband got me thinking — why do I love hockey so much and have loved it since I was old enough to cheer? At first glance, it's a bunch of imposingly large men chasing around a little black disk, but it's so much more. It takes concentration — even watching it takes concentration. Look away and you might miss something big. Nothing made me happier than when we got a DVR and I could rewind games, so I could see a play that I missed or just relive a great goal over (and sometimes over) again.

Hockey takes strategy — sure, there are those "ugly" goals where everyone is just jamming their sticks around the crease, hoping something squirts loose so it can be banged home, but equally often, there are those gorgeous tic-tac-toe plays or slappers from the circle or a spin and a rocket from the high slot. The beauty of the sport captured my imagination even more as I entered my teenage years. I possessed an encyclopedic knowledge of the Rangers. At my brother's wedding when I was fourteen years old, I was a sort of party trick. His friends rattled off jersey numbers and I told them the players who wore them — "#2 — Tom Laidlaw; #3 — Barry Beck" and so on. No one could stump me.

In seventh grade I cut out newspaper pictures from all of the games and wrote articles to accompany them, keeping all of the pages in a neat blue binder with a Rangers sticker on the front. While other girls read *Tiger Beat* , I read *The Hockey News* . When I went to the mall, I would head first to the newsstand to see if there were any hockey magazines I could snap up, praying that my favorite player, Don Maloney, would be featured.

I thought I had died and gone to heaven when the Rangers were featured in a Sassoon ad. That ad hung on my wall, along with a poster of Ron Duguay, his curls flying behind him, until I went to college. A button featuring Don Maloney was fastened to the cord of the air conditioner next to my bed, only because I couldn't find a poster of him.

Don Maloney was my first crush. I figured a mere ten years between us meant nothing, even though I was only fourteen years old at the time. I got to meet him twice. The first time he handed me a puck over the glass at a Rangers' practice at Rye Playland (I still have it) and the next time, he ran over my foot while I waited for his autograph. It's not really as terrible as it sounds—his car kind of rolled over my foot. When someone alerted him and he apologized profusely, I simply said, "I love you!" Poor guy must have thought I was nuts. I don't think I even felt the pain until I got in the car—the sheer thrill of Don Maloney actually speaking to me was a powerful anesthetic.

I still tell my husband that he should be thankful that I loved Don Maloney so much as a teenager, because his look—one of a fairly constant five o'clock shadow—formed the basis of what attracted me as I got older. I've always had a weakness for a stubble covered jaw, much to the happiness of my husband who hates to shave. I think that the boyfriend before my husband, my college sweetheart, appreciated my love of scruff too—my favorite gift from him was an authentic Don Maloney #12 jersey with a fighting strap. It didn't matter that Don Maloney had long since left the Rangers and was finishing up a tenure with arch rival Islanders. I loved that jersey and still have it.

Any guy whom I have ever been with needed to understand that hockey—and my fierce love of it—is as much a part of me as the blood flowing through my veins. They also needed to understand that they better not talk to me when the Rangers are on, because I likely won't hear a word they say and I may even turn the TV up to drown them out. On the plus side, I'm always up for watching Sports Center.

I've imparted a love of hockey to my boys and when they get mad at me, I pull out the trump card. How many of your friends' moms know what the difference between boarding and charging is? How many of them know the motions for a cross check penalty and a hold penalty? How many of them know all of the words to the Canadian national anthem and can recognize John Amirante's voice after a two second snippet of the "Star Spangled Banner" on the radio? I'm pretty sure the answer is, "None."

I feel grateful that I have hockey to bond with my boys over. Unlike my husband, I don't build rockets with them, coach them in baseball and basketball, collect baseball cards with them, ooh and ahh over baseball gloves and bats and basketballs with them. But, we have hockey and during the Rangers' exhilarating Stanley Cup playoff run, even my teenage son, Drew, has given me big hugs when our boys score. My older boys are usually a bit more into baseball and basketball, but not at this time of year and my youngest, Aidan, is always into hockey—as a toddler, he pulled out his "Sean Avery dance" whenever the Rangers scored. My boys and I watch the games together. We scream, cheer, give high fives and hug each other. I only wish that I could share with them what my dad and I shared—at least a few games a season throughout my teens, always sitting in section 314. I cherish those memories even more now that my dad is gone.

So, why do I love hockey so passionately? Is it because my brother dressed me up in hockey pads and shot pucks at me when I was merely four years old? Is it because I loved skating so much? Or did I love skating because of hockey? Is it the finesse or the adrenalin? Honestly, it doesn't matter why I love it, just that I do. Just like it doesn't matter that my husband thinks hockey is boxing on ice. He's entitled to his opinion, as long as he doesn't talk to me during a game.

THE NEW NORMAL

~ November 9, 2012 ~

THERE IS A HOUSE IN MY NEIGHBORHOOD completely decimated by Hurricane Sandy—the front crushed by a once towering, magnificent old tree; the white Toyota in the driveway flattened into a broken mess of glass and steel. Every time I drive by that house, there is someone taking a picture of the grim scene. Every single time, without fail—and, I drive by that house at least four times a day. Even now, when most of the tree has been cut away, with only the trunk left on the car and a gaping hole where the roof was, people are still stopping, jumping out of their cars, cell phone raised in front of them. I saw someone make a U turn this morning—in the middle of a busy road—just so he could get a better look. I've tried to figure out the magnetic draw to that particular house. I share in it, of course. My phone was broken, so I had my husband send me the picture he took. I posted it on Facebook as a symbol of the destruction this Superstorm has wrought, but also as a reminder that my family and I were very lucky. I wrote, "This puts things in perspective. Not having power and one downed tree which fell away from the house is not a big deal."

Someone wrote on the thread that the house has become a "must see" in our town and again, I pondered why. I think perspective—the feeling that someone has it worse than you do and you should just suck it up and be grateful for whatever you do have—has a lot to do with it. Thankfully, someone else wrote on the thread that no one was hurt in the home. So, there isn't a sense of morbid curiosity. It's not the sight of a makeshift memorial—no one perished, thankfully. People are undoubtedly drawn to it, simply because it is such a stark example of Mother Nature's power. It's humbling. We have been lucky in the New York metropolitan area that we have been relatively unscathed by natural disasters—at least in my lifetime. I think we may have gotten a bit complacent. I know that I for one completely and totally underestimated the power of Sandy. I completely underestimated the potential for such widespread destruction. Just a couple of weeks ago I could not fathom sitting in a line for gas for hours, nor could I fathom driving by my house and not even going in, because it was so cold and dark. I could not fathom toddlers being swept from their mother's arms and carried away to their deaths by a current of water so strong, even a mother's grip couldn't overcome it. I could not fathom that the beach my son played volleyball on this summer would be destroyed—parts of the boardwalk we strolled on smashed to pieces. I couldn't fathom any of these things, though I knew that they happened of course, especially running fundraisers for victims of natural disasters as Community Service chairperson for my kids' school for the past eight years. They just happened somewhere else—not here. New Orleans. Japan. Joplin. Haiti. Just not here.

On the eve of the hurricane my family and I were at the mall. The wind had started whipping discarded wrappers and coffee cups around the parking lot. A cold mist sprayed our faces as we walked across the asphalt. In Macy's the young salesman said that he couldn't understand why people were shopping for clothes when they should be buying candles and batteries, bottled water and canned goods. I told him, "We're New Yorkers, we're tough. We'll get through this storm, no problem. It'll be nothing—you'll see." We got through Irene—we spent twenty-four hours in my basement, because my neighbor's tree was leaning precariously over our house, waiting for the one big gust to finish the job. But, we emerged unscathed. Even those who lost power were frustrated, but not despairing that things would never get better. And, that's kind of how it feels now—that things will never get better. Our town seems very post-apocalyptic, with many areas still plunged into darkness at nightfall and I have to admit that I was dead wrong when I assured that salesman that Hurricane Sandy would be no big deal, that as tough New Yorkers we could handle anything.

Make no mistake, though—I'm not saying that New Yorkers are weak or that we won't recover. I know even the most devastated areas will spring back eventually, stronger than ever. I mean that right now—right while we are going through it—it feels like it will never end. It feels like it did after 9/11—like the world would never get back to normal, like we'd never be safe again. And, you know what—the world never did go back to the normal it was before 9/11. It became a new normal where security guards sat behind the locked front door of every school. It became a new normal where scores of children have become young adults missing the guiding hand of a parent who perished, where memorials dot suburban corners and grace town beaches. But, in that new normal we were able to feel happiness again and life post Hurricane Sandy will become the new normal, as well.

The new greeting is, "Do you have power?" We have become a town of haves and have-nots and it has absolutely nothing to do with money. This was, as Chuck Schumer stated, "an equal opportunity storm." If you don't have power, you really want to feel happy for those who do, but it's hard not to feel insanely jealous. And if you do have power, it's hard not to feel guilty and not to feel like you're not doing enough to help your less fortunate neighbors. Call it survivors' guilt. But, even with power, there is still the looming fear that it will go out again. During the nor'easter that battered our already battered island my lights kept flickering and then went out for just a few minutes. The power came back on, but those few moments were an eternity. My stomach was in knots wondering if we would be in the dark again—I knew too many people who had already lost power a second time to take anything for granted.

I think *that* is the new normal—to never take anything for granted again. A hot shower; a hot meal; a bed to sleep on, instead of the floor—these are all things that most of us don't even think twice about here in the middle class suburbs of Long Island. But, there are many people who don't have those things—even when they are not enduring the aftermath of Superstorm Sandy. To live in their shoes even for a short time is nothing short of illuminating, and I hope it will spur people to help those less fortunate long after this crisis has passed. Because now, we all know how it feels not to have something when you need it. Even having a full tank of gas in one's car feels like the ultimate luxury. The feeling of being trapped, because I only had an eighth of a tank of gas before waiting in line for two and half hours to fill up my tank was very anxiety provoking. When I put that nozzle back in the gas pump and turned on my car to see a full tank, it felt like the sweetest victory in world. If there could be a gift from Sandy, if there is a silver lining in the darkest of nights, it is surely the feeling of gratitude for anything that we do have. And, I hope that lingers long after the rebuilding is done.

WHAT IF? PART 2

~ *December 5, 2012* ~

I HAVE REALLY GONE BACK AND FORTH about writing this blog post for several reasons. For one, my son is on Facebook and I don't want him to know what I have been going through lately. For another reason, I am an intensely private person, especially when it comes to certain health issues. Now, that might sound strange, because almost all of my blog posts are extremely introspective. I plumb my psyche for most of my material and my readers know a tremendous amount about me, my family and my take on parenting. This subject has just been hard for me to explore—contemplating serious illness. But, then I went back and read "What If?" my blog about my breast biopsy three years ago and I realized that my reason for writing that blog post three years ago—to share, so people going through the same thing know they aren't alone—is still just as important today. So, I'll block my son when I post this and I'll just dig in and share—if you've faced something similar (or are facing something similar), now you know you're not alone.

It's incredibly ironic how I ended up where I am, waiting for biopsy results for the past week. I have been on what an oncologist called the "CA-125 treadmill" since July. CA-125 is an ovarian cancer marker, but not a very reliable one. In fact, it's one of the most unreliable screening tests out there—for any type of cancer. It can be elevated for no reason at all—perhaps the time of a woman's cycle bumps it up. Inflammation anywhere in the body can raise it. Sometimes the cause of an elevated CA-125 is never found. I was told in July that my CA-125 was high. I never wanted to take the test—I knew that with the high rate of false positive tests the chances that mine would be high, necessitating more tests was good. My gynecologist insisted that I take it, because my sister had ovarian cancer and my mother had uterine cancer. I had no choice, because it was bundled in with an anemia test on the prescription and I was pretty sure that I was anemic. Of course I needed to take a second test, which was also elevated. The doctor told me that I needed to see an oncologist. "You know, you've opened a can of worms," I accused him. He agreed, but said that he had no choice now but to send me to a gynecological oncologist. That was the last time I spoke with him. No follow up phone calls from him—nothing. He washed his hands of me after setting me on this path.

The gynecological oncologist—who happened to have treated my sister and my mother—was not worried at all about the CA-125, but he advised me that I have a complete hysterectomy as soon as possible. I told him that I have a good five or six years before menopause and asked if I could just wait until then. His response, "You likely have some very nasty things waiting down the line for you that could very well take your life. Why would you want to wait?"

When my husband, Jeff, and I left the office, tears rolled silently down my cheeks. Waiting for the elevator, he turned to me and asked why I was crying. "It's good news," he said. "You don't have cancer—the CA-125 doesn't mean anything."

"But," I stammered, "I don't want a hysterectomy. I'm too young. I'm not ready. I don't need it."

Jeff of course said that I could do whatever I wanted, but he pleaded with me to consider it. "I don't want you to be a statistic," he whispered.

My internist agreed with me that it seemed extreme to just rip everything out for something that might happen somewhere down the line—but, also might not. She referred me to the top gynecological oncologist at Memorial Sloane Kettering Cancer Center and very likely the top in the country. At first I was told that he might not even see me. He only takes on patients with advanced ovarian cancer or the BRCA gene. I had neither. But, they called me back after the doctor went over my case and said that he would see me. The day of my appointment I waited for three and a half hours—most of which were spent wearing an exam robe, waiting in a room. I was literally losing my mind. But, the wait was worth it when the doctor finally came in. He was kind, understanding and most of all he assured me that he didn't think I needed surgery. But, he said that I should see the gynecological geneticist at Sloan just to be certain. He promised that he would only do the surgery if the geneticist said that I need it. "Even if you beg, I won't do it, if he says you don't need it," he joked.

"Believe me, I would never beg for this surgery," I countered. "I came here because I wanted to be told that I don't need it, not that I do."

So, I went to the gynecological geneticist—also the tops in his field—in a fairly optimistic mood. That mood darkened quickly when I was on the sonogram table. Before seeing the doctor, I needed to have a sonogram and a follow up blood test to check my CA-125 level. And here's where the irony comes in—my CA-125 level was perfectly normal and not only that, the doctor assured me that it was normal all along for a woman still in her child bearing years.

Unfortunately, though, the sonogram wasn't normal. I knew something was wrong right away. The radiologist came in after the tech finished and spent quite a long time staring at the screen. I asked if everything was all right; she answered that she took a lot of pictures and she had to look closely at them. Then, she assured me that the doctor would take good care of me. I was shaking by the time I went back to Jeff in the waiting room. Of course, he laughed off my anxiety. I insisted that I had had enough of these tests—every six months for more years than I could count, thanks to my family history—to know when something is off. The radiologist always says, "Everything looks fine," while I'm still on the table. This radiologist seemed clearly uncomfortable with my question and her assurance that an oncologist would take good care of me didn't make me feel any better.

I have to say the six hours that I waited to see the geneticist were some of the longest of my life. I went back to Jeff's office and did a bit of work on my laptop. I looked out the window with some of Jeff's coworkers at Justin Beiber's car being swarmed by screaming girls outside of Madison Square Garden. I contemplated doing some shopping at Macy's Herald Square. In the end we just went back to the office and waited two hours for the doctor. He apologized profusely for the wait, but I almost didn't want to know—as long as I was waiting, I didn't know if there was something wrong for sure. But, it just felt inevitable that there was indeed something not quite right.

Walking up out of the bowels of the E train subway station at 53rd Street and Lexington Avenue, the notes of Pachelbel's "Canon" floated out to meet us, played amazingly well by a couple of buskers. I love that piece of music—I even walked down the aisle to it at my wedding. I felt like I was in a movie, walking slowly up the stairs with pictures of the skyline in between the risers, knowing that I was very likely going to hear bad news, news that could change my life. Before the doctor came in I shared my concerns with Jeff. He said, "Why so many bad thoughts going through your head? You'll be fine. Don't worry."

I told him that I hoped he could say, "I told you so," to me, but that I had a bad feeling that I would be the one to say that and for once, I truly didn't want that honor. "I'd rather prepare myself for the worst," I told him, "than be blindsided by bad news that I don't expect." I wasn't surprised at all when the doctor said that he saw something on the sonogram that he needed to biopsy and that he needed to switch hats from geneticist to oncologist—but honestly, it didn't make it any easier. It's a particular kind of fear when you're given bad news at a doctor's office. It's almost primal. Which makes sense—it's a fear of not surviving. He assured me that it might not be anything at all, but he also said, "If you weren't scared, I would be worried about you," which really was so much kinder than it sounds here. He had loaded up a lot of information on us, particularly information pertaining to my genetic makeup and the fact that my feeling like I'm always waiting for the other shoe to fall—cancer wise—might not be so farfetched.

In looking over my mother and sister's pathology reports (which I had faxed him earlier), he noticed a few things that could point to Lynch Syndrome, an awful genetic "predisposition to cancer" that can rocket one's lifetime risks for certain cancers to sixty percent. Because of this and some other symptoms that I've had, coupled with the abnormal sonogram, he had to do a biopsy. He gave me the choice to wait for a week and come back, but he said that if he were in my shoes he would want it done, instead of losing sleep over it.

So, I did it and I was sure by now I would have heard—it's a week, seven days of anxiety wondering if it's good or bad.

The few people who know about the test say no news is good news, so I Googled that to see if there was any truth to that saying when it came to biopsies—that maybe malignancies take less time to show up, giving quicker results. This is what I found—"The Anxiety of the Biopsy." Apparently studies show that once a woman hits day five of waiting for biopsy results her levels of cortisol—the stress hormone—are equal to that of a woman who has already been diagnosed with cancer. I believe it.

Waiting is excruciating. I imagine different scenarios. I imagine happily telling my few friends and family who know about the biopsy that I don't have cancer. I also imagine telling my kids that I have cancer. I imagine surgery. I imagine not being able to take care of all of the things that I need to take care of and that brings me back to that "what if"—the most insidious phrase there is, as I said in that last blog post about my last biopsy. That breast biopsy was good—great, nothing wrong, nothing there, everything suspicious removed, sent out and everything came back negative. But, during that biopsy, the doctor who performed it assured me that it looked totally benign and that she was able to remove the whole lump. I truly don't know what the answer will be with this biopsy. So, I'm left to play the "what if" game and play out every scenario in my head, no matter how frightening. Every time the phone rings my heart jumps out of my chest. I know one of those calls will be the doctor—I can't go on waiting forever, but I don't know if I want to even know the answer.

Postscript (2016): That biopsy was benign, thankfully. And the four or five I've had since then (I've lost track), were also benign. I still don't know if I have Lynch Syndrome three and a half years later, but we are getting closer to an answer with the testing of tissue from my sister's tumors, still stored two decades later for specifically this purpose.

BRAVE

~ *December 22, 2012* ~

I ALWAYS DREAD PARENT TEACHER CONFERENCES A BIT— ever since a conference when my son was in second grade and a school psychologist made me cry, saying, "You don't even know what's wrong with your son. How miserable you must be." Well, we did eventually find out what was "wrong"—Joshua has Obsessive Compulsive Disorder (OCD). You probably already know that (and if you don't, you can go back and read two previous essays about it—*Twice Exceptional* and *Crime and Punishment*). What you may not know, though is that in the years since his diagnosis (he was diagnosed at the end of second grade, he is now in sixth grade), he has grown into an incredibly brave young man who will tell anyone interested about his OCD.

Still, I did not know what I would hear when meeting with Joshua's teachers earlier this week and I certainly couldn't have anticipated his English teacher's report. As soon as I sat down, she gushed about Joshua's presentation on having Obsessive Compulsive Disorder. She said that he was very confident and answered all of his classmates' questions. She said that he really enlightened the class and she was so happy that he shared his story. When Joshua initially proposed doing his essay and presentation on having OCD, his teacher called me to make sure that it was okay with me. I told her that as long as it was okay with him, it was fine with me. I did worry that he might be judged or change his mind at the last minute, but I was so proud that he was even willing to try.

Late last night I was neatening up my den before going to bed and came upon Joshua's essay. It was in a pile of schoolwork that I had started to go through earlier in the day, but never finished. It pulled me in right away, and even though it was after 1:00 am, I read through the whole thing. I quickly decided that I needed to share it—that it could help other kids (and even adults) going through the same thing. so here is what it's like to live with OCD, in Joshua's own words:

"Almost four years ago when I was eight years old, I was diagnosed with OCD. OCD stands for Obsessive Compulsive Disorder. This is the first time I'm telling a big group of people, because I've always been kind of embarrassed about it, but now I know it's nothing to be embarrassed about. OCD is a disease that makes you do stuff multiple times, like washing your hands many times, turning on and off the lights, opening and closing the refrigerator and other things. It also makes you do something a certain way every time, like walking into the house a certain way, getting into bed a certain way, brushing your teeth a certain way and other things.

Have you ever noticed that I'm really skinny? Well, I'm only about sixty pounds, because of OCD. It makes me worry that if I eat too much, I'll get sick. I know won't, but I can't help it. I also have to tap my fingers a certain way a lot during the day and it gives me symptoms of ADHD.

One day, my mom was reading the newspaper and saw a little ad that Zucker Hillside Hospital was doing a study to see if a person with OCD has a different brain than someone who doesn't have it. At first I didn't want to do it, because you need to have an MRI to participate. Then my mom said that I would get paid $410 for my time going. They would pay me $80 twice to do an interview and $250 for the MRI. Of course, I said yes after hearing that. This was in fourth grade, by the way. I had to get picked up early twice to go to a doctor in Queens for the interview—then I got paid $80 each time.

Then the big day came. My mom picked me up from school at 12:45 and drove me out to Zucker Hillside Hospital for the MRI. I had to wait for an hour. Then a doctor came out and took me to the MRI room. They told me to lie down on a bed. Then they put heavy duty headphones on me, because the MRI is really loud. Then they gave me a rubber ball to squeeze, in case something happened and I needed them to stop the MRI. The MRI took an hour and a half, but at least they had to pay me $250 by law.

The doctors have now scientifically proven that people with OCD have different brains from people who don't. I feel very proud that I was a part of this research. I've also learned that having OCD is nothing to feel bad or embarrassed about. It's just you. This disease will never stop me from doing what I want to do."

As I finished reading this essay last night, I had tears in my eyes. I can't really explain the emotions that hit you when you realize that your child—one who has struggled (and continues to struggle) with a disease as formidable as OCD—truly possesses the strength to overcome anything. It's a mixture of gratitude and awe—of course—but something else intangible, unnamable. Like a sigh of relief in an emotion. When I told Joshua my idea about sharing this essay because his story could help a lot of kids struggling with OCD (or many other mental health issues) to feel a lot better, a huge smile spread across his face. He said that he would love it if I shared it. I'm so proud of him and I'm honored to share such an authentic, brave voice.

SKIN DEEP

~ *March 8, 2013* ~

I'M NOT A SHALLOW PERSON. I care deeply about many important issues—the environment, animal rights, human rights and a myriad of other causes. Most importantly, I know that beauty is only skin deep. But, skidding towards my forty-fifth birthday has turned me into a shallow narcissist. I stare at myself in the mirror and wonder if I need a face lift or maybe just some Juvederm. I smooth my skin back and curse my fear of doing anything more invasive than applying night cream that promises to slough off dead skin while I sleep, leaving me radiant in the morning. I notice the little lines around my eyes and slather on "anti-aging eye treatment." I inspect my temples and wonder why a bit of gray is sexy on men, but haggy on women.

My husband tells me I look better than most thirty year olds and my kids insist I'm really only twenty-five. And it makes me feel incredibly ungrateful that I just can't believe them. I blame part of it on most women's inability to see themselves as others see them—we're our own worst critics—and part of it on the cashier at Michael's. About a month ago I informed her that the cart full of frames I was buying was for my son's artwork. "He's in honors art," I boasted.

"High school or college?" she asked reasonably.

I wanted to cry. Of course I'm old enough to have a son in college; I just don't want to look like I am. Right before I turned forty, a woman stopped me on my way out of a diner and asked if I was my kids' mother or their baby sitter. She said that I didn't look old enough to be their mother, but that I seemed too attentive to be a baby sitter. This happened often. More than once I was mistaken for my kids' baby sitter or even older sister. A couple of years ago the lady at the front desk at my kids' middle school yelled at me to stop as I walked out the door. I turned and asked if there was a problem and she sheepishly said that she thought I was a student leaving. I thanked her profusely, before slipping out the door. A year ago an elderly woman asked my mother if I still lived with her. My mother replied that I have my own home and family. The woman looked shocked. She thought I was eighteen. (And I thought she needed glasses.) But now—now someone had not only accepted without even a fraction of disbelief that I have a child the age that I do (fourteen and a half years old), but that I could have one four years older. I'm very disappointed in myself that this bothered me as much as it did.

The inescapable truth though is that I can't expect to look thirty for the rest of my life. I should just age gracefully and accept that everyone gets wrinkles and gray hair eventually, even if forty-five is the new thirty-five. This isn't the first time I've faced a birthday worrying that I'm looking older—when I turned thirty-five I decided that I suddenly looked old and that I had lines around my mouth, the dreaded parentheses. I dealt with it by getting blonde highlights—the new look cheered me up. That and the fact that people still thought that I was a teenager. This time I've been looking for solace at the drug store. No, I'm not buying over the counter drugs to concoct my own mood altering substances—I bought "Age Rewind" foundation. The ad clearly said it would make me look like Christy Turlington, who is just a year younger than I am. Only, when I put it on, it didn't make me look like Christy Turlington—it only made me look like I had slightly orange spackling on my face. In fact, even Christy Turlington probably doesn't look like the Christy Turlington in the ad, as gorgeous as she is.

I stopped searching for the miracle and went back to my Origins VitaZing tinted moisturizer, definitely not heavy duty, but it has antioxidants in it to wake up your skin and it gives a nice glow. I also use GinZing brightening eye cream and Halo Effect—a pinkish, shimmery highlighting potion. I use it as a very lightweight blush. It smells yummy and is very subtle, adding just the slightest sheen. I'm a bit addicted to Origins and have been since I was in my mid-twenties and my roommate gave me a basket of Origins goodies for my birthday. I'm planning my next purchase—I received my $10 off coupon for my birthday and every year I treat myself to something. I think this year it will be Starting Over "age erasing moisturizer." Will it really erase the little fine lines and tighten up everything? I have no idea, but I think it's really more about feeling like you're doing something, even if it's not as radical as a face lift or even a shot of Botox between the eyes.

I think more importantly though, is being easier on ourselves—I say ourselves, because I know I'm not the only one facing this milestone birthday worried that my age is starting to catch up to me. As women we are constantly bombarded with images of celebrities who defy aging. Celebrities who are over fifty now often look no older than when they were twenty-five, in fact they look younger than when they were twenty-five. It's an impossible standard. They either have had "work done" or they're air brushed to within an inch of being unrecognizable. Comparing ourselves to celebrities is just a recipe for disaster and a distorted self-image.

A few months ago—right after Hurricane Sandy—I was rushing through the mall. I had been sleeping on my sister's floor for days and had just waited at the overcrowded Apple store for two hours to get my broken phone replaced. A young guy manning a kiosk called me over as I sped by him. "What do you use for your skin?" He asked eyeing me up and down. I told him Origins and he said that it was doing a great job.

I nearly fell to my knees in gratitude. I told him that I was feeling very old and that it's great to hear that in your forties. He was incredulous and told me that I looked like I was in my twenties. He asked me why I felt like I looked old and why I didn't see myself as looking young. "You should be grateful and not complain about feeling old," he admonished. "I'm twenty-seven and you look younger. You obviously have a lot of energy too." I didn't tell him that I was running on pure post-storm adrenaline, I just smiled. Then, of course, he tried to sell me his line of skin care, but still—it got me thinking. Do I really see myself as others see me or do I see myself through the lens of impossible expectations and insecurity?

Fast forward to a few weeks ago—I was going to see my eye doctor who has known me since I was sixteen and has a front row seat to the crow's feet around my eyes. He always tells me I look young and I was sure that this time he wouldn't—it had been a year, an incredibly stressful year that aged me more than other years. But, sure enough he called me the "ageless wonder" and for just a brief moment, I felt like it. And, I think that's the key to accepting ourselves for who we are, instead of getting depressed every time we look in the mirror—just try to see yourself as others see you. Oh, and maybe a few blonde highlights.

SENSELESS

~ *April 16, 2013* ~

YOU NEVER FORGET THE MOMENT you hear about a tragedy. 9/11 is as clear and sharp as cut crystal in my mind. I was in my backyard on that cloudless September day, the sky almost shockingly azure. As I pushed my two little boys on the swings beneath the canopy of still lush green leaves, my phone rang. It was my husband, Jeff, on his way to New Jersey. "Turn on the news," he said urgently. "You'll never believe what happened—a plane hit the World Trade Center. I can see the smoke rising in my rearview mirror."

"I told you it could happen!" I answered. I had had a fear of low flying planes for as long as I could remember. Planes nose diving into the ground and bursting into flames haunted my dreams—I wasn't afraid of flying, just being on the ground when a plane plummeted to Earth. I think the seeds of my fear took root either as a baby living near Kennedy Airport or when as a child I saw a news account of a plane crashing into a bridge and decapitating a woman just driving along minding her own business. Whatever the cause of my fear, my husband's phone call didn't surprise me. It only seemed a matter of time before some reckless pilot smacked into a skyscraper.

What happened next shocked me though—my husband said, "Oh my God, it has to be a terrorist attack. Another plane just hit the second tower. Go turn on the news."

I turned it on and I didn't turn it off. Not for a while at least. I was glued to the images of devastation, to the sheer destruction. Living on Long Island, it was all too close. Jeff was stuck in New Jersey and I was alone with my babies—a newly minted three-year-old and a nine month old—trying to make sense of everything. My parents came over for a while to help me, but in the end I was alone with my thoughts trying to sort everything out. When I woke up the next morning it was a punch in the gut to realize that it wasn't all some crazy nightmare—that the planes bursting into flames were, in fact, quite real this time.

I felt much the same way when I woke up this morning, when I remembered everything that happened yesterday. Boston was my adopted hometown for nine years—from the tender age of twenty-three years old until I moved back to New York when I was thirty-two and pregnant with my second child. I evolved from a kid to a grown-up with a family when I lived there. We still have tons of friends and family there and it still holds a special place in my heart. In fact, twenty years ago, on a night when spring turned into the anticipation of summer, I ran into my future husband on the same street where yesterday's bombs caused such carnage—Boylston Street.

I don't think I will forget the moment I was driving—shuttling kids here and there—and my phone rang. I pressed answer on my steering wheel and my sister's voice came through the Bluetooth, "Did you hear the news?" I could tell it was not anything good. As soon as I heard the word, "bomb," my first thought, heart in my throat, was that it had gone off in Penn Station—right below my husband's office. It took me a moment to realize that she said the Boston Marathon. And then, it took another moment for me to register that one of my closest friends was there—very likely cheering from the finish line. I knew another close friend was watching, but she was miles away at the start.

"I have to call Scott," I said and rushed off the phone. A second later, my friend answered and assured me he was okay. Scott has been there for me, no matter what, for over a quarter of a century, for over half my life—I know I can call him when the worst possible things happen. He talked to me as I raced to be by my dying father's side before he slipped away and then stayed on the phone with me when I realized I was too late. He talked to me for half an hour while I wandered around the Christmas Tree Shops awaiting a phone call informing me of the results of a biopsy I had done. He also seems to have ESP and somehow knows to call me when I am having a particularly trying day—like that day at the Christmas Tree Shops. Then there was the day that I had gotten a devastating rejection from a literary agent and he called minutes after to tell me that I'm a much better writer than the author of a best seller he was reading. I still don't know how he knew I need a pep talk right at that moment. It was a scary few moments when I learned about the bombing in Boston, worrying if Scott and his family were in the path of destruction.

Everyone personalizes even the most public of tragedies—everyone thinks about it in terms of how it affects them or could have affected them. It's just human nature. Whether you're simply thinking about how quickly you can lose someone important to you or whether you're putting yourself in the shoes of a mom who lost a child the same age as your own child. It's the reason that after the Sandy Hook Elementary School massacre we all hugged our kids a little tighter. We all made sure to say, "I love you," before sending them off to school. It's the reason I can't stop thinking about eight-year-old Martin Richard who was killed in the blast. One moment he was cheering friends and family across the finish line, the next he was gone. I'm the mom of an eight-year-old boy. It is an amazing age—still sweet, but independent, often passionate about anything that catches their fancy. For my oldest it was dinosaurs—at eight years old his nickname was Mr. Paleontologist. For my middle son it was cars—he could tell you the make and model of every car, not only on the road—but, from the inception of the auto industry. And, for my youngest, now eight years old, it's meteorology. He's the class weatherman and he can rattle off the fourteen day forecast and what various storm patterns mean, as well as hurricane and tornado categories with ease.

So, this is what I ponder when I think about the devastation in Boston, when I think about the unimaginable becoming real, about the act of a cowardly terrorist filling a day of joy with fear and blood—I think not only about the possibility of having lost a friend, but about little Martin Richard's interests. Was it baseball? Was it dinosaurs like my son? Was it hockey? I saw an adorable photograph of him wearing a Bruins jersey and hat. I think about his injured mother—was she conscious? Did she know what happened to her son? I know there are so many other stories to come out of this horror—stories of heroes, of human resiliency, of kindness amidst the chaos—but these are the stories that are stuck in my head—how I could have lost a friend and how a mother lost her eight-year-old boy. A boy who probably wrapped his arms around her in a hug goodnight less than twenty-four hours before and whose arms she'll never feel again—all because of some blackened soul intent on stealing our joyous moments and filling them with fear and pain.

But, guess what? The terrorists don't win. Whether the terrorist is a domestic one, a lone wolf operating out of hatred for the government (making a statement on Patriots Day, on Tax Day) or a foreigner, here to bring death and bloodshed to our soil—they don't win. They don't win, because there are those stories of people running towards the blast, not away from it—risking their lives to help those who had fallen. There are stories of people listing a room for free for runners stuck with nowhere to go. There was one person who listed not only a space on his couch for those in need, but two Chihuahuas to cuddle with. People came together as they always will. So, I guess there is one more thing I'm thinking about today and that's the human spirit and how incredibly resilient it is in the face of tragedy and how incredibly supportive, giving and loving our world can be, even when all the evidence points to the contrary.

WHY DO I WRITE?

~ June 13, 2013 ~

ONE OF THE WOMEN IN MY WRITING GROUP posed the question to our loop, "What's your reason to write today?" I thought it was a great question and all of the answers illuminated the different reasons we put pen to paper. But, more than anything it got me thinking about something I had said earlier in the day. I was speaking with another mom while waiting for our kids at school pick-up. When she found out that I had written a novel and was working on my second one, she enthused, "That's so exciting," which is, by far, the most common reaction to that bit of news.

My response—"I wouldn't wish being a writer on my worst enemy." It was a knee jerk comment. I had been sitting in my car trying to fix my novel before sending it out to an amazing editor who is interested in it. I suspected that it might need work, a year after I thought it was done, simply because of agent rejections. Most have loved my writing, calling it "terrific" and "lovely" and more than one even asked me to send my next novel. But, they also had some issues with the plot of this novel. Just minutes before I got the full request from the editor at a networking luncheon, an agent whom I respect very much who rejected my novel explained to me that she found an aspect of the plot hard to believe. I took this comment to heart and mid-pitch to the editor decided on a plot tweak that I'm fairly sure will fix the issue and make it completely believable. I knew it was the right thing to do, even though it would be some work, even though the change in my pitch was completely by the seat of my pants. I explained that I had to make a minor change and it might take me a few days to get the manuscript out to her. She assured me that it was fine and that I should take my time.

I thought it was a quick fix, but the small tweak I made sent changes rippling through the rest of the manuscript. It's taken me days to rewrite everything that now needs to be rewritten, so it matches that one little tweak and there's still no guarantee that it will wind up in readers' hands. This is why I wouldn't wish being a writer on my worst enemy—not because of the act of creating art. Nothing makes you feel more alive. It is because of the chore of trying to get the art you've created out into the world. So, if that part of the process is so difficult, what makes me keep diving in? My writing peer's question left me pondering that ...

I write, because I can't help it. It's the only thing I'm good at. It's the only thing that I've ever cared about doing, since I was a little girl—writing words that make people feel. If I don't do it, I die a little inside. My first writing professor at the University of Massachusetts, Deborah Shea, inscribed this message in my creative writing notebook—"To be a writer is a truly honorable thing. You will be ostracized and rejected, but when success comes—and it will if you work long and hard enough—it will be sweet." I've never forgotten her words to me, even though they were more than half a lifetime ago. (I know I've mentioned that quote before, but that's how important it is to me.)

I never thought that I'd be working this long and this hard, but somehow I still believe that success will come and it will be sweet. And even if it doesn't, that's okay—that's not why I write anyway. I write, because I have no other choice. Stories need to be told. Emotions need to be conveyed, even though it is hard as hell sometimes and even though trying to get your words out there into readers' hands can be soul crushing, I'll keep doing it as long as I have something to say...

PASSAGES

~ July 12, 2013 ~

IN THE BACK OF MY NIGHT TABLE CABINET sits my past life. Behind a book light and my favorite novels and a folder of important documents, is a row of journals—their flowered and paisley spines tempting me to crack them open and revisit the moments that made me who I am today. I don't often give in, but in researching my next book (and hoping for some dialogue sparks for the one I'm revising now), I pulled out a slim harvest gold book with red and black blooms and pretty green scrolls on the cover. I hit the jackpot with it. Encompassing 1992 through the middle of 1993, it started just days before my boyfriend of two and a half years broke up with me and ends a couple of weeks after I ran into my future husband on the street.

Kafka couldn't have penned a bigger metamorphosis. I went from a girl—an insecure, depressed girl who was sure she'd never be happy again, crying herself to sleep every night and living on soup and Little Debbie Snack Cakes—to a confident young woman. I worked out at the gym again after abandoning my gym rat lifestyle for a few years. I knew exactly what I wanted in a relationship and refused to settle for anything less. I could even fill six journal pages with a bulleted list of all the things I liked about myself (before assuming arrogance, it included things like "I love the color green," but more on that later).

I was twenty-three years old, just one month shy of my twenty-fourth birthday and living on my own—four hours from home—when I started the journal. I was two months past my twenty-fifth birthday on the last page. There were, of course, pages and pages about how much I loved and missed my boyfriend, and pages and pages about how much I hated him. It included details of our almost nightly phone calls (apparently we spoke often in the months after our breakup, which probably didn't make things any easier for me.) But, there were also plenty of passages about my friends and family rallying around me—about the hours on end one friend (Scott, mentioned in my essay, *Senseless*) listened to me—we'd talk every single night until the wee hours of the morning. I'd like to think I listened to his relationship woes as much as he listened to mine, but I don't know if that was even possible. I do know that we made each other laugh—a lot.

There was an entry about how my roommate sat next to me with a tissue box when I finally broke down sobbing, realizing that the boyfriend and I were never really meant to be, even though I was sure that we were forever and I picked up my entire life and moved for him. Suddenly I saw that I truly was better off without him and that it wasn't all my fault. It wasn't his fault either—we were simply young and had some difficult circumstances. I realized at that moment that nothing I could have done would have changed the outcome. And then—I was free. It was literally turning the page on my life. I met my future husband, Jeff, three weeks later.

I had two other boyfriends between that break-up and my epiphany. But, I don't think I ever really gave my heart to either of them, even though they were both perfectly nice and handsome and ardently professed their love for me. I broke up with each at the three month mark—the time when you either move forward into something more serious or you walk away. I had to walk away. I was still tethered to the past. I dated other guys as well, and most were good distractions. Some weren't—there was the guy who picked me up with a "booger hanging out of his nose and dragon breath." I know—I was a bit vicious in the journal, but I knew no one would see it. More importantly, he was rude to the waiters; he ordered a dish for me that I didn't want—and boasted that he was a bad boy. I took great pleasure in turning him down for a second date. I did have a great time with some dates—still, for over a year I couldn't move forward (or maybe I just didn't want to).

And then… I could. I was over the pain. I was over everything. There were things about myself that I needed to fix before I could move on (that's for another essay) and once I did that, it was easy. But, this essay isn't really about getting over a break-up—it's about the gift of being able to revisit the person I was before I became the person I am. It's about getting a glimpse of myself as I evolved and grew. I felt everything so deeply and recorded all of those feelings.

Even if I hadn't been dumped, 1992 still would have been one of the darkest years of my life. My grandparents both died on the same day. My dog died and I never got to say goodbye. My weight, which was always a struggle for me to keep on, plummeted further. My apartment complex was riddled with drug dealers and other unsavory types, one of whom tried to break into my apartment. The gold and diamond necklace my parents gave me for my twenty-first birthday was stolen. And to top it all off, I had such a terrible ear infection that I lost hearing. But, out of that darkness rose hope. Everything was still in front of me. I just knew I would "make it big" according to one entry. I talked about wanting babies and dogs. (I might not have made it big, but I did get the babies and the dogs.)

I knew that I had hit bottom and emerged a stronger and no doubt better person for it—and that brings me back to those six pages of things I liked about myself. Most still hold true—some good and some bad. Apparently I thought it was a good thing that I always believed I'd start balancing my checkbook, even though I never did. And I must have thought it was charming that I had no sense of direction (and still don't!). Or how about this one: "I can never throw anything out." My husband got a good snicker out of that one. I have no idea why I thought that was a good thing, or maybe it was when I hardly had anything to throw out.

And then there were these in the bulleted list:
"I can write." (The very first thing on the list.)
"I love hockey."
"I am honest."
"I am down to earth."
"I love Mel Brooks movies."
"I am strong."
"I am loving."
"I am loyal."
"My favorite woman on TV is Elaine from Seinfeld."
"I always like the book better than the movie."

And two of my favorites: "I have really good intentions," and "I love it when a dog licks my face." There were so many more listed and I was relieved to see that most still hold true. Not all—can't say I've gone out dancing in quite a while. But on the whole, it was kind of amazing to be reminded of all the things I liked about myself when I actually had time to contemplate such things.

There was one more gift—just as amazing as remembering what I liked about myself: remembering what first drew me to my husband. For one thing, I said that he was the first guy I spent time with "that didn't make my uh-oh alarm go off." My friends who knew him better than I did (I had a crush on him after seeing him play the drums in a battle of the bands in college, but had only met him once or twice) warned me that he was trouble and was probably not even interested in me. I always had a weakness for bad boys and Jeff definitely gave off a bad boy vibe, but there was a sweetness to him. The night we ran into each other I wrote in my journal, "My gut reaction was that a) he's a good person and b) we clicked and he felt something too. Why am I always wrong?" But, I wasn't wrong.

A few weeks later, on the last page of the journal, I wrote that I liked the "juxtaposition of creative (a musician) and solid (getting his MBA) in his personality." I also wrote that he was "multi-dimensional." And a few lines below that—"It just scares me, because I get the feeling that this could turn into something big. He's a sweetheart and really cute." I wrote that I didn't want to be disappointed again, but I also wrote, "Maybe I won't be." And that is the heart of the most important thing I learned during that year of transformation—to believe in myself and believe in my gut; to take a chance and love openly. I was absolutely right—it was the start of something big. It's pretty wonderful to be reminded of that twenty years later.

THE BOOKSHELF

~ October 22, 2013 ~

IT HAD TO BE DONE. I've known this for a long time, but I made every excuse in the book not to do it. I didn't think they were excuses, though—just facts. I've been too busy working on my novel revisions. I'm always running to my kids' schools for one thing or another—forgotten gym clothes, PTA meeting, class party. I had to clean the living room, kitchen, bathroom—someplace seen if guests stop by. But, this afternoon it came time to face the fact that it just must be done. So, I did it. I went down into my basement—slowly, tentatively and purged a huge chunk of artifacts of my three boys' "little kid" years. My youngest just turned nine and I'm forty-five—it's time to realize that my dream of a fourth child is dead in the water. Never going to come true. I can't keep holding on to wooden puzzles and sweet little board books. Boggle Junior with my son's name and first grade classroom number on the box cover? He's fifteen now and in tenth grade. It's time to let go.

There are some exceptions—there had to be. After all, I started with the bookshelf. I would not dump anything by Shel Silverstein, Eric Carle, Graeme Base or the book *What Moms Can't Do*. The book, *I'll Love You Forever* by Robert Munsch had to keep its place on the shelf, as well. And since I'm always brutally honest in this blog, I'll admit that I burst into tears as I pulled the books off the shelf and placed them in a neat pile on the floor. It was the kind of cry that leaves puffy little pillows under your eyes and a rosy sheen to your nose.

There are so many memories in between all of the covers, not just my favorites. The many dinosaur books reminded me of when my oldest son was nicknamed, "Mr. Paleontologist," thanks to his deep love of the pre-historic creatures. He had to have every dinosaur book he saw and he read them cover to cover. Now his love of sneakers has replaced his love of T-Rex and a $6.99 book can't even touch the joy a pair of fancy kicks that can cost twenty times more brings him. I miss those simpler days so much sometimes—a child on my lap; a book open. Maybe he's pointing. Maybe he's dozing off to sleep. Either way, there was a closeness that reading a book together brings that can't be duplicated by any other activity.

My kids still read, of course. My youngest, Aidan, can spend hours immersed in a good science book, trying to unlock the secrets of the universe—or at least the hows and whys of various weather patterns. My middle one, Joshua, would prefer his iPod to a book and it can be a battle getting him to read, but if he loves a book, he can read it three times. My oldest, Drew, is taking honors English and gets to read all the great, meaty stuff that goes along with it. When he read *Romeo and Juliet* we had an in-depth discussion about the end and I have to say it was a very special moment in parenting for me. I was an English major and getting to relive my student days is more fun than I would have thought—and makes me more than happy to lend a hand with homework.

But, and of course there's always a but, it's not the same. Keeping your child on the path to being a life-long reader is not nearly the same as setting them on that path. Setting them on that path is wondrous. It is magical—it is the best kind of bonding there is. And that's why I was crying. I'll never be there again. It's not just the books that hold memories—it's the toys too, of course—but the books, those are the most cherished.

As sad as it is though, there's something liberating about getting rid of things you never use. There's something liberating about seeing white space on what was once a ridiculously overstuffed shelf. There's even something liberating about acknowledging that you're ending one chapter in your life and moving on to another. I'm done with the "young mom" chapter. I probably have been for a while. I'm in the thick of things—teenagers (one already there and one almost there) and a fourth grader—only one year left of elementary school. At this time next year, I'll have only middle and high schoolers. Perhaps most astoundingly, I'm exactly equidistant from my last child being born to that child leaving home for college—nine years in either direction. Nine years has gone by in the blink of an eye, although in some ways it seems like a lifetime ago.

As I surveyed the piles of books, puzzles and games on the dark green carpet, I catalogued all of the things I've done that I couldn't have if I had a baby or toddler now. I wrote a novel—that's the big one. I started it when my son was in nursery school, but didn't finish it until he was in elementary school. (Immediately I thought—well, what if it doesn't get published? Was it worth not having another child then?) I've gone to writing conferences and have spent hours researching agents and publishers. My husband and I went to the Atlantis resort in the Bahamas—just the two of us—on an all-expense paid trip. My mom could never have watched a baby in addition to a thirteen, eleven and seven-year-old. I adopted three dogs from the time that I started thinking about having another when my youngest was two. I probably wouldn't have been able to save all of them if I was overwhelmed with a newborn. And I shudder to think what the third dog I adopted—after our first dog passed away—would do to a curious toddler. He's not patient and I'm not the type to dump a dog—so we'd be in an impossible situation.

But, all of that doesn't really matter—they're just things I tell myself to feel better. The only thing that matters is that you need two people to want a child and my husband just didn't want a fourth. I always joked that if I wanted another kid, I'd have to find a new husband and I was far too lazy for that. But, the truth is I could have tried to push him to add another child to our brood. I talked him into the others. Not that he didn't want them, but he wasn't ready when I was.

Right before we started trying for our first child I told him, "You get ready" when he expressed his concerns. I was twenty-nine years old; we had been married for a year and I felt it was time. I told him he'd never regret it. I was right. I told him the same thing with the second, when he expressed concern about having another child while our first was still just a baby himself. But, when my oldest turned eighteen months old and started saying, "No" all the time, I was sure that a new tiny bundle would cure my longing for easier days. "You'll never regret a child," I told him and I was right.

With our third, he asked me, point blank, "How can you possibly take care of three when you can barely take care of the two you have?" That wasn't exactly the right question—I took care of my kids just fine. It was myself I barely took care of. I was run down by chasing after a five and a three-year-old. Even worse, that three-year-old had numerous health issues, including severe asthma and sleep apnea. And both kids had already had surgery, Drew for sleep apnea and Joshua for adenoidectomy. We knew surgery for Joshua's sleep apnea loomed in the near future.

I was exhausted and anxious and absolutely certain that having a new baby would bring the joy back into my life that seemed to be slipping through my fingers like grains of sand. "You'll never regret a child," I told my husband for the third time—and of course, I was right. But ... would I be right a fourth time? Or would he regret it? Would caring for a baby and then a toddler while managing the hectic schedules of three school age children—sports, Hebrew school, after-school science programs—while in our forties put us over the edge?

I didn't know the answer. As much as I wanted another baby, I wasn't confident enough to utter those words, "You won't regret it." I wasn't confident enough to push. Somewhere inside I knew I wouldn't regret it, but would he? Perhaps. Maybe if we had a bigger house, I would have pushed. There's really no room for another child, although as I always say—babies don't take up much room. But, as they get older they do. And babies might not take up room, but all their stuff does. And that's why I'm cleaning it all out. I don't have babies anymore and I've finally accepted the fact that I won't. It's hard to say goodbye to that dream, but I'm hoping to replace it with other dreams. Maybe the next chapter of my life will hold lots of promise, even without a bundle of joy. And I'm hoping that there will be babies again a decade, or more likely, two down the road—I've heard that being a grandparent is just pure joy, untainted by the angst of parenting. Now, that's something to look forward to...

HUNGRY

~ *January 17, 2014* ~

WHEN I WAS GROWING UP, my mother often said to my brother, "Just wait until your children do the same thing to you!" if he was late getting home or didn't call when he should have. She never said it to me, though—she didn't need to. I came home when I was supposed to. I did my homework. I dated nice boys. I obeyed. Always, I obeyed. But, in my early twenties I put them through something no parent should have to go through—watching me slowly starve myself. Well, they didn't really have to watch, being that I was living four hours away, but when I came home skinnier and skinnier, I know they were alarmed. I thought I was fine, though and couldn't understand why they would ask me to move back home. Now, watching my child eat less and less and weigh less and less feels like the worst possible karma. It also feels like somehow it's my fault.

Now, there are probably some of you who know me who are thinking, "I knew she had an eating disorder!" or maybe, "I was right when I told her she needs to eat a steak!" But, it's not what you think. I didn't look in the mirror and see a rotund person staring back at me as I zipped up my size zero jeans. I hated how skinny I was. It wasn't always like that—I was "curvy" by the time I was ten (my nickname was Dolly Parton!) and all I wanted was to be flat and skinny like the other girls. I got my wish when I was eleven years old and lost fifteen pounds due to an illness. I learned to be careful of what I wish for—for the next several years I was terribly insecure about my weight. But by the time I graduated high school, I weighed about what I do now. I had a boyfriend who took me out to dinner a lot and out for ice cream and out to the movies with vats of buttered popcorn. Gradually the weight crept on and I looked healthier. By my sophomore year of college I weighed five pounds more than I do now. I'd like to think it was the weight training I was doing, but I'm sure it was the late night pizzas and giant chocolate chip cookies from the student center.

But, then something happened—I can't really get into it here for a few reasons. Let's just say that I was a mess of anxiety for a good reason, but I hid it very well. The only thing that suffered was my appetite. I just couldn't eat. Well, that's not exactly true—I could eat a lot my junior year, but I would be in pain and nothing really appealed to me. Slowly, I started eliminating the things that made me feel like someone was knifing me in the stomach. I was left with plain pasta, vegetables, fruit and corn muffins. Oh—and English muffins. I lived on English Muffins with jam. It was like I could only handle the simplest of foods—comfort foods that you'd eat when you have the flu.

It was my psyche that was distressed, but I acted fine. And to tell you the truth, being hungry blurred the edges of the pain a bit. Sure at first it's an uncomfortable sensation, but after a while that slightly hazy feeling when you haven't had enough to eat felt almost like a buzz from a glass of wine or a couple of beers. Any study on nutrition will tell you that you're just not as sharp if you're living on fumes and that's what I was doing. An English muffin with jam for breakfast, a cup of soup for lunch or maybe just a baked potato with a bit of cheese, a bowl of pasta with margarine and some veggies thrown in for dinner. I ate enough to barely stay upright and I was almost pleasantly out of it at times. Being hungry turned down the volume of the noise in my brain. I'm sure that's hard to understand for the average person, but I wasn't average. More importantly, I got used to the feeling of fuzziness. But, by the time I turned twenty-four I was ill all the time—bronchitis, sinusitis, any germ that walked past me I caught—and I had lost more than weight.

You see, I had a boyfriend—whom I thought I would marry—but he couldn't stand to watch me starve. He dangled the carrot of an engagement ring in front of me—saying that if I gained ten pounds, we'd get engaged. I tried. I went to therapy. I learned what was behind my not eating and gradually I was starting to fix it. But, it was just too late—it was too painful for him to watch me destroy myself when he knew that the solution was so easy. Just eat. Eat everything. Eat anything. Just eat. But, I couldn't. Not at first at least. So, he walked. Watching my son now, I completely understand it and even feel bad about what I put him through. I also feel bad about all the family dinners when I'd come home to visit and be like a deer caught in headlights as everyone exhorted me to put more on my plate. Put more in my mouth. I thought I was fine though. Now, when I look at pictures from that time it horrifies me.

I tell my son, Joshua, that I understand. I tell him that I know what it's like when food seems like the enemy, because of how it makes you feel. He's scared to eat, because he's scared of how he'll feel, not because he wants to be skinnier. If you read my previous essay, *Twice Exceptional* , you know that Joshua has Obsessive Compulsive Disorder. His stomach pain is caused by anxiety, not the food he's eating, but he can't see that. I couldn't see it either when my head and gut were inexorably linked. So, I tell him I get it. But, it still scares the crap out of me because I know how incredibly hard it is to get past it.

There are times when I really feel like my husband, blames me for Joshua's eating problems—little comments here and there. He'll take his words back after, but it's still hanging there. Dark and damaging. There are times I blame myself. I'm a picky eater—part of it is self-preservation. I'm allergic to two things that are in so many foods. I over-analyze the menu when I eat out and worry that something will be cooked on a shared surface and I'll have a reaction (it's happened more than a few times). I also still fall into the trap of no-appetite when I'm stressed. Like the other night—I had a half of a bagel with butter and cheese for dinner. Last night I had a bowl of cereal. Sometimes I'll eat a cup of yogurt with a spoonful of peanut butter for dinner. But, I'm at a healthy weight now. I weigh ten pounds more than I did when my ex-boyfriend dangled an engagement ring in front of me.

It all worked out just fine, of course. I met my husband a year after that break-up. I had been going to therapy and the gym and I was happier and healthier than I had been in a long time, even if I was still a little underweight. But, when we were newlyweds I hit a stressful patch and food became the enemy again. I had a wake-up call, though. I fainted while waiting for a table at a restaurant. I had only eaten an apple and a cup of yogurt since breakfast that day and when my husband took me to the emergency room my blood sugar was dangerously low. I realized at that moment that if I wanted to have a healthy pregnancy at some point that year, I had to start taking better care of myself. I went to a nutritionist and did the hard work of making myself eat more. I know, some of you are surely snickering, "How hard could it be to eat fattening foods?" The answer is very hard — when your brain is telling you not to eat it.

I know this is the problem with Joshua and I feel completely helpless. I've taken him to the doctor — he showed us Joshua's weight (about sixty pounds) on his iPad on a chart with blue and red lines. His weight wasn't even anywhere near the curves. If his weight was the same percentile as his height on that chart, he'd weigh thirty pounds more — he'd weigh almost what I weigh. But, it's not. It's way below. I've told him that I'm going to take him to an eating disorder clinic, which he was not happy about. We've offered to buy him a tablet if he hits seventy pounds. Nothing works. So, I just try to let Joshua know that it will get better. That he can get through this and come out on the other side. He won't always be afraid to lift the fork to his mouth. Sometimes you just need someone to listen. When I hit rock bottom on the scale — my lowest weight was seventy-nine pounds when I was just shy of twenty-four years old — I only told one person, my friend Scott. He didn't judge me. He just listened.

I try to do that for Joshua. I try to listen without judging. It's incredibly hard when you just want to scream, "Eat something! You're making yourself sick!" But, talking about it just makes it worse. Talking about it guarantees the food will sit on Joshua's plate, rather than wind up in his stomach. But sometimes, the best medicine for an eating disorder is just knowing that someone understands what you're going through – just knowing that you're not alone.

"Eating disorder" is a thorny label, though. The doctor said that Joshua doesn't really have an eating disorder, because he doesn't think that he's fat. I disagree with that. I think any time one eats too much or too little, it's an eating disorder. And, an eating disorder is a wily opponent. It makes you feel like things will never get better. Like things are hopeless. Joshua tells me that he wishes he were someone else. He wishes that he could be like our dogs and eat everything in sight. He wishes he could just shovel the food in. I tell him that he can be that person. But, only he can hack through his food fears. The first pediatrician we ever went to as new parents told us that there are three things you can never make your child do—poop, sleep and eat. "Don't even bother trying to control those three," he said with a sigh. And that's got to be the hardest part of this whole shitty situation—I can't make Joshua eat. Only he can do the difficult work of realizing that food is not the enemy. Only he can hit the bottom and claw his way up. I can only let him know that I'll be beside him every step of the way and will give him a boost out of the shadowy depths whenever I can.

I didn't really want to write this post—or at least I didn't want to share it. But, as a writer you have to be willing to shine a flashlight into the darkest corners of your life. If not, you may as well step away from the laptop. Plus, if my son was brave enough to let me share his story (I asked his permission), I could certainly be brave enough to share my story. I had two other reasons to write this—one selfish, one not. The selfish one—this essay has been pinging around my brain for a long time. If I didn't write it, it would probably keep playing in an endless loop, keeping me from getting my other work done. The unselfish—I know there are other people out there going through similar things. And while I can't offer a solution—unfortunately there isn't an easy one—I can say the same thing I say to Joshua, "You're not alone." And sometimes, that can make all the difference in the world.

THE PUZZLE

~ February 27, 2014 ~

"IT'S LIKE FITTING TOGETHER THE PIECES OF A PUZZLE," the psychologist tells me and I swear, his eyes light up. Not that I can blame him for his excitement. My son, Aidan, is an extraordinarily interesting subject and I'm not just saying that because I'm obviously biased. I'm saying it, because he really is.

Aidan was brilliant from an early age. At two years old he asked me out of the blue as we were browsing in a book store, "Did you know that 2 + 3 = 5?" Not long after that I found him sitting on the floor of his bedroom crying. When I asked what was wrong, he wailed, "I can't read!" His solution? He memorized the books that I read to him, so he could "read" them himself. At four years old he came home from camp one afternoon and announced, "The square root of forty-nine is seven," and then proceeded to rattle off several other square root problems. Apparently his counselors thought it was fun to teach him square roots, because he already knew basic math in and out. "I feel like I'm talking to a twenty-seven-year-old," one counselor told me. "I have to remind myself that he's four."

He could recite every single state in the union and the day it earned its statehood by the time he was six. Every state. My sister had given him a book, *Fifty States of America* and he memorized it. When we visited Plymouth Rock, Aidan overheard a couple say that the first state was Connecticut. He corrected them, piping up in his little voice, "Actually it was Delaware. It entered the union on December 7, 1787. Connecticut was January 9, 1788." (And yes, I had to Google that, because I couldn't remember the dates. He's way smarter than I am.)

The presidents were no different. Aidan memorized every president, thanks to a set of flash cards I bought him, and could tell you the date of each president's birth and death, as well as the order of presidency. Forwards and backwards. He can start with Washington and go forward or Obama and go back. Either way, he never misses one. We were at a party and someone was wondering when Gerald Ford died. Aidan had the answer ready. I Googled it on my phone and he was right, of course.

So, now you know—Aidan really is an extraordinary child. But—and there's always a but, isn't there—he has a hard time functioning in school. He aces every single test. He's hasn't gotten a word wrong on a spelling test since first grade—he's in fourth now. He doesn't study and brings home high nineties. But, he doesn't pay attention either. He daydreams, because he knows everything and he's bored. Or at least that's his take on it. When I asked him why he doesn't pay attention, he answered, "I'm bored out of my mind."

The psychologist found that he has "an extremely high fund of knowledge," which he explained probably means that he already knows a lot of what's being taught. He also said that Aidan informed him that he daydreams when he's bored, but he "doesn't do it as much anymore." One time Aidan told me that he really is listening to his teacher; he just doesn't always look at her.

Aidan's teacher, a lovely woman who is rightfully concerned about him, filled out all the little circles on a behavioral scale that I had passed along to her as part of the psycho-educational evaluation Aidan was undergoing. According to her answers, Aidan has a 91% likelihood of having Attention Deficit Disorder (ADD) or Attention Deficit Hyperactivity Disorder (ADHD). According to my answers on the parent scale, Aidan has very little likelihood of having ADD or ADHD, but may have an anxiety disorder of some sort. I see him work with incredible focus when a subject interests him. When I picked him up one day from his after school science program, the teacher called him a "genius." I asked her if he had trouble paying attention. She immediately answered, "No."

At science camp pick-up when he was seven years old the program leader told me that he worked on his robot the entire session, even when the kids around him (much older kids) were getting wild, jumping around and throwing things. He just sat at the table and meticulously put together his robotic arm. At home he can easily entertain himself, reading books, drawing detailed, correctly scaled maps of the United States and using train tracks to construct a replica of area highways. He has built volcanos and Frankenstein hands. He read a book I bought him on experiments cover to cover and eagerly carried out many of them. I just don't see the attention issues that his teacher does. And yes, I know that neither ADD nor ADHD preclude paying attention to enjoyable things, but this is different.

So, when the psychologist's first suggestion was a trial of stimulant medication to test if he has ADD or ADHD (if it helps him pay attention in school, he has it—if it does nothing, he doesn't), my immediate reaction was to politely decline. "Did you find any evidence of an attention disorder in your evaluation?" I asked.

"Well, no—not really. But, it might be the fact that it's quiet. There are no other distractions." I told him about the after school classes and camp—both places with all different age kids and plenty of distractions and he agreed that being able to pay attention in a situation like that is telling.

"Look," I said. "I don't want to be rude, but I don't want to medicate my child just because he's bored. He's doing fine academically. I really hesitate to fix something that's not broken. If he was suffering academically, that would be a different story. I'd be perfectly willing to try medication. But, he's not."

His teacher did report that he "moves slowly throughout the day and needs many reminders to stay on task." I just don't think that medicating him for that is a good idea—as difficult and frustrating as I'm sure that is. I move slowly and would forget every single thing I had to do if it wasn't for my iPhone calendar. Perhaps it's hereditary.

"Will it fix his social issues?" I asked. The one area Aidan's teacher and I rated Aidan similarly was the social skills scale. We both reported problems there. And of course, that's the most heartbreaking finding and the one that can't be fixed by all the meds in the world. Even though Aidan has two good friends and seems perfectly fine with that, he has at times been bullied (thankfully the situation was remedied) and has had social difficulties—enough that he's in the social skills group at school. And that little nugget of information is what brought the psychologist to perhaps finding that one piece of the puzzle that's been missing for most of Aidan's life — or at least since early toddlerhood.

After I mentioned that Aidan has an encyclopedic knowledge of many topics, the psychologist asked, "Does he learn everything there is to learn about a subject and then move on to the next thing?"

When I answered, "Yes, but he retains the knowledge," he inquired, "You know what that's a sign of?"

"Asperger's?" I asked, knowing the answer.

"Yes, it's a very common sign of it — an intense interest in a subject and the desire to learn everything about it. Then again, it could just be his scientist's mind — but, there are enough other signs that it should be investigated further."

I wasn't really surprised — not at all in fact. But, I still felt the heat creep up my cheeks and my stomach knot up. I know that it's entirely possible to live a normal, rewarding life with Asperger's, even an extraordinary life. It's been contemplated that Bill Gates may have Asperger's; Albert Einstein and Abraham Lincoln too. Surely many people with Asperger's (which as of recently is no longer an official diagnosis — it's now considered an "Autism Spectrum Disorder" or ASD) accomplish amazing things. It's just hard to think about my brilliant, kind boy possibly facing a lifetime of social challenges.

The first time I brought Aidan to be evaluated for Asperger's was almost a year ago. His gym teacher informed me that she had first-hand experience with someone close to her who has Asperger's and she saw a lot of those traits in Aidan. I really appreciated her input, because she saw him in a more social setting than academic teachers. Plus, I had my suspicions already. But, within a few minutes of speaking with Aidan, the psychologist ruled out Asperger's. "He makes eye contact. He has a conversation. There's no way this child has Asperger's." This new psychologist said that plenty of kids with Asperger's make eye contact. There are varying degrees. But, at the time I breathed a sigh of relief and packed that theory away. I still didn't have answers for why things are harder for Aidan than other kids, though.

Aidan has always had sensory issues — at his kindergarten graduation he alternately covered his ears and covered his eyes. It was heartbreaking to watch. At his fourth grade concert, he spent most of the time trying to push up the sleeves of his button down shirt, because he was warm. When he was a baby, he hated if his feet touched sand or even grass. He'd scream bloody murder if I tried to put footed pajamas on him. Lotion on dry skin was an impossibility. Occupational therapy helped, but didn't cure everything—like his food aversions. No fruits, except for applesauce. No vegetables, except for corn (which he informed me is really a grain). Frosting on a cupcake? No way. Mashed potatoes? Not even a fork-full.

As a toddler, Aidan wouldn't give anyone hugs except close family and if someone he wasn't very familiar with picked him up, he screamed. At the toddler gym he attended the owner—a large, muscled man—picked Aidan up and after that Aidan cried every single time we went to his class, he was so traumatized. We ended up dropping out. Aidan even mastered the "foot five" a few years ago, a trick my friend taught him, because he didn't want to give high fives.

When I think about all of this, I realize that a diagnosis of Asperger's wouldn't be the end of the world, because maybe it would let us get him the help he needs and perhaps help his teachers to understand him better. He's the proverbial square peg that they are trying to fit into a round hole. It's just not going to work and medicating him to smooth down his edges so he'll fit in seems to me the worst possible idea.

I guess only time—and some more testing—will tell. So far, all we know is that his IQ is in the superior range (and in some areas the very superior range). On one part of the IQ test he did much worse than the others, which may indicate a visual tracking problem—which could certainly affect his ability to keep up and pay attention in school. But, in another area that generally suffers in ADD and ADHD he scored in the 99% percentile. So, clearly there's something else going on. And, I will get to the bottom of it.

Whether he's just a quirky future scientist (he wants to be a meteorologist) or on the autism spectrum really doesn't matter—all that matters is that somehow we (Aidan's educators and my husband and I) come up with a plan that will maintain his thirst for knowledge while helping him fit in better in the classroom setting. Because if his curious spirit is beaten down by an educational system that wants him to learn like everyone else before he gets to accomplish great things, it will be a loss for everyone.

THE MIRROR

~ *April 7, 2014* ~

NOTE (2016): I WROTE THIS ESSAY a little over a year after *Skin Deep* (a few essays previous) and there may be some overlap of ideas. Clearly, this is an issue that I will revisit many times over the years ...

People tell me I look young—it's my thing. I've looked younger than I am since I was a teenager. A thirteen-year-old boy asked me out on a date when I was seventeen years old. I told him that he was far too young for me (and that I had a boyfriend), but he would not give up until I produced my driver's license. When I was thirty-four years old I was at the library with my boys, two and four years old. They were, as usual, making a bit of a ruckus. When the custodian approached me, I was sure he was going to kick us out. Instead, he asked, "Are these your kids?" When I answered, "Yes," rather than replying, "Well, get them out of here," he simply said, "You look way too young to have kids that age." I thanked him profusely, though I wasn't quite sure if he meant it as a compliment or an accusation.

People often told me I looked too young to have kids as I tried to wrangle two toddlers and it was generally said with an air of hostility. During those moments, I realized how it must feel to be a teen mom—this was way before MTV glorified getting knocked up before the age of twenty—and it wasn't pretty. I probably looked as if I popped out a few kids before I was even legal to drink. I even got carded going to see my husband's band play at a huge club in Boston. I had just turned thirty years old and was pregnant enough to show, but the bouncer carded me. I may have hugged him—I can't remember.

You might be thinking right about now, "Geez, she's just bragging for two whole paragraphs. I don't need to hear this. I'm done." But, wait—don't stop reading. That was just the set-up. I promise there's more to say that won't make you hate me—I hope. Like this—when I turned thirty-five I decided that I looked old. I hated the parentheses lines around my mouth and a few grays had sprung up at my temples. For my thirty-fifth birthday my parents got me a gift card to a fancy salon. I used it to get blonde highlights woven through my hair. I loved the blonde, but couldn't keep up with it—not with two little kids. Pretty soon I started looking like a reverse skunk, so I went back to brunette (from a box) and that pretty much sums up my beauty maintenance. I basically do very little and hope for the best.

I color my hair from a box still (actually, my husband does it and I have to say, he does a great job). I've been a bit adventurous with even the box color—like doing an ombre. But, I recently went back to my original color (or at least a close approximation)—Feria Espresso from L'Oreal. It's way cheaper than a salon, quicker and, most importantly, I kept having allergic reactions to salon hair color. I'm violently allergic to sulfites and I didn't realize that hair color is chock full of sodium metabisulfite. I just chalked it up to an anxiety attack when my heart would start racing and my head would suddenly feel like everything emptied out of it, I was so dizzy. Sometimes even the box color makes me dizzy and feel like my head is on fire, but I can cut the time short and wash it out at least. I'm sharing all of this, because it leads me to my next point—I often wonder if I'm doing enough ...

Now that I'm forty-six years old I wonder if it really is time to start using something more potent than Origins skin cream. I get like this every year around my birthday. In fact, writing this paragraph, I had a flashback to another post I wrote as I "skidded toward my forty-fifth birthday" last year. I revisited it and realized that it covers a lot of the same territory. This bit of writer deja-vu made me realize something—I clearly don't follow my own advice. That essay ended with "...I think that's the key to accepting ourselves for what we are, instead of getting depressed every time we look in the mirror—just try to see yourself as others see you. That and maybe a few blonde highlights."

So, why do I still get depressed when I look in the mirror and realize those fine lines around my eyes aren't going anywhere, no matter how much eye cream I glob on? Why when people say to me that I look way too young to have a sixteen-year-old, do I put my hands to my face and mutter self-deprecatingly, "I feel like I look old," instead of just smiling appreciatively and expressing my gratitude without a disclaimer? Why when a security guard at the airport in February pointed to me and told my kids that their sister was waiting for them did I wonder if he needed glasses? Rereading my essay from last year, *Skin Deep*, I realize that this is something I've pondered for quite a while. Why indeed can't I take my own advice and see others as they see me?

I explore this theme in my novel, *Goddess of Suburbia*. What if a regular mom with all of the body insecurities that go with the job finds that her naked form is suddenly zipping around the Internet for everyone to see? Would she die of shame or would she emerge stronger, finally able to believe it when someone tells her she's hot? Of course, I can't share the answer — that would ruin the book. But, it was really interesting for me to explore her psyche — because perhaps it's a bit of a mirror to my own. (Not that I want a naked video of myself zipping around — EVER.)

Not that long ago an older woman said to me, "If I looked like you, I'd kiss the mirror every day." I walked away from her thinking, so what's real — what she sees or what I see? More importantly, when I'm this woman's age, will I be beating myself up for my insecurities now? I'm pretty sure the answer to that question is, "Yes." When I look at pictures of myself from when I first started to worry that I was looking older, I want to kick that thirty-five-year-old's ass. My skin was dewy and fresh — I don't know why I was so hard on myself. Even when I look at photos from last year, I think — well, I looked better then. This past winter was so stressful and it shows.

That's when I start thinking about doing a little more than slathering on a rich cream every morning and every night and rubbing coconut oil into my face a couple of times a day. (I swear, it makes your skin feel amazing and smells so good!). I start thinking about how my friend told me that way more women than I thought are all using Botox and using it in their early forties. I think about all of the lip plumpers and the resurfacing lasers that women my age take advantage of. I think about eye jobs and facelifts …

But, that's all that I do—I think about it. As much as I would love to consider these fountain-of-youth promises, I know that I'll never do any of these things – not that I judge those who do. I won't do these things, because I never put anything in my body unless it's absolutely necessary. Having an anaphylactic reaction to a medication can make you a bit paranoid about meds in the future and as much as anyone would like to think that Botox is not a drug, it is. According to Wikipedia, it was first used therapeutically to correct strabismus (crossed eyes), blepharospasm (uncontrollable blinking) and achalasia (a spasm of the lower esophageal sphincter). And, even though the amount used to erase wrinkles is widely considered safe, it's still comprised of "the most lethal toxin known," also according to Wikipedia. I just can't see shooting that into my face, no matter how young it would make me look.

Then there are all the other injectables and procedures—maybe I'm a baby, but I just can't bring myself to even consider anything invasive. So, I can either age gracefully and hopefully to start seeing myself as others see me or I can be miserable and notice every little line every time I look in the mirror. I of course know the right choice—I'm pretty sure that in ten or fifteen years, I'll look at pictures of myself from now and wish I could kick some forty-six-year-old ass for not appreciating what I have when I have it...

THE POWER OF KINDNESS

~ *June 3, 2104* ~

SIXTY-SEVEN POUNDS. That's a number I never thought I'd see when my thirteen-year-old son stepped on the scale. Sixty, yes—maybe sixty-two or even sixty-three soaking wet. But, sixty-seven pounds, a mere three pounds away from seventy, seemed unreachable. That is until my son met John Giannone, the New York Rangers sportscaster from MSG Networks. The change in him since their first encounter is nothing short of remarkable. Simply put, this connection that he's forged with John and the ripples of change it has sent through his life have renewed my faith in humanity.

I "met" John two years ago on Twitter during the Rangers' fairly unremarkable cup run. It was nothing like this season—it was over way too soon—but, we started "talking" hockey and writing and our kids. I'm a Rangers nut and to have a hockey insider with an incredible store of knowledge and a brilliant take on the game to discuss my favorite team with was (and still is) something I truly enjoy. He's also a great writer and has been incredibly supportive of my work, reading my book more than once—and my synopsis and essays, etc. He has an eagle eye and has been a great help.

Add to all that the fact that John is totally down to earth and incredibly kind and you know why I consider him a true friend, even though we've only really met a few times. So, this is why the night before the first time we finally met in person at the Rangers' Hockey House (a fan festival located just outside Madison Square Garden), I confided that my son, Joshua, suffers from severe Obsessive Compulsive Disorder and an eating disorder. At thirteen years old he weighs only a few pounds more than my nine-year-old.

He's my height, but weighs about twenty-seven pounds less than I do. You probably read about his battle in the essay *Hungry* .

I told John how Joshua looks up to him and was so excited to meet him and he promised to spend some time chatting with Joshua. He not only made good on his promise, talking to Joshua and his brothers about sports and their lives, while a line of autograph seekers built up behind us, but he also gave Joshua his email address, so Joshua could write to him during the playoffs.

My son has spent five long years in therapy, not counting the time it actually took us to find a therapist. It's been a process of two steps forward, three steps back—always ending up somehow worse than he was before any breakthrough. We met with five therapists before one finally figured out what was wrong. The process took three months—I started searching for a therapist right after the school psychologist made me cry during Joshua's second grade parent-teacher conference. He was asked to sit in and his contribution was this: turning toward me with a look of mock sympathy and saying, "How miserable you must be; you don't even know what's wrong with him." Joshua's teacher handed me a box of tissues as she saw my eyes well up.

So, you can figure out that it's been a long, arduous road—often feeling as if we've hardly made any progress at all. OCD is usually just portrayed as a person being neat or a control freak. In reality, it's like a prison—the person suffering from it is trapped in a vicious cycle of routines, usually quite elaborate. These elaborate OCD routines were like a noose around Joshua's neck, choking the joy out of his life. His teachers reported that he simply stared vacantly in class, not taking notes—seemingly not there at all. Going out to dinner was such an anxiety provoking ordeal for Joshua, that we avoided it. He was terrified of new places, new foods and even familiar foods in new places. He lost weight while we were in Disney World in February, because there was so little he would eat. He lost even more when he came down with the flu in March, which quickly escalated into pneumonia a few days later—his weak body a prime host for a secondary infection.

The worst of Joshua's routines and fears revolved around food. They are the routines that are the hardest to break and the ones with the most devastating physical and emotional impact. Not eating was leaving Joshua vulnerable to both serious physical ailments and emotional instability. How many of you find yourself moody and unable to focus after skipping a meal? Now imagine eating hardly anything day after day. We begged Joshua to eat. We threatened to take him to the hospital and have a feeding tube put in. We took him for regular weight checks and made him drink Boost, a nutritional supplement. But, nothing worked.

That is until he met John. Back to that meeting at Hockey House—Joshua felt incredibly special to be the focus of John's attention while so many people waited to chat with him. He felt even more special when he received his first email reply from John. We were in the drop-off line at school and he couldn't wait to go in and tell his friends. But, there was something bigger going on than just feeling special. The day we met John, Joshua ate an entire slice of pizza for dinner and didn't do a routine before it (the first time in years). The next morning, he ate a new food for breakfast—and again, no routine. I couldn't believe it. We had brought both pizza and new foods to Joshua's therapist's office to no avail. Those times he'd promise not to do the routine, but the next day he was back at it.

I asked Joshua what was allowing him to quit something that had become so ingrained in him, even though it was so detrimental to his health. He explained that the day we met John he was so excited, that he forgot to do his breakfast routine. So many good things happened; he decided not to do it the next day. His budding friendship with John was such a great distraction that he didn't do it the next day nor did he do it the next.

After four days of being routine free I sent John a novel length email thanking him for the profound impact he had on Joshua's life at that point already. This is part of that treatise, "I was sure that the effect would wear off and he'd be back to his eating routines in a day or two—but, today's the fourth day and he's still routine-free. Just thinking about it, I tear up. Raising a child with a mental illness is an arduous, sometimes soul crushing task and I can't thank you enough for giving us a glimmer of hope." Well, those four days have turned into just over six weeks. From the first round of the Stanley Cup playoffs to the finals. And, Joshua still isn't doing food routines. It feels like some sort of miracle every day. I marvel at how sometimes the simplest things can have a profound impact—like kindness.

John certainly didn't have to give my son the attention he has. Some people are only nice to those who have something to offer them—furthering their career, a chance at publicity. A symbiotic relationship is the driving force behind a lot of acts of kindness. You scratch my back, I'll scratch yours. But, my son—a thirteen-year-old boy—has nothing to offer in return for everything he has received, except the feeling of making a huge difference in a young boy's life. It's gone beyond even eating. The week before Joshua's bar mitzvah we brought his sign-in book to Hockey House. John penned the most thoughtful, encouraging inscription and I really think it had a lot to do with Joshua's sudden confidence. He chanted his Haftorah perfectly. He embellished on his D'var Torah on the fly, adding in an entire passage about my dad who passed away three years ago. There wasn't a dry eye in the house. He even winged his candle lighting speeches, calling friends and family up to light candles with snappy invitations that sounded as if he worked hours on them. And all thanks to a connection forged through hockey and Twitter—the most unlikely of catalysts for such a profound change.

I told John that this amazing connection reminds me of the starfish story. It's about a wise old man who happens upon a boy throwing starfish into the ocean—the old man tells the boy he can't possibly make a difference, there are too many starfish to save. The boy throws a starfish into the ocean and says, "I made a difference to that one." And, that's what John has done—made a huge difference to one person. And for that, we'll be eternally grateful.

Note: I made sure Joshua read this essay and approved of it, because it's his life I'm laying bare. He was more than happy about it and said that he doesn't have anything to hide. He wants to help others feel not alone and I'm so proud of him!

TIME BOMB

~ *June 4, 2014* ~

THE OTHER DAY I HAD REVISITED AN OLD ESSAY, *What If? Part 2*, because I've had a similar post rattling around my head for over a week and I didn't want to repeat anything. But, finding myself in almost the same exact situation—waiting for biopsy results—a year and a half later, I guess I'm doomed to repeat something. Especially this—I really don't want to write this essay. I'm intensely private when it comes to certain things (and as I've mentioned, I know that may come as a surprise with all of my psyche plumbing essays), and this is just something that I don't want to share. But, I know that it will help other people going through the same thing. I also know that when I write about something, it usually defuses it in my brain. And lastly, I'm ridiculously superstitious and since I blogged before receiving my last two biopsies results and they were negative, one little part of me thinks— well, you better blog before this one too. Silly, right?

Only—is it like the Budweiser commercial, it's only weird if it doesn't work? Who knows—people employ all kinds of good luck charms. I guess I'll know if it works soon enough—my doctor was supposed to call me two days ago. Actually, she said that she might have even had the results five days ago—before the weekend, but definitely by Monday. It's now Wednesday and my phone hasn't rung. I know I should call her, but I just keep putting it off. No news is good news, right?

I'm really not surprised to be in this position again. For years I have felt like my girl parts—at least my ovaries and uterus—are ticking time bombs. My sister and my mother both had reproductive cancers. My aunts on either side had breast cancer, sometimes considered a reproductive cancer. My grandmother passed away from cancer one week after she was diagnosed, it was so advanced. Her bones were lacy from the invasion of cancerous cells, but it likely started elsewhere. All of this is why a gynecological oncologist geneticist (quite a mouthful, if that's even the right term) at Sloane Kettering told me a year and a half ago that the ticking time bomb analogy isn't quite so far off (maybe not in those exact words, though). I may have Lynch Syndrome. Lynch Syndrome causes a genetic disposition to more cancers than I care to share here and they are the worst ones (not that any cancer is good). It's not a death sentence, but it's surely a "lifetime of worry" sentence.

The only way to know for sure if I have it is to have my sister's tumors from almost two decades ago tested. I called the genetics office at the hospital where she had her surgery more than once and they never returned my call. I've now found out that her tumors may be long gone; many are kept for only a decade. I did speak with a genetic counselor at another hospital when I went to get an ultrasound the other day. She told me that they have newer tests that may be able to give me an answer even without the tumor.

As I lay on the table for that ultrasound, feet in stirrups, staring at the ceiling and counting the slightly cratered tiles above me, all I thought about was what kind of a deal I could strike with God. I've had a lot of ultrasounds and struck a lot of deals. I had run out of things. I couldn't really promise to be more charitable—I already run the charity drives at my son's elementary school. I post homeless animals on my Facebook rescue page. I could have promised to continue to be charitable after my son graduates elementary school this month, but I didn't think of that. Instead, all I could think of was that I'd be less anxious. Ha! Like that was going to happen, especially since I knew that something was wrong.

Once you've had enough of these tests, you can tell when something's not quite right. I could tell, because of a few very kind comments the radiology tech made. She didn't give anything away — the technicians can't. I'm just hyper-attuned to people's words and the way they say them, perhaps because I'm a writer. They were just general sympathetic utterances and not anything specific to my situation, but I knew.

And then, I had to wait for the doctor to come in and take a look. She usually just pops her head in and says, "Everything looks good. You're fine." Or maybe, she'll take a quick look herself and then offer reassurance that everything looks as it should. But, this time she lingered. In one spot. For a while. It felt like an extremely long time that I was lying there in that dark room, looking at the ceiling, but it may have only been five minutes or less—or it could have been ten. I have no idea. It seemed like an eternity until she told me that it could be nothing, but maybe I should get another—more invasive—test just to be sure. There was definitely something there, probably polyps (which are most likely benign, but could be pre-cancerous or cancerous). Whatever it is, the course of action would be a biopsy, which is exactly what I had done. So, I felt like I was one step ahead of the game. I won't have to wait another week to see if it's nothing to worry about. But, waiting is waiting, regardless that part of that time was before I knew that something is indeed there—it's still been eight days without an answer. At least I have my beloved New York Rangers to distract me. Their thrilling Stanley Cup run has come at the perfect time.

The distraction of hockey or not, I kind of get the feeling that perhaps a good chunk of people—friends, family, even doctors— feel like maybe I've brought all this stress upon myself. I get it, I really do. I'd probably be thinking the same thing. If I had just gotten a hysterectomy when it was first suggested to me, I would be off this stupid treadmill of biopsies and ultrasounds. But, it was suggested by only one doctor—an oncologist at a different hospital, and then my regular gynecologist conferred. I don't see either of them anymore—not only because of that. The other doctors have said that yes, I should consider it, but I really need to know the whole story before making a decision. If I don't have Lynch Syndrome—my risk is just like everyone else's. I tested negative for both BRCA genes several years ago. It's not really worth major surgery for something that might not even be a risk factor. I have another sister—no one has ever told her to get a hysterectomy and she's several years older than I am.

And that's the thing that trips me up—a hysterectomy is major surgery. Most doctors won't do it via laparoscopy anymore, because of the risk of spreading infection—at least that's what I've been told. Plus, the doctor who suggested it said that he'd have to slice me open, because I'm too small, to remove anything any other way. I don't really have time for the recovery from that, unless it's absolutely necessary. Of course, I don't have time to be gravely ill either and if I do have Lynch Syndrome, of course I'll get rid of everything—good riddance! And, if the worst should happen and the biopsy is positive, I'll be the first one to rush to that surgery. But, until I have some answers it's just a waiting game – and I'm left hoping that time bomb doesn't go off

Postscript: That biopsy was negative, as were all the others so far (knock on wood!).

HOCKEY AND HEART

~ June 9, 2014 ~

DURING MY SON, JOSHUA'S, RECENT BAR MITZVAH, the rabbi mentioned that Joshua had overcome many obstacles to get to where he was that day—up on the bimah*, having just perfectly chanted his Haftorah**. Then he added, "Just like Joshua's beloved New York Rangers, he has faced adversity and prevailed." Little did the rabbi know that just a few short hours later the Rangers would trounce Montreal 7-2 – best Bar Mitzvah gift ever.

I was actually pretty thrilled that the rabbi brought up the Rangers during such a solemn moment. You see, I've cultivated a love of hockey in my kids since they were old enough to—well, since they were born. I don't really remember a time that I didn't push my hockey agenda. I told my Boston born-and-bred husband that he could get our kids for all the other sports—baseball (Red Sox), basketball (Celtics) and football (Patriots), but I get them for hockey—the most glorious sport of all. Plus, I could never raise Bruins fans.

If you read *Ice Dreams*, you know about my lifelong love of the New York Rangers. But, it's about more than hockey. The Rangers have made my life better in more ways than I could have imagined when I first became obsessed as a little girl decades ago. For one thing, I learned to skate. First I took up figure skating, but abandoned it for "power" skating when I was sixteen years old. It was faster, more exciting and being adept at it let me work as an intramural hockey referee in college. I still have my hockey skates somewhere, even though I had to give up skating twenty years ago, due to an autoimmune disorder—Raynaud's Phenomenon—and some circulation complications (it sounds worse than it is, but giving up skating was tough...).

Some of my best memories are of the many afternoons I spent at the rink in high school. I was a volunteer and taught little kids to skate. My payment was ice time on a wide open, empty, smooth rink—I still have dreams that I'm skating on that expanse of ice, my hair flying behind me. I skated at the rink where the Islanders practiced and I would wear my Rangers jersey just to make a point— they really could have flattened me. Instead, they jokingly teased me about my skate rags and sometimes pretended that they were going to check me—perhaps my ire was ill-placed. I wouldn't have had any of those ice rink memories, including skating at 8:00 am at Amherst College with a hockey class there, even though I was a University of Massachusetts student. My intramural hockey boss was the teacher and let me join his class for some free ice time. Of course, without my love of hockey, I would never have been the only female referee—still probably one of the coolest jobs I ever held.

I wasn't uncomfortable being the only girl referee, because of one other gift my love of hockey bestowed up me—as a teen and in college I always felt comfortable around guys, because I could talk hockey. I'm naturally shy (even if I talk a lot), but discussing my favorite team made me gregarious, without any of the awkward babbling I often fell prey to when I was nervous. I've always "known my stuff" and that let me feel comfortable talking hockey to anyone who wanted to listen. One of my favorite compliments I ever received was tossed out by a male friend while we were watching hockey at a bar, "You're a guy with boobs," he said, with more than a bit of admiration lacing his voice.

Along the same lines, hockey has been a bridge to new friendships—rabid Rangers fans automatically have a lot in common. It's not that easy to make friends as an adult, especially when you don't have little kids anymore, but I've made friends in the cyber world and even in the real world, thanks to a shared love of hockey. There's nothing like watching a game together and suffering or celebrating to cement a new friendship. Even commiserating online about our favorite team forges deep friendships, albeit in the virtual world. I have a whole "Rangers family" on Twitter and I've become friends on Facebook with fellow Rangers fans from my town whom I never would have met if we didn't discover our shared Rangers passion through social media. If you read *The Power of Kindness* , you know the remarkable effect Rangers sportscaster, John Giannone's, friendship has had on my son and our whole family.

Hockey also taught me that in order to achieve greatness, you need to practice, work hard and sometimes endure more than your fair share of setbacks and defeat. This knowledge has served me well as I try to sell my first novel, *Goddess of Suburbia*. All writers receive rejections and I'm no exception, but I know that I'm lucky that just about every rejection has been positive. I've received page-long emails with positive comments and more often than not, it just wasn't what the editor or agent was acquiring at that moment. Even so, it's still easy to get down. But, watching hockey for decades has taught me that what's in the past doesn't matter—not one bit.

In hockey, each game is a "clean slate," even in the playoffs. At the beginning of this magical season—which didn't seem so magical at first, hence proving the point that the past doesn't matter—Alain Vigneault handed out t-shirts at training camp that read, "Clean Slate: Grab It." That mentality and coaching philosophy has served the Rangers' well during their spectacular Stanley Cup run. Up until two nights ago—Game 2 of the Stanley Cup final against Los Angeles—every single defeat was followed by a victory. (In my opinion, Game 2 should have been the Rangers—the lack of a whistle on the third goal when Lundqvist was clearly hampered by the bodies on top of him is reprehensible. Every single time I watch the replay, I feel physically sick—but, it's like the proverbial train wreck, I feel like I have to look at it.) They need to bring that clean slate tonight—they need to forget about the blown leads and the officiating injustices and just know that they have it in them to be champions.

And this is why I was so happy that the rabbi brought up Joshua's "beloved New York Rangers" and the lessons he can learn from them about overcoming obstacles. Lord knows my son has a lot of obstacles, but really—who doesn't? Everyone has something and everyone is the underdog at some point in their lives. I for one would prefer to root for the underdog, which is exactly what the

Rangers are in this series. Imagine the sheer joy if they overcome a 2-0 series deficit to win it all—something only five teams have done in the history of the Stanley Cup—on the part of both players and fans. It's an incredible storyline. Starting in Game 5 against the Penguins, the Rangers' improbable run couldn't have been scripted any better. I read somewhere that it's Disneyesque—that's completely true. Martin St. Louis showed such courage and heart showing up to play a day after his mother passed away, that it inspired the rest of the team. Dominic Moore, returning to hockey in September after taking a year off to grieve the death of his young wife, scored the game winner in Game 6 against Montreal. I tweeted that it seemed like they were skating on the wings of angels. It's been incredibly inspiring to witness this team's resiliency and fortitude through so many hardships. And, the way they rallied around Martin St. Louis speaks to the character and heart of this team.

Which, brings me back to my point—why am I so happy that the rabbi made the connection between the Rangers and my son's struggles? How many other sports can kids watch—forget about sports, how many other teams can kids watch—and take away lessons in courage, heart, resiliency and never giving up? To me hockey is so much more than just a game—it's a way to live your life. Let's go Rangers!

MY WRITING PROCESS
(OR—UNINGED AND EATING CHIPS...)

~ *June 18, 2014* ~

MY AWESOME WRITER FRIEND, Debra Druzy, was kind enough to invite me to partake in a blog hop, for which I'm a week late. And, I feel terrible. The assignment was simply to answer questions about my writing process. To be honest, I was a little intimidated. Debra has a kick-ass process (that has resulted in the sexy, sweet and totally satisfying *Sleeping with Santa* stories) and I have none. None to speak of, at least—unless you count eating potato chips and other greasy (and preferably salty) snacks a process... Disclaimers aside, here are my answers ...

What am I working on?

Let's see—I recently finished the final, final revision of my first novel, *Goddess of Suburbia*. It was a long road—six years and many, many revisions—but, I think it's the best it can be now and it's off in the world on submission with some pretty amazing people. So, now I'm working on my next project—a novel that spans three decades and is told in present tense, flashbacks and journal entries. It is the story of three best friends, Josie (or Josephine to her mother), Alec and Caleb, who are inseparable from the moment they meet at college orientation. A love triangle that endures through college and beyond, Josie chooses Cal over Alec, marrying him with Alec as the best man. But, there has always been that tiny nugget of doubt, leaving Josie wondering if she chose wisely. Twenty years later, Josie finds her marriage to Cal crumbling just as she needs his support the most. Facing a cancer diagnosis, Josie reaches out to Alec while Cal escapes into a bottle of whisky. It's only then that she realizes that a miscommunication years earlier changed the entire course of her life. Is it too late to alter her path now, or can she reclaim the happiness that should have been hers just as she's about to take on the biggest battle of her life?

Note: Keep reading and you'll see how long it took for the above paragraph to take shape. Hint: Josie, Cal and Alec were simply — "two guys and a girl" at first...

How does my work differ from others of its genre?

Well, for one thing — my heroines are real. They have gray hairs and some cellulite. They may be beautiful, but they're also insecure — but, not in an irritating, weak way. They're insecure in the way that we all are. Many women, especially moms, feel like they're not quite good enough and Max, the heroine in *Goddess of Suburbia* and a mom of four, is no exception. Her house is a mess, dinner often means pizza, mac and cheese or a take-out rotisserie chicken, because they're always rushing somewhere — just like real life. Most of her day is spent acting as a chauffeur or a referee. Her teenage daughter wants nothing to do with her. Probably the number one comment I get from readers is that they can relate to Max — that reading *Goddess of Suburbia* feels like going out to lunch with your best friend and gabbing for hours. I couldn't think of a better compliment, even if I tried.

Why do I write what I do?

I've wanted to be a writer since I was eight years old, because I've always had an overwhelming desire to make a reader feel something with my words. Plus, when I was eight my second grade teacher told my mother I should be a writer, after reading the "book" I wrote about the friendship between a mouse and an elephant. I still remember how happy I was when she said that. I idolized that teacher, Mrs. Hewsenian, and it was a heady feeling knowing that she enjoyed my writing.

In sophomore year English class at the University of Massachusetts we had to choose another student's essay that spoke to us and write a note to the author explaining why this was the case. A big chunk of my classmates chose my essay about how hard it was to break up with my boyfriend of three years just a couple of months earlier. I remember one girl wrote to me that she felt like she was reading about herself. I was hooked. So, this is why I write women's fiction about moms, "Mom Lit" — if you will. That's the genre that makes me feel like I can relate — like I'm reading about myself. Sure, sometimes I want to read a book to escape, but more often — I want to feel like I'm understood, like someone gets me. That's why I write fiction that, hopefully, makes others feel that way too.

How does my writing process work?

Like I said above, I don't have much of a writing process, so I'll describe my process in answering these questions:.

1. Sit down with my laptop and really good intentions. Get a couple of paragraphs down in a speedy manner. Feel pretty good about myself and my creativity.

2. Decide the best way to describe *Goddess of Suburbia* would be a link to the sneak peek. Insert that link. Feel clever. Try to think of a snappy way to describe my next book, tentatively titled, *The Ties that Bind* or maybe I'll rename it just *Triangle* or maybe *The Road Not Taken*, or *The Bend in the Road* . Get distracted by trying to think of a new attention-grabbing title.

3. Read the synopsis I wrote for my next book, whatever the name may be, in "Notes" on my iPhone. Realize that it's way too complicated and somewhat rambling. Look at time the note was saved and see 2:13 am. Realize this makes perfect sense. I had to meet a deadline for the contest I was participating in, so I wrote it dead tired in the middle of the night on my phone, after falling asleep on my laptop. Feel momentarily proud that I made that deadline and took second in the contest. Then remember that I still need to think of a quick snappy way to summarize it, because the current synopsis is neither quick nor snappy.

Panic that I can't think of a hook for my next book, whose title I'm really not so sure about anymore. Even worse, the characters don't have names — they are just X,Y and Z at this point. Coming up with names for characters is the hardest part for me — often I'll be halfway through a short story or novel and a character will just have this: [ ], instead of a name. It has to fit. It has to be perfect. Make a note to go to baby name website and see what hits me.

4. Decide that I absolutely must vacuum and mop the floor right at that very minute (well, at least vacuum and wet Swiffer it),

because my three-legged rescue dog has been shedding all over the place. Sit on the nice, clean floor and rub both of my dogs' bellies (thereby creating more fur). Notice two buckets of laundry. Start folding one. Bring laundry upstairs to put away and decide there's no room in my dresser, so I pull out a stack of shirts I haven't worn in a while to try on. Decide perhaps I should shower before trying them on, being that I've been doing all this cleaning.

5. Try to think of a snappy description in the shower—no luck. Feel a little light headed after the shower, so eat some potato chips. Still feeling lightheaded—heat up a slice of pizza. Realize that I haven't taken my iron pills for anemia in at least two weeks and that's probably why I'm lightheaded. Spend half an hour searching for the iron pills in my cabinets. Grab stool and take everything out of cabinet. No luck. Put it all back. Resign self to feeling lightheaded. Eat a cookie.

6. Fortified with pizza and sugar (even if not iron), sit down with laptop and decide to just skip ahead and answer the other questions and go back to the description of what I'm working on now when I think of something clever. My mother stops by fifteen minutes later to pick something up. Chat with her for a few minutes. Tell her I've been working. She comments that my living room looks so clean and neat. Decide that perhaps procrastinating is good for something. Kids get home from school as she's leaving. Empty all the barely sipped from water bottles by my front door onto plants in our tiny garden. Wonder how three children can amass at least a dozen water bottles over a few days. Place said bottles in a bag to recycle.

7. Finally sit down again with laptop under a tree in my backyard—five hours after I started. Try to write while kids play hockey in front of me. Insist I can't tell if a disputed goal was actually a legit goal, because I'm working. Notice a Facebook notification. Click on Facebook. Notice twenty-four Twitter notifications. God help me. Check phone. Answer texts. Try to figure out what to make for dinner. Eat more potato chips. Go back to blog post. And, here I am—seven hours after I started, still with no snappy description. And now I have to drive my son and his friend somewhere. And, none of my kids have eaten...

So, that's kind of my general writing process. Not too impressive, huh? If I had to say how I come up with ideas, it would be this—an idea comes into my head, usually something I've seen or maybe even something that's happened to me. It knocks around my head for a while. I take it and extrapolate it out into different scenarios—best, worst, craziest. Sometimes, one will stick and then it kind of hounds me until I write it. I know that sounds crazy—but, I'm a "pantser" through and through (a writer who flies by the seat of her pants, rather than plotting everything out before putting the proverbial pen to paper). I do like to have an idea of the end of a book before I write it, but how the characters get there is often up to them. My characters tell me how to write them—it's just very organic once I start typing and sometimes they surprise me. I was adding in a scene to *Goddess of Suburbia* during this last rewrite and it ended up not being at all what I envisioned at first, but it was so much better than I could have planned. I expected the character to act a certain way, but as I was writing it, I realized she just wasn't ready. It was too soon after her husband betrayed her for her to be so vulnerable. And, that scene ended up packing much more of an emotional punch than I ever anticipated—it was just supposed to add a bit of heat. I can't say any more, because it would give too much away.

To summarize—my writing process involves eating chips, jumping in full-on with an idea once it's driven me to the brink of insanity by pinging around my brain for weeks or even months (or sometimes years—see below) and letting my characters tell me what they should do next. Occasionally, I simply imagine an alternate reality to the life I'm living (in *Goddess of Suburbia*, I imagined what it would have been like if I had started dating my future husband/former bad boy musician in college, instead of at twenty-five years old and he was "the one that got away"). I'm fully aware that everything above may make me sound more than slightly unhinged—does that mean that I'm not actually crazy? You know, because crazy people never actually know they're crazy, right? Or maybe the crazy people who know they're crazy are just writers …

Postscript: About that summary above—it's now exactly forty-eight hours since I started this post and I just finally finished it. For two days I couldn't think of names, even with a visit to the top baby names of the 1960's database. These characters had names when I first wrote about them twenty-four years ago. They were the main characters in the novel I was writing during my senior year Independent Study in Creative Writing. (I can't use those names anymore, because I know too many people with them, including a niece and nephew.) For my final project I wrote forty pages—all handwritten on loose leaf paper—and proudly handed them to my professor/faculty advisor in the program. He read them, loved them and awarded me an A for my Independent Study program, but lost the pages before returning them to me. I was heartbroken, and I asked for a computer for graduation, determined that would never happen again. I said, "goodbye" to those characters for decades. I just couldn't think about what I had lost—and how I could possibly try to replicate it.

But then, a conversation with a friend made me think of them and I thought—wow, they'd be pretty interesting to get to know as adults, to see where they ended up. Because, I loved them—that was really my first novel and they were my first fully formed characters. I still have a plastic bin in my basement with pages and pages of my writing from college. They must appear in some of those pages—the ones that weren't lost—and I'll sprinkle those in as flashbacks. That's the other part of my creative process—if characters stick somewhere in my brain, even just in a remote corner, they deserve to have their stories told. And, I'll do my best to honor that.

Postscript #2 (2016): I have no idea what happened to the above novel, but now it sounds really good to me ... I think it got absorbed into another novel I was working on before this one and ultimately went back to—the husband's name in that one is now Alec, instead of the original Dan... This example just shows how completely disorganized and haphazard my writing process is and probably explains why until *Goddess of Suburbia*, I had at least three or four unfinished novels floating around (including, of course, the one that my professor lost)...

NO JOKE

~ *July 30, 2014* ~

RAISING A CHILD WITH A MENTAL ILLNESS—any mental illness—can be a soul crushing task, but sometimes I feel that raising a child with Obsessive Compulsive Disorder (OCD) must be the most soul crushing of all, partly because it's so misunderstood. There's a misconception swirling around OCD that it's really all about being neat and organized. Celebrities toss off in interviews and those often irritating "Twenty-Five Things You Don't Know About Me" lists that they have OCD. "Oh, I'm definitely OCD," they claim and then go on to explain that everything needs to be in its place or perhaps they like everything—from books to spices— arranged alphabetically. Um, that's called being neat. And organized. Maybe even anal—I'll give them that. But, OCD it's not.

Because of this misconception, it's difficult for people on the outside of your immediate circle to understand that for a child with OCD activities that engender excitement in a typical child (I won't use the term "normal child," because really, who's normal? And what even constitutes normal?) causes a tidal wave of anxiety in one with OCD. Summer camp trips for example—a trip to the amusement park can lead my son, Joshua, to become so riddled with anxiety that he loses weight. Not a few ounces—a few pounds. If you've read *Hungry*, you know why this is a problem. Add in a stay at a hotel and the panic that sets in is off the scales.

His camp has been great in trying to soothe his fears. His counselor assured him that no one would make him go on any rides. The nurse said that he can come to her room during the night if he has anxiety. I told him he can call me any time—even in the middle of the night and I'd answer my phone and talk him down from whatever fear is haunting him. I told him that he'll be so, so happy if he does this and has fun. We even talked to his therapist about it. We came up with all the reasons that he should go, especially the fun he'll miss if he doesn't. But, most importantly—I told him that if he gives in to the fear, the OCD wins. Nothing I said really mattered, though. He had made up his mind before camp even started that he wouldn't be going on this trip.

Complicating matters, a boy in his group has been quite mean to him. He's not singling Joshua out—he's mean to other kids too, but Joshua probably suffers more than the others, because this boy's poor behavior centers around invading Joshua's personal space and touching his things (grabbing his lunch, reaching into his backpack, throwing his shoe down the hall, etc.). Actions like these are often major anxiety triggers for Joshua. If he's already anxious, it's just a million times worse. (And yes, the counselors have talked to this boy.)

And so, instead of my dropping him off bright and early in the morning to climb on a coach bus, he'll sleep in. He'll have a bowl of Cocoa Puffs and watch *Zoey 101* or *Victorious* reruns. He just went to sleep and it's after midnight—12:04 am to be exact. He feels terrible about not going—he feels like he's disappointing his buddies who were hoping he'd go and room with them. He feels self-conscious about his decision too, like he'll be judged. We told him whatever he decides to do, it's okay—but, it's a delicate balance. You want to really encourage him to go and get out of his comfort zone, but you don't want to make him feel bad about his limits.

Already, he's done more this summer than last summer. He went to a water park almost an hour away and saw *Wicked* on Broadway. He was so nervous about both trips, but we talked him into going. I can't take full credit for the water park trip, though. In *The Power of Kindness*, I wrote about the extraordinary effect John Giannone, the New York Rangers sportscaster, has had on Joshua. He really helped him turn his life around this past spring, allowing Joshua to gain eight pounds and shoot up two inches in just a few short months. If you skipped ahead and haven't read the essay, read it—it will restore your faith in the kindness of people when the world can seem very unkind. (That last statement may risk coming across as hubris—I'm not speaking at all to my writing, just the amazing story itself and the effect it has had on those who have read it.)

It was, quite frankly, miraculous and I started believing that perhaps the worst of Joshua's OCD was behind us. But, that was pretty Pollyannaish of me, I have to admit. While Joshua's has not gone back to the food routines John helped banish—a HUGE, HUGE accomplishment—he is still hounded by other fears. The important thing though is that those fears won't kill him, but not eating could. So, I owe John more than I could ever possibly say. (I mean, really, how do you thank someone who pretty much saved your kid? It's just not possible, but I'll keep trying.) He is an incredible person—perhaps the kindest, most selfless person I know. And, he's the reason Joshua went to the water park.

The night before the trip Joshua was a mess. He had been spiraling downward for three days, not sleeping, not eating and lost three pounds, something he could ill afford. I reached out to John in desperation at 12:30 at night and he wrote Joshua a lengthy email as soon as he got my message, even though he had just returned from a trip and was no doubt exhausted. It made a world of difference.

Joshua was so excited to wake up to an email from John and looked forward to showing the email to his friends. It distracted him just enough to go. So, I can't really take credit for talking him into going to the water park and I certainly wasn't able to talk him into going on the overnight, no matter how hard I tried. (And, if you're wondering why I didn't enlist John's help this time—I've dumped far too much on the poor guy already, including enlisting his help in my own professional conundrums, since he's also a fantastic writer. He deserves to spend time with his family during his summer break and relax—not put out our fires.)

Plus, I don't really know if even an email from someone Joshua looks up to so, so much could have convinced him to go—the fear was so palpable. I'm sure there are some reading this who will shake their heads and wonder why I didn't just force him to go. I'm pretty sure his friends won't understand. They're still young, after all. And, I wouldn't be surprised if the camp staff doesn't quite get why he's not going. To tell you the truth, I don't blame them. It's really not their faults. It all goes back to those misconceptions—to the fact that most people don't realize exactly how much of a prison OCD really is.

To be honest—I thought I would end this essay right here, but in searching for images to pair with the post, I realized something quite disturbing that just solidifies my feelings that OCD is regarded as somewhat of a joke. I'd say four-fifths of the images I found were "funny." I put funny in quotes, because they really weren't. Supposedly funny t-shirts popped up, even comic strips with names like OCD Girl and titles like Hallo-clean poke fun at this extremely serious mental illness. And, there were more cartoons than I can count.

Would you wear a t-shirt that says, "I'm bipolar" with a funny punch line under it? How about a shirt referencing schizophrenia with a witticism making light of the illness? No? I didn't think so—it would be terribly politically incorrect and yet, people continue to find OCD funny. They continue to trivialize it. When I introduced my son to his fifth grade teacher, she said that they'd get along great, because she had OCD too. "Everything in my room needs to be in its place," she chirped and I seriously wanted to smack her.

So, the next time someone says, "I'm so OCD—I have to vacuum my living room every day," enlighten him or her. Say, "That's not OCD. That's just being neat." (Of course, the exception is someone like my grandmother. She would stay up cleaning every single night until 3:00 am. I'm fairly certain she had OCD, but was never diagnosed. After all, OCD does have a genetic component.)

And, if you see a cartoon or t-shirt that says something like, "I'm CDO, it's like OCD, but the letters are in alphabetical order—as they should be!" realize that OCD is no joke—it's a serious disease that robs even children of the happiness they so deserve...

THE POWER OF KINDNESS PART TWO

~ August 26, 2014 ~

"I CAN'T THANK YOU ENOUGH." That phrase is thrown around a lot, but how many people actually mean it? How many people are lucky enough to know someone whom they feel they truly can't thank enough? I would imagine not many. But, my family and I are lucky enough to know someone who makes us feel like that—New York Rangers reporter, John Giannone. My husband thinks my "mushy-gushy" (his words) essays are a bit over the top and may even make John, a really humble guy who truly feels he hasn't done anything special, feel a little uncomfortable with my profuse expressions of gratitude.

While I would never in a million years want that to happen (and thankfully, it turns out nothing could be further from the truth), I can't help but find myself pondering this: How can you possibly thank someone who has lightened the burden of your child's struggles—even in his darkest moments? And, I also can't help but try to do just that with the only tool I possess—my words. Although, I suspect even the most eloquent of words couldn't quite convey the depths of my gratitude. One reason I'm so grateful to John and feel compelled to thank him again is the fact that when he participated in the ALS Ice Bucket Challenge, he nominated Joshua to take on the challenge (along with legendary New York Rangers player and television analyst, Dave Maloney—a huge thrill for Joshua and me). I had to figure out how to thank him. (On a side note, my kids say thank you in their own way, including my almost fifth-grader writing "John Giannone is awesome" in whatever medium he can—sand, clay Bananagram tiles.)

This is the third version of this essay (according to WordPress, it had twenty-five plus revisions, but that doesn't count all the revisions I made on my phone—emailing myself changes). I'm trying to avoid over-the-top, maudlin sentiments and convey my gratitude simply. But, I'm not only writing this to say thank you, I'm also writing it because too often we only hear about people with nefarious motives. We only hear about those who would throw someone under a bus (figuratively and quite possibly literally), if it would help them reach their goals. It's refreshing, touching and inspiring to read about someone doing something just to benefit another. I learned this when I posted *The Power of Kindess* on my blog. People I'd never met before told me that it made them cry. Over and over I heard that it gave my readers hope and made them feel less alone. You can't ask for more than that as a writer.

I'm assuming by now you know the remarkable effect John has had on Joshua. He's accomplished what five years of therapy hasn't— he got Joshua eating again after years of suffering from an eating disorder and looking absolutely skeletal. After he met John (whom I had become friends with on Twitter a couple of years ago) at the New York Rangers' Hockey House fan festival Joshua started eating. That very night he ate a whole slice of pizza, something he hadn't done in ages. Every time John emailed Joshua, he made leaps and bounds. And, John was able to get him to break past his fear and go on a summer camp trip to a water park (as I wrote about in *No Joke*). But, things spiraled quickly for Joshua this summer. He had a lot of anxiety surrounding camp, mostly because of the trips his group took.

I didn't want to reach out to John every time Joshua had a setback, because it was becoming a regular occurrence and I didn't want John's relationship with Joshua to become a burden. Plus, it's summer—John's time with his family and I felt that asking him to email Joshua would be an intrusion. So I refrained from sharing when things got even worse—when we found out that Joshua needs a second surgery to correct a problem that we thought was solved with a surgery two years ago. Thankfully, it's not life-threatening, but it absolutely needs to be done. So, we have no choice and Joshua was, understandably, shaken by learning that he needs to go through this painful surgery again—with another week of school missed and another one to two months spent sitting on the sideline during gym and intramural sports.

I was shaken too. It seemed a couple of weeks ago as if everything was falling apart. Joshua lost almost all of the weight he had gained in the spring. And he grew almost two inches since then, so he seemed even more skin and bones—a good thirty pounds underweight and then some. I was having my own health issues—a mysterious allergy that left me with my arms and legs bright red and hot to the touch and even made my mouth swell and a few hives pop up after eating a burger with zucchini and tomato on a sesame seed bun (I rarely eat anything with sesame seeds, because I don't like them). Yet, no doctor has been able to figure it out (though, they've narrowed it down to sesame seeds, aloe, polypropylene glycol, sulfates, benzoates and a few other unpronounceable chemicals) and the allergist advised me to carry an epi-pen. But, all that didn't even matter to me—if Joshua was happy, I would have been too. I also had other things weighing on my mind—but, this isn't about me and I don't like to have a pity party for myself, so I'm not going into it here.

I will say that every so often during this difficult summer I've made a mental checklist of all of the things worrying me in order of importance and every single time Joshua's struggles came out on top. And every single time I've decided that that's the only thing that matters. Watching him so racked by anxiety and wasting away was painful and blotted out any other problems (even though it likely made any health issues I had worse—without my even realizing it).

Because I was so wrapped up in worrying about Joshua's mental state, Robin William's death hit me—as it had so many others—hard. Not just because he seemed like a genuinely lovely person and I loved him as a performer (especially having grown up on *Mork and Mindy*), but also because it really drove home the fact that mental illness is quite often an insurmountable challenge, no matter how much money you have, no matter if you're famous and are showered with the adoration of millions. Those things don't matter when there is a darkness that envelopes you, when everything seems hopeless and it seems like the world would be better off without you, even though nothing could be further from the truth. As the parent of a child with mental illness (and having faced my own twin demons of anxiety and disordered eating two decades ago), I found this terrifying and unspeakably sad. I'll admit that I cried over it—over everything—sneaking into my basement to sit in my big, cushy rocker, so no one would notice. And, no one did notice when I came back up five minutes later—my eyes red-rimmed. The mom can't fall apart, even if I felt like I was inside.

It was not long after this nadir that I got a tweet from John saying that he was challenging my "awesome son Josh" to do the ALS bucket challenge that's been sweeping social media in recent weeks. I couldn't hear the audio on the video when I first listened to it, sitting in the parking lot at Kohl's, but just the fact that he challenged Joshua made him (and me) so happy. That night when I kissed Joshua good night he whispered, "I feel so special." It was the first night he fell asleep with ease in weeks, maybe even since the beginning of the summer.

That would have been enough to make things better. Joshua actually ate a whole slice of pizza again that night and a garlic knot—something he hadn't done in weeks either. But, two days later—our first night in Hampton Bays on vacation—we were at a restaurant with excruciatingly slow service. To pass the time I brought up John's video and handed the phone to Joshua, telling him to play it and see if he could hear the audio. I watched him—head tilted, phone to his ear—as his countenance transformed. He broke into a huge smile and his face lit up. He was shaking as he handed the phone back to me.

"Did he mention you?" I asked.

"Oh my god! He said I'm the best Rangers fan he's ever known!" was his incredibly excited response. I was floored, as well and had to watch it. Well, watching that video and knowing how Joshua struggles every day and knowing how hopeless things have seemed at times lately, I just started to cry—right in the middle of the little restaurant. People glanced at me. I probably embarrassed my kids. But, I didn't care one bit. This was one of the nicest things that anyone has ever done for me and my family. And most importantly, it caused a seismic change in Joshua—he started eating again. He started smiling again. He gained back the weight he lost. He even grew an inch—a whole inch—since he was measured two and a half weeks earlier at the surgery consult. I know that seems crazy, but the doctor said he's hitting a growth spurt.

The best part—this video is better than any psychotropic drug out there. It is the ultimate panacea. Every time Joshua gets anxious, I tell him—"Remember, you're 'the best Rangers fan' John has ever known!" and we watch the video for the millionth time. A huge smile crosses his face. His heart rate slows down and the knots in his stomach ease up. So, that's why I'm immeasurably thankful and not sure if I'll never be able to adequately convey that.

My 80-year-old mother (who does not dole out praise indiscriminately) summed it up nicely after watching the video. She said, "There are very few human beings like that in this world. He should be greatly rewarded in his life." I couldn't agree more.

SILENCE

~ *November 24, 2014* ~

I'VE BEEN THINKING ABOUT SILENCE A LOT LATELY—not the absence of sound, but the absence of disclosure. The silence we keep after we've been violated—the tamping down of the urge to right a wrong, because of a fear of blame the victim mentality. I started thinking about this even before the whole firestorm surrounding Bill Cosby. If you've somehow missed it—say you've been without internet service for a while (or perhaps living under a rock, because it's also been in the newspapers)—sixteen women have now come forward claiming that Bill Cosby sexually assaulted them decades ago.

The biggest argument from those in Bill Cosby's camp is this: Why didn't these women come forward when the crime was committed? Why did they keep their mouths shut for decades? Surely a secret like that would have to come out somehow—it just couldn't sit festering for thirty years without seeing the light of day...

Well, actually it could. I'm not saying he's definitely guilty—I'm neither judge nor jury. I'm just saying that it's entirely possible that these women kept quiet so many years ago because to speak up could have very well meant that they would become the pariah, rather than the perpetrator being the pariah. There was a prevailing attitude then that the victim had to be proven innocent more than the accused. Was she drinking? Was she dressed provocatively? Did she give any crossed signals? Only if the answer to all of those questions—and sometimes more—was an unequivocal "no," could the process of finding the true criminal guilty begin. The only women held above this were those raped on a dark street at night by a stranger—but, even then the thought very well may have been,

"Well, why was she out by herself on a dark street at night? Shouldn't she know better?" And, the saddest thing is that these crusty, outdated attitudes still prevail today. How often is someone who is sexually assaulted completely immune to the speculation that she somehow brought it upon herself? Not very often.

And yes, I know all about Affirmative Consent laws that are becoming more of the norm on campuses. I know that under these stringent guidelines a young man—or woman—must receive a clear "yes" before proceeding. No letting things evolve naturally, because you might find yourself accused. But, I'm not entirely convinced that this will change the culture of blame. Plus, if you take away the possibility of crossed signals by requiring an affirmative yes—then does everything else become rape? And is this the solution? I think educating young men to recognize no or, even more importantly, the sometimes subtle signals that equal no might be a better approach. But, I digress...

Back to silence—as I mentioned, I've been thinking about it for a while, well before people have been arguing on internet threads and in forums about whether or not a true victim would stay silent for decades. My next novel, *Feel No Evil*, is about just that—it's about what happens when the price of silence becomes too great and the allure of revenge beckons. Kate was sexually assaulted in college and two decades later her attacker shows up as someone she may know on Facebook. She realizes that he's living his life, happy and carefree, while she suffered for years before finally burying the memories as deep as she could in order to get on with her life. Here's an excerpt from the synopsis:

Kate Brown, a rape survivor, knows that in life there's "...such a gossamer line between well and unwell, between balanced and on the edge, ready to tumble over the precipice." She's worked so hard to leave the past behind her, but seeing her attacker, Vin, decades later as "someone she may know" on Facebook threatens the "normal" existence Kate has built as a wife and mother.

Kate becomes obsessed with Vin and the crimes she's convinced he's committed. There's the murder of her college friend, among others. As Kate puts the pieces together, her carefully crafted existence unravels. Early on, Kate says, "I work hard to make sure that the sinister thread of darkness woven through the fabric of my existence never wraps itself around my brain again."

Do I have anything in common with Kate? Well, I'm not trying to solve decades old murders—but, I'll leave it at that. I'm a writer—if I shared what's real and what's not, it would be like a magician showing the audience exactly how to do a trick. But, I'll say that I get it. I get why these women have stayed silent for decades, especially when leveling accusations against someone so well-known and so loved. The fact that other accusers have been paid off to keep quiet, just makes the whole she's doing it for the money argument seem ridiculous. If these women were doing it for the money, wouldn't they have at least tried to get a payday years ago?

They're not speaking up now in the hopes of a windfall, or even in the hopes of garnering fifteen minutes of fame. No, I believe they're speaking up now, because they think someone will finally believe them. And yet, they're still being judged and doubted. They're still being held up for scrutiny as money hungry whores. For as many people who think Bill Cosby should rot in a prison cell for his heinous crimes, there are just as many who believe these women should be burned at the stake, ground up in the media frenzy and spit out a shell of themselves.

Is it possible that all these women are making it up? Is it possible that they read the descriptions of the other alleged assaults and said, "Hey, I see an opportunity here!" and crafted an eerily similar tale? Of course it's possible—anything is possible. But, is it likely? Not at all...

VERY SUPERSTITIOUS

~ February 2, 2015 ~

IN MY ESSAY, *TIME BOMB*, I talked about waiting for biopsy results and the fact that I might have Lynch Syndrome—a ticking time bomb of a disease if there ever was one. It was written just shy of eight months ago and it's extremely frustrating that I'm still in the same situation—waiting for biopsy results again, still not knowing if I have Lynch Syndrome or not.

In that essay I wrote:

"…I really don't want to write this post. I'm intensely private when it comes to certain things (I know that may come as a surprise with all of my psyche plumbing essays), and this is just something that I don't want to share. But, I know that it will help other people going through the same thing. I also know that when I write about something, it usually defuses it in my brain. And lastly, I'm ridiculously superstitious and since I blogged before receiving my last two biopsies results and they were negative, one little part of me thinks—well, you better blog before this one too. Silly, right?

Only—is it like the Budweiser commercial, it's only weird if it doesn't work? Who knows—people employ all kinds of good luck charms…"

So…now I kind of feel like I have to write an essay every time I wait for biopsy results. Yes, I know that ventures from simple superstition into possible OCD (Obsessive Compulsive Disorder) territory. And I'm not bandying about that term casually—by now you probably know my son, Joshua, has OCD and that I take it very seriously. But, my feeling the need to write an essay does follow the tendency for people battling OCD to imbue a completely unrelated activity or event with the unrealistic power to change the outcome of another event. For my son it translates into food routines generally. For example, up until last spring Joshua was convinced that he had to do certain routines at breakfast or he'd have a terrible day at school. Meeting New York Rangers broadcaster, John Giannone, fixed that—Joshua didn't do his breakfast routine, and yet he had such a wonderful day, so he realized he didn't need the routines. Of course, other routines sprung up in its place, but that was the worst one. But, I digress ...

Why do I feel the need to write an essay now every time I wait for biopsy results, since the last three biopsies I posted essays about were negative? (For any biopsies before those—there were one or two at least—I didn't have a blog to post on.) I think it's because when you're faced with the unknown, mitigating the circumstances (or trying to) feels like exercising even the tiniest bit of control—though, my rational self knows full well this control is simply an illusion, at best. The entire situation is out of my control. A sonogram I had recently was "suspicious for the finding of multiple tiny ... polyps." (I left out all the confusing med-speak in the middle.) Polyps are usually benign growths that can also rarely be precancerous or even malignant. I've had them before. They generally come and go, but if there's a chance I have Lynch Syndrome, they have to be looked at more closely. I took the word, "tiny" as a good sign. But still, they can't be ignored.

There is one way to see if I have Lynch Syndrome—if my mother and my sister's tumors get tested. For whatever reason, that hasn't worked out. I'm not laying blame, I never would. I did actually call today to make an appointment for one or even both of them to accompany me to see a cancer geneticist at St. Francis Hospital, but she's no longer taking new patients. So, I'm going to go back to Sloan Kettering and tell the doctor it's time for Plan B. He said he could do some tests on just me—they might not be as accurate, but at least they'd give me an idea. I've been on this "cancer treadmill," as my old gynecologist called it, for two and a half years now—since I had an elevated CA-125 result in July 2012. That test—which really never should have been done, because it's not accurate—opened a can of worms.

I know that it's probably gotten to the point for friends and family that my biopsies are just routine, so I hardly told anyone. I've had so many it feels like why should I keep telling people? Plus, it's almost like I'm The Boy Who Cried Wolf, but I'm not the one asking for the biopsies. I'd be happy as can be if a doctor never ordered another one for me. Plus, I really do prefer to keep my medical issues private (which is why I'm so conflicted about posting this ...).

I'd also rather not tell people about the biopsy, because I'm pretty sure, as I mentioned in *Time Bomb* , that more than a few people feel I've brought these tests on myself—that I could easily get off the cancer treadmill if I had a total hysterectomy. And, I totally understand that. But, it's not minor surgery. It's a long recovery and it changes everything. Sudden menopause is a lot harder to go through than gradual menopause from what I've heard. Unless I know for sure that I have Lynch Syndrome, I'm not putting myself through that. After menopause is a different story. I'll cross that bridge when I come to it.

Watching the Super Bowl last night I reflected upon a Super Bowl eleven years ago—on February 1st also—when I stole away from the game to do an ovulation test. I desperately wanted to get pregnant with my third child, so I wasn't leaving anything to chance. Of course, even though it was positive, my husband had to finish watching the game—so, I didn't have a Super Bowl baby, but my amazing son was born the following October, so it worked out for the best. Remembering that time and the Super Bowl six years prior to that when I called friends during halftime to tell them that I was pregnant with my first child made me long for the days when the answers I was waiting for involved babies, not illness. But, there's no way to turn back the hands of time. And there's no way to guarantee that I'll get the answers I want now—even by indulging my superstition. The only thing this essay will really accomplish is letting others who are going through the same thing know they're not alone, which is all I could ask for as a writer.

Postscript (2016): I'm very happy to report that my sister's tumor was finally tested for Lynch Syndrome in March 2016 and in June she got the best possible answer—it did not show Lynch Syndrome. I am finally off the treadmill—knock on wood!

A SEASON TO REMEMBER

~ June 5, 2015 ~

NOW THAT I'VE HAD A WEEK to let the disappointing end to a remarkable New York Rangers' season sink in, I've come to the firm conclusion that it was NOT a failure. Actually, I came to that conclusion the second the final buzzer sounded at the end of game seven, and it was clear there would be no eleventh hour, thrilling comeback. We had plenty of those in the 2015 playoffs. We were graced with a plethora of moments that made fans jump up and down like lunatics (at least I know I did) and wonder with awe how in the heck they could pull out a win when it looked like all was lost (Capitals series, anyone?). They were the first team in NHL history to bounce back from a three games to one deficit two years in a row. How anyone—any true fan—can say this season was a failure, is beyond me.

I was talking to a dad at my son's baseball game about this, shaking my head in disbelief that anyone could actually be such a fair weather fan. And OK, I may have gotten a little riled up. "Have you punched anyone?" he asked with a chuckle. "Maybe punched a wall? You might feel better."

"I know," I admitted, "I am really angry at the fans ranting on Twitter and Facebook about this season being a disappointing disaster. Maybe they should be Islanders fans or Capitals fans. Then they'd see what it's like to experience true heartbreak in the post season."

Really, think about the success the Rangers have had in the post season compared to those teams. They've gone to the Eastern Conference Finals three out of the last four years and last year they played in the Stanley Cup final. Not to kick those other teams when they're down, but the Islanders haven't made it out of the first round since 1993. In fact, they've been playing golf after the regular season comes to a close far more often in the last two decades than they've skated onto the ice for a playoff game. The Capitals, even with Alex Ovechkin's fire power, haven't escaped the second round in almost as long. Definitely not in this century—it was 1998. All the fair weather fans lamenting the Rangers' lack of success in the playoffs would do well to remember those numbers, and be grateful that our team has kept us entertained well into May for more years than not recently.

Even better, the Rangers treat their fans well during the playoffs. They host an amazing, free fan fest that's more fun than a day at Disney World (at least for my family)—Hockey House. We loved jumping on the train and spending a few hours playing games; watching Blueshirts United Live; taking "virtual selfies" with Rangers player holograms; filming videos of ourselves doing our best Sam Rosen imitation; and best of all hanging out with our favorite person, Rangers announcer John Giannone (notice I didn't just say, "favorite announcer"—John is really our favorite person). Hockey House is always more fun with John there, even if he is mobbed by autograph and selfie seekers.

Everyone associated with the Rangers organization is just so, so nice. My son lost his drawstring backpack (won that day at Hockey House) with his $50 Rangers sweatshirt in it—a gift from his aunts— and the nicest Madison Square Garden employee, Kirsy, managed to find it the next day. I love the players, yes, but I love the culture of the organization too. Even the attendant in the bathroom at MSG during the games is friendly and sweet. It's a pleasure going to a game.

In addition to Hockey House, the Rangers run a free program for kids called "Go Skate." My ten-year-old, Aidan, had a fantastic time learning to play ice hockey from Rangers alumni Brian Mullen. And, the people running the program are very kind. They gave me a stick for my thirteen-year-old, Joshua, because he was recuperating from surgery and couldn't attend the program. And, one of the guys running the program remembered us at the next event we attended at our town rink, where we got to meet goaltending great Gilles Villemure. I'm grateful that my team is so involved in the community and gives back to fans with fun events, like Hockey House, Go Skate and Blueshirts Boulevard (at which my oldest son was invited to dance on the stage with the band performing).

There are more variables than stats that make a team worthy of fans' adoration. There's heart, character and involvement in the community. The Rangers possess all of those things in abundance. This is why I'll never turn my back on them—whether they lose a game seven after clawing their way back into a series or don't even advance at all. Considering all of the injuries that came to light after the playoffs (Rayn McDonagh, Marc Staal, Dan Girardi, and Keith Yandle all played beaten and battered- through serious ankle injuries, a torn MCL and a shoulder sprain, respectively) and the very serious and scary injury to Zuccarello, it's a miracle they made it as far as they did. Zuccarello's creativity with the puck, speed and precision passes were all sorely missed. Hopefully his skull fracture and brain contusion will heal quickly and he will be back on the ice racking up the points next season.

And, that's the beauty of hockey—if a team goes deep into the playoffs, the next season is only a few months away. Camp starts in September with a clean slate and second chances. Soon enough I'll be dreaming of a Stanley Cup in 2016, because I believe in this team. I bleed blue. So...to all of the naysayers calling for blockbuster trades and Glen Sather's head, I say, "Chill out." It was a good season, an amazing season even. They were the best team in the NHL, the President's Trophy winners, until injuries took a toll. And even with those injuries, they were a mere twenty minutes away from reaching the Stanley Cup final two years in a row. They're so close; it's only a matter of time. Remember, there's always next year...

HERE WE GO AGAIN

~ *July 13, 2015* ~

BUT MY BOOBS ARE MY BEST FEATURE—that was the first thought that went through my brain when the mammogram technologist informed me that the radiologist needed more views, "because she saw something that changed from last year." I know— incredibly shallow and probably conceited sounding, but you can't help the thoughts that career through your brain while your breast is squished painfully between two glass plates and you're wondering what that magnified view the doctor ordered will show. And if I'm going to write this, I better be honest. How else could it help others going through the same thing, if I only share the thoughts I'm supposed to have, not the ones I actually do have?

I know there's someone else out there who's had the same shallow thought, and maybe my sharing it makes her feel not that bad. I told myself that not wanting to lose my breasts really shouldn't be my biggest worry (especially since reconstructed boobs are bouncy forever and look awesome—I know from friends and celebrities), but still...that was stuck in my head. You see, improbably, they actually got better as I got older. People who knew me in my younger years have actually asked me if I had work done. I haven't—I just was always underweight and when my weight crept up into a healthy zone as I got further into my forties, my body morphed into the shape it was intended to be if I never abused it by not eating enough.

When I was a kid my nickname was Dolly Parton. I was curvy when I was still in elementary school. I hated it back then. I wanted to be skinny and flat chested desperately. I had no use for hips and breasts. They didn't help me skate faster—if anything, I was less aerodynamic. They drew unwanted attention. I got my wish when I was eleven and lost fifteen pounds due to an illness. I didn't gain it back until I was sixteen. And by that time I had grown a little, not much, but enough that my curves were no longer so curvy. I lost weight again in my early twenties. I remember when I was twenty-four years old, someone I worked with told me that I had the body of a twelve-year-old boy. I did. Having kids changed that. And so did getting older—my metabolism slowed down and I was able to gain weight. Someone told me a couple of years ago that I looked like Jessica Rabbit—a much more flattering comparison than a twelve year old boy and one that actually made me really happy. Over the years, I've embraced being curvy more so than when I was young, but like most women I often have a love-hate relationship with my body. And there are things I scrutinize way too much.

But...I'm happy with the sweater puppies. I've gone up two cup sizes from before I had kids (or sometimes one, if it's a fuller cut bra). I fill out clothes I never filled out before. So...this was the shallow train of thought that went through my head. I really couldn't think about surgery, treatments or any other truly scary stuff. It's easier to contemplate losing a favorite body part than possibly losing your life. Plus, I just don't have time right now to deal with an illness and all the unpleasantness (an understatement) that goes with it. I have a book coming out soon, as many of you know, and I have a launch party and hopefully a mini (very mini) book tour. I'll also be doing a blog tour. And I'm going to a huge conference in a couple of weeks that I paid a lot of money for and that I've been looking forward to. Much of my energy goes to my son's struggles and just trying to keep him happy and healthy. (Again, you probably know about this.) I don't have time for any of this—but really, who does?

So, when the doctor gave me a bit more of an explanation and told me that she just didn't like the look of one area on my mammogram—there was a cluster of microcalcifications, deep and on the outside, an area cancer apparently likes to hang out in—my next thought was, boy, am I grateful that I go to a state of the art hospital (St. Francis Women's Center in Greenvale, NY) and I see a really good doctor (Dr. Patricia Barry) and she caught something so tiny on the mammogram. She assured me that it probably isn't cancer—if anything, it would more likely be precancerous changes. Still, I'm so grateful for that—precancerous cells morph into cancer without much warning. Or it could be early stage cancer. She said two or three times a year mammograms that look like mine turn out to be malignancies. Or it could be nothing. I of course, stupidly, consulted Dr. Google. Big mistake. According to a few sites, clusters are generally a cause for concern, especially where mine are located.

But, somehow I'm calm. And that scares me, which is completely ridiculous. I'm never calm before a biopsy. I just keep thinking, Okay, I'll deal with whatever it is. I have too many breast cancer warrior friends who have shown me what it's like to "fight like a girl" and not only survive, but thrive. Plus, this isn't my first breast biopsy. You probably read about my last one over five years ago in the earlier essay, *What If* . That biopsy was different—a 9 mm complex cyst. Dr. Barry did that biopsy too and removed everything. She assured me it would be benign as soon as she saw it on the ultrasound screen. She was right.

This biopsy will be a bit more complicated, or maybe just a bit more uncomfortable. I have to lie on a table on my stomach, with a mammography machine beneath me. And I have to lie perfectly still like that for ten to fifteen minutes. Should be loads of fun. My husband said that it sounds like I'll be a car up on a lift at the garage with the mechanic working below me. He's not entirely wrong. The table is high up and they'll have to give me a lift onto it, thanks to my diminutive stature. But, as uncomfortable as it is, I'll get up at 6:00 am tomorrow to get ready for it. My husband will drive me— fighting morning rush-hour traffic—because I had to sign something saying I wouldn't come alone. Who would want to go alone anyway?

And...I'll feel grateful after, even when I've got steri-strips sealing me up and a bag of frozen corn draped across me to ease the soreness, because whatever it is—I'm lucky. If it's benign, I'm really lucky. If it's not, well then I'm lucky that it was caught and that I wasn't late scheduling my mammogram this year, like I usually am. Either way I'm just lucky. And I won't forget that when the doctor calls me with results in a few days...

Postscript (2016): The biopsy was benign, thankfully. I feel like the luckiest person, because two more biopsies (stomach and esophagus) were benign after this (knock on wood!!!).

INSPIRED BY REAL LIFE...OR NOT...

~ October 12, 2015 ~

WHEN MY NOVEL, *GODDESS OF SUBURBIA*, was published in August, I had the honor of hosting a book launch party at Book Revue in Huntington, NY. Book Revue hosts all sorts of literary luminaries, sports figures and pop culture phenoms—from Hillary Clinton to J.K. Rowling to Dennis Rodman to Snooki. I spoke about my book and read a selection to a packed house. I was touched and amazed that the line waiting for me to sign copies of *Goddess of Suburbia* wrapped around the bookshelves. There were eighty-five chairs set up and it was still standing room only. Here's my book talk from that night (August 27, 2016)...

"In case you're wondering—this book is not autobiographical. Even my editor asked if I had endured the same things as Max—and she said that she was sorry for me if I had. She said that it seemed so real, she had to think that maybe it was. She offered sympathy, saying that she felt terrible for me, before I assured her that it was not true at all. She said, 'Can you blame me? Poor Max, I'm so happy you hadn't gone through this'!

I couldn't really ask for a better compliment as a writer than that I created a world on the page that feels so real, readers feel bad for me. Although, I'm not sure my husband is too happy about it! He doesn't want to be associated with the husband in this story, Nick, that's for sure! What husband would? And of course he wouldn't want to think that I'm pining away for my college boyfriend. I can assure you, this is a world completely sprung from my imagination.

There are some things inspired by reality. People might recognize the neighborhood of postage stamp sized lots as pretty similar to my neighborhood of postage stamp sized lots. Town of Oyster Bay residents will probably recognize the beach Max goes to as Centre Island Beach on the North Shore and the amazing ices shack she talks about as Bonanza's in Oyster Bay. And East Hollow may seem just a bit like Plainview. Though, East Hollow is populated with people who are far meaner. In fact, at the eighth grade dance I sought out my son's very kind principal to specifically tell him that the principal in the book is absolutely nothing like him. I also stood up at the end of a PTA meeting to make sure that everyone in attendance knew that the vicious PTA president in *Goddess of Suburbia* was not based on any past or present PTA presidents (or even members for that matter!).

So, what is inspired by real life? The feeling that you don't always quite measure up or belong. Like everyone else has some secret key to keeping their lives running smoothly and their houses neat and their laundry under control. Max's worry about what other people think of her is probably my way of working out the very same flaw that I have. I think a lot of readers have related to that.

A blogger who interviewed me told me that she saw a lot of herself in Max. She then asked me if Max is a lot like me, as well. I had to answer that yes—Max is indeed like me in many respects (one big way in which she was not like me when I wrote this book has changed—I gave her blonde hair, thinking that I'd never be a blonde and therefore, no one would think I was describing myself—who knew I'd become allergic to my espresso hair color and have to go blonde?. Now we have one more thing in common.

So, how else are Max and I alike? Well, we share a love of Target. We both don't get our hair cut often enough. We both prefer skinny jeans and flowy tanks for going out, fleece lounge pants for staying in and sweats of any kind the rest of the time. And as I alluded to earlier, we're both always behind on laundry. We both put our kids before anything. We both love animals. We both have hyperventilation syndrome—though I don't need to carry around a paper bag with me (I do, however carry a rescue inhaler for my asthma). I was diagnosed with hyperventilation syndrome in college and breathe too shallow when I'm stressed or nervous or speaking for a long time (like tonight—I was a bit nervous about fainting up here on the podium). I took that feeling of not getting enough oxygen and spun it out with Max. And that's a lot of what writing fiction is—taking a familiar feeling and spinning it out to a more intense scenario.

I've always loved books that are about ordinary people in extraordinary circumstances or conversely, extraordinary people in ordinary circumstances. Max is more the former—she's your typical running around ragged, living on fumes, mom. She feels a bit restless and always has this slight nagging suspicion in the back of her mind as she's shuttling her kids around in the minivan that perhaps there's something more. And then she's thrown into this situation where her life is just out there. Her stuck in a rut, boring life is suddenly anything but. The video was really just my vehicle for that to happen.

People become famous so easily now—I was really struck by how someone could put up a video on YouTube; it can go viral and suddenly, that person is on the *Today* show. Or a Facebook post goes viral and suddenly this person who never asked for attention is hurled all sorts of vitriol. Like the woman who posted the photo of her baby with an orange face after she nursed him too soon after a spray tan. I'm not saying she was right or wrong—I'm just using that as an example. Though, she did put that photo out there, unlike Max. A better example would be the courtroom artist who drew Tom Brady. All of the sudden, she's on the receiving end of such hate—she was just doing her job. Max was just trying to save her marriage.

As an aside—it's been very interesting to me that some women reviewing the book are angry that Max made the video—'How could she be so stupid?' they ask. In kind of a meta moment, that just confirms to me many of the insults hurled at Max from behind the anonymity of a computer screen are completely accurate. She would be subject to that kind of abuse, because people are angry at her for doing it and she's only a fictional character. That was another thing I wanted to explore—how it's so easy to fling hate, when one isn't face to face.

In the version before the one you hold in your hands, Max's life was much more tumultuous. She was framed for murder and the whole media circus was even bigger. She had to race to find the killer, before losing everything important to her. I loved that story, but an agent asked me to rewrite it. She said too many bad things happen to Max and the reader takes the hits right along with her. She told me that the situation was too 'larger than life.' It wasn't believable to her. The agent asked me to rewrite the book without the murder and with a bigger emphasis on her relationship with her ex, Ben. She wanted it to be happier, lighter, more hopeful. She wanted more Ben—a lot more. I took her four pages of notes and spent three months rewriting it. It didn't work out between me and the agent (after eight months with no response to my rewrite on her part, I politely let her know that I was no longer seeking representation), but I think that happened for a reason. Beta readers really embraced the feel-good story. And now, you have it in your hands.

I have to think that all of the rewrites, all of the bumps along the road led to this moment. One reviewer wrote, 'I couldn't love Max more if she were my own real-life best friend.' And one blogger tweeted that the book was her favorite book this year. It all worked out in the end. I have a great publisher, Booktrope, who didn't worry about whether a book about a tired everywoman PTA mom was marketable—they only looked at whether it was good or not and figured it would find an audience who loves it. I'm forever grateful for that."

Postscript (2016): *Goddess of Suburbia* is now out under Gold Coast Press, my own imprint. Booktrope closed its doors on May 31, 2016, two weeks after *Goddess of Suburbia* hit best seller status in the Women's Fiction: Romance category. (You can read more about that in *Paralyzed*—a bit down the road in this book.)

ON LIVING PASSIONATELY

~ October 14, 2015 ~

I WAS TASKED WITH BESTOWING THREE BITS OF ADVICE for women looking to reconnect with their passions and live authentically—not an easy feat, even though I wrote a novel about just that, *Goddess of Suburbia*. I'm grateful for it, though. Writing this essay offers me the rare opportunity to focus for a moment on how, at forty-seven-years-old, I finally realized a dream I've had since I was eight—becoming a published author.

So...my first key to reconnecting with your passions: think about what captivated you as a child; what you loved in high school; and what you were passionate about in college. Is there a thread? Did a creative pursuit; academic subject; sport or philanthropic endeavor capture your heart when you were very young and continue to bring you joy throughout young adulthood, only to be abandoned when the realities of grown up life—marriage, kids, day job—got in the way? If there's something you've always loved, do it. It's that simple.

For me, writing is the thread that's woven through the tapestry of my existence—from childhood through today. As I mentioned, at the tender age of eight I decided I wanted to be a writer. My desire only grew over the years. By the time I had my first child, I had written about forty articles for various publications and studied creative writing in amazing workshops with renowned authors. I was on my way. But, one baby slowed my writing down a bit and two stalled it altogether. By the time baby number three came along, I rarely put pen to paper. I wrote here and there, but nothing that I submitted.

I started writing seriously again when my youngest was in nursery school, launching a blog to showcase my personal essays and working on a novel. The day he started full day kindergarten, I set a goal and made my husband a promise... If I didn't get published by the time my little guy graduated kindergarten, I'd get a "real" job. Writing felt like a hobby, even though it was the only subject I ever studied, the only career I knew I'd ever be good at. Not making money at your job can do that. But...before my youngest donned his tiny graduation cap, my essay, *Kicking Superwoman to the Curb*, was published in *Long Island Parents* magazine. After taking off ten long years, I was convinced that it was time to fully return to my passion.

It took another five years (almost exactly) before I got my first book contract—for *A New Life* , a short story e-book (during that time I posted many personal essays and had a few articles published). I had written it right before my decade long hiatus, during the last workshop I took when my oldest son was a year old. A few months after *A New Life* came out, Booktrope Publishing accepted my first novel, *Goddess of Suburbia* (the novel I started while my son napped in the minivan after nursery school). This brings me to my second key to rediscovering your passions and living authentically...

Don't ever give up. Even if it seems like you'll never get to where you want to be, even if it seems like the road ahead is so daunting—surely paved with rejection—don't give up. There were times for me that it seemed like it would be so much easier to just throw in the towel, just raise the white flag. I was done with the rejection or even worse, no response at all. I never even heard from some publishers who requested *Goddess of Suburbia*—not slush pile submissions, actual requests for my work. It took me a few months to work up the courage to submit to Booktrope—I didn't think I could handle one more endless wait for a response that may or may not come. But, it was about two weeks from the time I submitted to the time a contract landed in my inbox. You just need one yes, and then every no you've ever received won't matter.

My last bit of advice, which has been the hardest one for me to actually follow, is to not worry about what others think of you. This is something that Max grapples with in *Goddess of Suburbia*. She worries deeply what everyone else thinks of her. It's her worst nightmare when she's judged harshly by the other moms. I think in writing about learning to let go of the preoccupation with others' perceptions, I was perhaps trying to work out that issue for myself. It's very hard to just do something and not worry about being judged, but it's the secret to living authentically. If you're always trying to be what others expect you to be, you'll never be true to yourself. One of my favorite quotes is, "No one can make you feel inferior without your consent," by Eleanor Roosevelt. So true—the most important key to living passionately and authentically is to do what makes you happy, free from the crippling fear of being judged.

I'M A PANTSER

~ October 28, 2015 ~

NOTE: THIS WAS A GUEST POST for my *Goddess of Suburbia* blog tour. There may be a few overlaps between this and the previous essay about my writing process, but there was enough new material, to warrant including it in this collection...

I'm a pantser. That's the best way to sum up my writing process. I don't plot. I just can't, though Lord knows I've tried. In fact, I took a plotting workshop with the fabulous and prolific Cherry Adair—it was so incredibly informative. I took all the different colored Post-Its, markers in every hue of the rainbow and a giant poster board and plotted my little heart out. I went from start to finish, outlining an entire novel called, *Out of Nowhere*. I had layers and layers of neon Post-Its, all scribbled with different colored markers, detailing scenes, characters, motivations—you name it, it was on that poster board. Cherry was impressed.

I was amazed at how easily I came up with the intricate plot about a single mother of a son who's battling Obsessive Compulsive Disorder. She and her son witness a hit-and-run not long after her husband has committed suicide (the hit-and-run is mysterious, with the body disappearing by the time the police arrive and the husband's suicide wasn't quite what it seemed).

In the days following the workshop, the story was really shaping up to be a tense thriller that readers just might have gobbled up. And then... I stalled. Sixty pages or so in, I hit a brick wall. Weeks passed and still the document hovered around sixty pages. That was when I realized that having the entire plot in front of me squelched my creativity. The once flowing creative juices slowed down to barely a

trickle. I realized that I needed my characters to evolve organically—
I needed them to tell me where to go next. I couldn't dictate the flow,
without getting to know them first.

Letting my characters write themselves might seem crazy, but
that's often just what they do. A scene I added to *Goddess of Suburbia*
during revisions ended up being not at all what I envisioned at first,
but it was so much better than I could have planned. I expected the
character to act a certain way, but as I was writing it, I realized she
just wasn't emotionally ready. It was too soon after her husband
betrayed her for her to be so vulnerable. And that scene ended up
packing much more of an emotional punch than I ever anticipated—
it was just supposed to add a bit of heat. I can't say any more,
because it would give too much away.

I have to admit, although I prefer to let my characters lead me in
their journey, I do need to know where that journey will end. I must
know where the story is heading, so I often write the last scene right
after I write the first scene and then I fill in the middle. In *Goddess of
Suburbia*, I knew where Max was heading. I knew the lessons she
would learn and with whom she'd find her happily ever after. How
she got there just kind of worked itself out as my fingers flew over
the keyboard night and day.

One of my favorite tricks to spark creativity during the writing
process is creating a Pinterest soundtrack board for the book I'm
working on. Music is always a huge inspiration to me and I've found
that gathering songs that capture the journey my characters are on
make it that much easier to get the ideas out of my head and onto the
page. I have soundtracks for each of my books and short stories, and
they are packed with the music that fits each story perfectly.

One thing I don't use Pinterest for is to generate story ideas. I
don't browse boards looking for my next hero. The one time I
decided to find photos to inspire my hero, he ended up looking
completely different anyway. I can't look for story ideas—they just
come into my head, usually an idea is sparked by something I've
seen or maybe even something that's happened to me. The idea
knocks around my head for a while. I take it and extrapolate it out
into different scenarios—best, worst, craziest. Sometimes, one will
stick and then it kind of hounds me until I write it. Sometimes, an

idea will drive me to what feels like the brink of insanity, by pinging around my brain for weeks or even months, until I have no choice but to write it. Occasionally, I simply imagine an alternate reality to the life I'm living (in *Goddess of Suburbia* , I imagined what it would have been like if I had started dating my future husband/former bad boy musician in college, instead of at twenty-five years old and he was "the one who got away").

Every once in a while it's a character who sticks in my brain, rather than a full story idea—like Tessa, that single mom to the son with Obsessive Compulsive Disorder. I didn't end up finishing her story in *Out of Nowhere*, but she still needs to be written, simply because I haven't forgotten her. I have another story for her and it's perfect. I know exactly where she's headed, but I trust my process enough to know that she'll surely make some unplanned detours on her journey to happily ever after. I know there will be a happily ever after because even though I write women's fiction and not romance, I always want my readers to close my books with a satisfied sigh. And that's really the most important part of my writing process— making sure that every scene I write makes a reader feel something. For me, that means writing from the heart, rather than just writing what I think will sell, because if you write from the heart, your words will always touch your readers.

A LIFE CUT SHORT

~ November 23, 2015 ~

I'VE BEEN THINKING ABOUT EZRA SCHWARTZ A LOT. He keeps invading my mind. I see his face when I'm arguing with my seventeen-year-old and I take a deep breath and tell him whatever stupid thing we're butting heads about just doesn't matter. A post with his mom's Facebook profile tagged pops up in my news feed and I can't help but click on it. I feel like I'm invading a mourning mother's privacy, but all the posts are public and none are recent. All I can see is the similarities between us—the gossamer line that separates us. We both love our sons, but I can hug mine (kinehora*, knock on wood and all that superstitious stuff). We are both mothers with sons who embraced USY (United Synagogue Youth), but my fifteen-year-old son just joined two months ago and hers went off to Israel to study and volunteer, only never to return, killed by a terrorist's bullet as he sat stuck in traffic, returning from delivering food to Israeli soldiers.

If you haven't heard of Ezra Schwartz, that's not really surprising. There hasn't been a lot of mainstream media coverage about his death at the hands of terrorists. You'd think an eighteen-year-old American college student slain in a burst of violence while studying abroad would garner more attention. In the wake of the tragedy in Paris are we immune to such horrifying news? Is Ezra now just another young person killed at the cusp of spreading his wings and gliding off into freedom and an uncharted exciting new world? Or is his death not all over the media because he was killed in Israel and some people think any violence in Israel is deserved? Or perhaps it's simply that any violence in the Middle East is just a fact of life, and as long as it's not on Western soil, it's not all that shocking? All of these possibilities are dangerous and heartrendingly sad.

I mourned with everyone else over the deaths in Paris. I changed my Facebook profile to the French flag layered over a photo of me signing a copy of my novel—somber despair layered over a happy moment. I posted the Eiffel Tower peace sign graphic on my writer page. I tweeted about my prayers for Paris. I thought about what it must have been like watching a concert (my favorite night out over all else, except maybe a hockey game) and suddenly being plunged into an unimaginable nightmare. I was a music journalist before I had kids and my husband played in a band. I spent so many nights watching live music in my younger days, of course I felt a thread to those killed and even those who escaped, traumatized for life, no doubt. And of course I felt grief over everyone who lost their lives—whether at a café or a stadium or an arts venue. I felt grief for children left without a father or mother, for the spouses left widows and widowers, for parents grieving the loss of a child. It's all horrible. But, so is Ezra's death—and I felt an even greater connection to his loss. I could so easily imagine it being my own loss.

Many people have told me that my essays make them cry. Well, this one is making me cry. In fact, it's hard to see the screen through my tears. Maybe it's because, as I mentioned, my middle son belongs to USY and has long professed a desire to travel to Israel. Maybe it's because Ezra was from Sharon, MA, a Boston suburb in which my husband and I spent many weekends house hunting back in 2000, before we decided to return to my native Long Island. We have both friends and family who live in Sharon and we have visited it many times. If my husband didn't get a job in Manhattan and I wasn't suffering from home sickness, along with morning sickness, during my second pregnancy, I have no doubt we would have ended up raising our kids there. And we very well may have ended up friends with the Schwartz family, perhaps attending the same synagogue. Or maybe Ezra's murder has affected me so, because I have several friends who opted for a year in Israel, before transferring to a more traditional university on US soil. Some of those friends even returned to Israel to make a life there. I have family in Israel.

This essay isn't about politics. It's not a condemnation of anything or anyone (except, of course terrorism). It's simply an essay about the emotions wrapped up in trying to make sense of the senseless, a Sisyphean task if there ever was one. There's just no way to wrap one's mind around an eighteen-year-old cut down before he really had a chance to live, especially when he was gunned down while helping others. It's even harder when you're the mother of three boys—all eerily similar to Ezra. Patriots loving, philanthropic-minded, mischievous boys with open smiles and good in their hearts. This is what makes me cry...

Kinehora—a Jewish phrase to ward off the evil eye. If you say something good, you quickly add kinehora to keep it that way.

HUNGRY PART TWO

~ December 22, 2015 ~

YOU'VE READ MY PREVIOUS ESSAY *HUNGRY* , so you know that watching my son battle an eating disorder has been the worst possible karma. If you skipped ahead and haven't read it, please give it a read or even just a skim now—so you can understand the magnitude of what I'm about to write... My son, Joshua, is doing better. (Knock on wood. Kinehora. And every other incantation meant to keep away the evil eye.) He's far from perfect, but he's better. He's only in fourth percentile for weight, but he's on the chart—for the first time in years, perhaps even for the first time since he was a chubby cheeked infant, the biggest of all my babies at a whopping eight and a half pounds. (I'm barely five feet and weighed one hundred and twenty-four pounds nine months pregnant—with the biggest belly you've ever seen—so eight and a half pounds was quite whopping.)

I nearly cried when the pediatrician showed me the little dot that marked his current weight on a curved line—an actual curved line, not below. He still needs to gain a good twenty pounds, but his life is no longer in imminent danger and the eating disorder clinic no longer wants to send him off to Wisconsin, to an in-patient clinic better equipped to deal with the severity of his illness.

Joshua's journey toward a healthier weight began with a trip to the asthma doctor this past spring. Joshua's breathing was labored and he suffered from chest pain. I was worried that his early childhood asthma returned. Only, the doctor said his small airways (the area affected by asthma) were perfect—it was his large airway, the sturdy muscles needed to push air in and out, keeping his body oxygenated, that was woefully inadequate. At fourteen years old, he had the lung capacity of an old man.

The doctor put his hand on Joshua's chest and pushed. "I can push right through. There's no resistance, no muscle," he told me, concern lacing his voice. Joshua's body was using his muscles for fuel, because he wasn't giving it what it needed through food. The body is very smart; it will do what it needs to do to survive. But, it can only use itself for so long, before there's nothing left. And that was the grim possibility we were looking at. It was terrifying.

Dr. Bruce Edwards is Joshua's asthma doctor (and mine, as well) and I'm naming him, because I have no doubt that he saved Joshua's life. He was the first doctor to say, "He needs help. He has an eating disorder and he needs treatment right away." Over the years, there had been some concern—translating to weight checks and bottles of Boost (which Joshua would drink inconsistently)—but no true alarm. And since no doctor seemed overly concerned (I was told years ago by one that obese children are far more worrisome than too skinny children), I thought that Joshua's fear of going to an eating disorder clinic was more important than getting him help. But I was wrong. And I finally realized it.

I made an appointment that day with the Eating Disorder Treatment Collaborative (EDTC). The first psychologist and nutritionist we saw at EDTC told us that they would give Joshua five weeks to show improvement (for that I was extremely grateful), but if he didn't gain at least a little weight in that time frame, it would be dangerous to keep him in an outpatient setting. They recommended sending him to Wisconsin for treatment at a clinic specializing in treating boys with eating disorders. I was also told that if he was dizzy at all or had a racing pulse, we should take him to the hospital. That's how dire his situation was. Joshua did not want to spend his summer in Wisconsin, so he vowed to get better in the outpatient program.

He reached out to our friend, and favorite cheerleader, Rangers sportscaster, John Giannone. John told him that if the Rangers could come back from seemingly hopeless situations, he could beat this thing, no problem. I'm forever grateful for the kindness John has shown Joshua. John's encouragement, coupled with Joshua's resolve not to go to Wisconsin—plus his desire to play ice hockey, a sport nixed by the doctors—gave him the push he needed to slowly start to gain weight. But, we needed more ammunition to win the war.

When I took Joshua to a psychiatrist, Dr. Stanley Hertz (again—giving credit where it's due), I never anticipated that his diagnosis would resonate so deeply with me. ARFID. That one little acronym, uttered by Dr. Hertz, brought tears to my eyes. ARFID stands for Avoidant/Restrictive Food Intake Disorder and it meant that there's a name for what my son has been suffering from, in addition to Obsessive Compulsive Disorder, for years. If you read *Hungry*, you know that it also gave a name to what I had battled in my early twenties. I beat it through talk therapy with a social worker, but Joshua needed more. He finally acquiesced to taking medication—I finally acquiesced to giving him medication.

After a while on the medication, Joshua was eating Chinese food (with his therapist, Dr. Jay Saul) and strawberry Greek yogurt (with his nutritionist, Kerry Fannon). And then suddenly, he didn't need their support to keep eating all of the new things on his plate outside of their offices. He'll now grab a slice of pizza out of the box on pizza night, instead of opting for a bowl of spaghetti and ketchup. He'll try new things—like miso soup and sweet and sour chicken, instead of sticking to steamed chicken and rice. He looks forward to his therapy sessions with Dr. Saul, not only for the support Dr. Saul gives him, but also because on the way to every appointment, we pick up a new Chinese dish to try.

It was slow going at first—everything, from medication to a nutrition plan—takes time to work. There were still anxieties lingering over eating in new restaurants for a few months, and then like the fog suddenly lifting, there weren't. Probably the best moment was when his pediatrician, Dr. Maggie Chalson, said the words he had been waiting to hear, "You can play hockey."

It felt like the biggest victory I had ever witnessed watching Joshua skate out onto the ice with the rest of the junior varsity hockey team. He hasn't been medically cleared to play in a game yet, but he's practiced with the team almost every Saturday, and even a few weeknights, since October 18th—just over two months ago. I must have looked like a loony that first time, taking a million photos of just a practice. But, I wanted to record a moment I never thought I'd see.

There have been setbacks to be sure—he hasn't gained any weight since he started playing hockey and this past week he lost weight. It's concerning, but he's still light years ahead of where he was. In fact, when Joshua went back to Dr. Edwards last week, the doctor walked back into the exam room after Joshua's breathing test and said, "I can only say, 'Wow!'" Joshua's lung function had improved by 20%. He's still not perfect—his lungs are functioning at 80%, but he's out of the danger zone. Even better, when Dr. Edwards pressed on his chest, he said it felt normal. He felt muscle, not a tissue thin covering over major organs. When Joshua takes his shirt off, I can't count every rib. He's got some heft to him, some meat on him. Since he first started this journey, Joshua has gained fifteen pounds (and lost one and a half this past week, for a net of thirteen and a half pounds). And... He's grown two and a half inches—at nearly 5'6", he towers over me. And he's not even close to being done growing at a week shy of fifteen—he's only had two growth spurts.

It's been a long battle—one step forward and two steps back, but the glimmers of hope every time we've thought that we hit rock bottom has kept us going. And the battle isn't over, but we relish every small victory along the way.

LETTING GO

~ *February 23, 2016* ~

I WAS WOKEN UP RUDELY, ABRUPTLY, ONE MORNING—yanked from such a sweet, amazing dream a mere four and a half hours after finally finding sleep, that it just added insult to injury. In the dream, my son, Drew, was a toddler. He sat on a low ledge, or maybe a bench, while I kneeled in front of him. His plump little arms wrapped around my neck and I believe he was laughing—an infectious laugh, his baby breath intoxicating on my face. I think we may have been at a book store. And then…then my alarm went off, erroneously set for thirty-five minutes before I needed to wake up. I was tired, exhausted really, when I finally climbed into bed the night before—that combined with an unfamiliar new phone led me to set three alarms by mistake. I couldn't fall back to sleep—even for the short time I had. Instead, my mind spun around and around, thinking about what the day would hold and how perfectly symbolic being awakened from that particular dream was, even if it was monumentally annoying.

You see, the dream was especially symbolic, since that day was the one in which one more figurative apron string tethering Drew to me would be cut as he speeds breakneck towards complete independence. And perhaps this was the most significant one in terms of freedom—it was the day he took and passed his driver's test. And now…now he doesn't need me to go anywhere. I won't hear, "Mom can you give me a ride?" I won't get texts, "Come now." Or even sometimes, "Please come now," if my exhortations to be more polite were remembered. Sure, I bemoaned playing taxi—but sometimes I relished it. Actually, often I relished it. Trapped in the car with me, Drew had to engage—he had to at least give clipped answers to my questions. Sometimes we even had full conversations.

Watching Drew pull out of the driveway the first morning he drove to school, was bittersweet. Tears spilled down my cheeks as a memory juxtaposed over him heading down the street to pick up his friend. I could picture that moment so many years ago perfectly... We were waiting in front of my house, standing at the very same curb he drove by, Drew barely able to contain his excitement, as my excitement was slightly tempered with a bittersweet sadness. I had to let my baby go—he was heading off to kindergarten, away from me for a full day for the first time. It was rainy and cool, so Drew was wearing a bright yellow slicker over his navy polo shirt and crisp khaki pants. I was wearing a track suit, my usual uniform back then. This one was black with white stripes down the legs and sleeves, and by the time I went back in the house after watching the bus drive away, the thin material was rain-streaked, leaving me shivering. It was hard then to let go, but I had no idea how much harder it would get.

Sending him on a bus for a day at kindergarten for the first time was a huge step, of course—he had never taken a bus anywhere before. I drove him to nursery school. I drove him to camp. For the first time, someone else was responsible for my baby. But, I still had a child in nursery school and was hoping to get pregnant again in the next few months. I wasn't "all out of babies," a line I'd read in an article once about a father deciding it was time to try for another child.

Now, I'm all out of babies. In addition to Drew driving, the tooth fairy just visited for the last time a few nights ago (and left $20 for four stubborn baby teeth that had to be pulled out at the dentist). My eyes welled up with tears as I drew on the envelope I slipped the $20 into. I've always drawn a tooth fairy on every envelope I placed under my kids' pillows, gingerly lifting the pillow, so as not to wake a slumbering child. Three kids equal a lot of tooth fairy envelopes (though I'm sure they stopped believing long before the last envelope was placed under each of their pillows). I couldn't believe it was the last time. Not only does my youngest, Aidan, not have any baby teeth left, but he doesn't want me to come to the bus stop to meet him anymore, though he didn't come right out and say that. He simply said, "I just think it's not necessary anymore." He's probably right, but that won't stop me from watching him from my porch. He's eleven, but it's all the way down the street ...

And that's part of letting go—you have to do it, but you'll try mightily to hang on just a bit longer. Like still watching our kids walk down the street, whether they think it's necessary or not. I've been thinking about letting go for a long time now—at least since last year when we started looking at colleges for Drew. But, I think it was even before that. There was a small moment that stands out in my memory—just another moment in a mundane day of doing chores. I was in my basement sorting laundry and I picked up a pair of Drew's pants—khakis he had worn to a science fair the day before. I actually started a blog post about that very moment. It was on September 29, 2014. For some reason, I never finished it. But, here's the beginning...

"Sometimes there's a moment that just drives home how big your children are truly getting. Oh, the signs are always there, but there's often just this tiny moment—one of many in a mundane day—that makes you say, 'Wow, they're growing up so fast.' Mine came while I was doing laundry. I always hold up every item of clothing and inspect it for stains that I need to attack with my trusty spray bottle of Resolve. I held up my son, Drew's, khaki dress pants and even with the cuff hitting the floor, the waistband was at my chest, or maybe even a little above. And, all of the sudden I had this flashback of holding up his impossibly tiny clothes—little onesies and sleepers—right before he was born. I had just washed everything in Dreft—all yellow or green or white, since I didn't know if I was having a boy or a girl—and was folding it to put in his dresser, a changing table with a pale yellow pad fastened to the top.

I lowered my hugely pregnant body onto the creamy yellow rocker—festooned with pastel dots, I fell in love with it the minute I saw it at a cavernous baby store in New Hampshire. Sitting in the cushy rocker I held up a mint green quilted sleeper and just imagined my baby wearing it. It was getting so close, I could barely wait to meet him or her ..."

That was all I wrote. I must have gotten distracted by kids, dogs, life and just never went back to finish. But I remember that moment I was doing laundry so clearly, even though it was almost a year and a half ago.

Now when I think about it, I should have realized that just because Drew was getting physically big, he was still a young kid. Having just turned sixteen years old, he still needed me to drive him everywhere—he hadn't even gotten his permit yet. He still was far off from making decisions that would affect the trajectory of his life. College acceptances hadn't started rolling in. We hadn't visited any campuses yet. In fact, college applications weren't even on the radar at that point. Now, I feel like I'm on a runaway train speeding towards my oldest leaving home. It's an important step, it's an exciting step, but no matter what—it will be a bittersweet one, as well. Just like putting my five-year-old on the bus to go to kindergarten for the first time all those years ago, it's time for me to let go…

A NEW PAGE

~ May 9, 2016 ~

YOU ALWAYS REMEMBER WHERE YOU ARE when you get really bad news—the moment is burned into your memory. On the last night of my family's spring break vacation, we were walking over the footbridge at Broadway on the Beach in Myrtle Beach, South Carolina. There was a lovely balmy breeze, the sun still bathing us in its glow even in the early evening—an idyllic setting if there ever was one. My three boys had just finished feeding the hungry catfish mobbing a spot of gently rippling water beneath the wooden bridge. We were light and happy, heading to dinner. And then—well, then I glanced at my phone after snapping a photo and saw a message from my book manager asking me if I knew that my publisher, Booktrope, would be shutting down at the end of May.

My hand flew over my mouth. "Oh my god. Oh my god. Oh my god," I stood motionless, repeating the phrase over and over and then I burst into tears. Right in the middle of a throng of tourists on a footbridge in South Carolina, I burst into tears.

"What happened?" my kids and husband chimed?

I was barely able to get out the words. "My publisher is going out of business next month," I whispered.

My son blew out a sigh of relief. "Oh, I thought someone died!" he exclaimed.

"Something did die," I wailed. "My dreams!"

You see, in addition to my novel, *Goddess of Suburbia*, I had a second book coming out soon from Booktrope—*Boys, Dogs and Chaos*. It was in the proofing stage and I expected it to be published by July. I was planning launch celebrations in Boston and New York.

It has been my dream to publish a collection of essays for years, but no publisher was willing to take on an essay collection from an unknown voice—no one, that is, until Booktrope. Other publishers required a writer have an established platform as a prerequisite to accepting a work of non-fiction. I have a decent platform now— just over 4,200 followers on Twitter and just under 630 Facebook likes. It's not huge, but perhaps it's enough for my book to be considered. But truthfully, I have no idea what to do with this book that's just waiting to be published, because after the fall of Booktrope, I feel like I'm adrift at sea without a life raft at times.

I will be honest, I wrote that line six days ago and haven't been able to finish this essay until now, though I've gone back to it several times. It's not entirely that I didn't quite know what to say after admitting that I feel like I'm adrift at sea without a life raft. I also was really busy with a completely craptastic week. I spent all of Monday at doctors' offices with my son who had a terrible eye infection. (And he had appointments with the nutritionist and the psychologist, as well – four appointments in one day sucked up any writing time.) The week continued with a death in my extended family, and of course the funeral and shiva calls (a Jewish condolence call) for this and another passing. During this time one of my dogs had a very messy stomach bug (sorry if that's "TMI"); I volunteered at my son's school and I tried to catch up on the post-vacation detritus—half unpacked bags, mounds of laundry—all while my husband was in Las Vegas for a conference. (He got to see Duran Duran and Lenny Kravitz in private concerts—my envy sucked up energy too). So, I had plenty of good excuses for not finishing this—and they all played a part. But… I also wasn't quite sure what else to say.

I needed to let my feelings percolate a bit—I didn't want to post when my emotions were running high. I wanted to process everything and make sure my words are measured—I'd never want to speak ill of anyone. Could the closing of Booktrope have been handled better—rather than announcing it on a Friday evening with the weekend stretched ahead of hundreds of us who were left pondering suddenly very uncertain futures? Yes, it could have. But, I'm not going to even try to guess why it was done that way. I'm sure there must have been a valid reason. Although some speculated otherwise in first days of high emotion, I don't think the owners of Booktrope enjoyed dropping this bomb and watching the ripples of dismay, anxiety and sheer unbridled panic spread out—not even one bit. This was their dream, their baby, and it's crashing—just as much as it is for the rest of us. I understand that they tried to do something revolutionary and sometimes revolutionary ideas fail. There is inherent risk in doing something that's never been done before.

Now, the future is spread out before me and I have no idea where to head next. Some authors already have their books waiting to be reissued—all laid out and just waiting to be self-published. I'm so impressed with them. I however need a bit more time to figure it out. Do I want to self-publish? Do I want to throw my book back into the traditional publishing ring? It garnered some amazing rejections—an oxymoron, if there ever was one. But more than one editor loved it—it just didn't fit into the publisher's acquisitions list at the time – or their marketing scheme.

Goddess of Suburbia is a tough book to market—no billionaire playboys; no vampires or otherworldly creatures; no sexy star athlete. No one seemed to know what to do with a book about a tired forty-something mom on a journey to living more authentically, even though they all found it well-written. This is precisely why I fell madly, deeply in love with Booktrope when they accepted *Goddess of Suburbia* a mere two weeks after I submitted it.

The editors—and agents—before tried to meld it into a marketable property (some of those changes were for the better—it's A LOT steamier now) or simply rejected it, but Booktrope took it on as it was, not worrying about how to market it, only worrying if the book was good. Perhaps Booktrope was doomed to fail—choosing quality over marketability is so very noble, but probably not the best way to succeed in our *Fifty Shades of Grey* world. People love brain candy—crap that's flashy, but lacking in substance. Actually, as bad as I feel saying this, I have to be honest—it was a bit of a relief to realize that my book wasn't the only one with suffering sales. I worried that I didn't do enough, but I have put so much effort into marketing that I've hardly written anything new in ages, besides the few essays that rounded out my essay collection. Do I regret working that hard for no return—or at least no monetary return? No, not at all. Do I regret being a part of Booktrope? Never. *Goddess of Suburbia* would have never gotten out into the world—and I might not have had the confidence to finish my essay book, if I didn't think I had a publisher ready and willing to put it out into the world. I don't regret anything, not one bit...

The opening line on *Goddess of Suburbia*'s acknowledgements page is this: "Thank you to Booktrope for taking a chance on this book about a regular mom whom readers can relate to—I'm forever grateful." And I am forever grateful—as I mentioned above, without Booktrope, *Goddess of Suburbia* would not have seen the light of day, because no one was willing to take a chance on it. I have a BookBub promotion coming up in a few days, and if it goes well, I just might have a chance to find a new home for this novel and hopefully, my book of essays. That one hurts even more than the fact *Goddess of Suburbia* is disappearing from the world on May 31st—even temporarily. I have to stay positive and believe that my words are meant to be out in the world. So many readers have not just loved *Goddess of Suburbia*, but connected with Max, a PTA mom embroiled in an Internet scandal. (One of my most rewarding moments—a friend told me that her women's therapy group discussed my book.) But even more than *Goddess of Suburbia*, readers have been touched by my essays. I have received messages from readers of my blog telling me that reading my essays made them feel less alone and given them hope when things seem hopeless. A writer can't ask for any more than that.

I know my essays need to be in front of more eyes than just my blog audience. I know that they will make a difference, so I need to find a way to get them out there—whether that means self-publishing or trying to sell to a traditional publisher or even maybe another indie publisher. (I'll admit I'm now a bit gun-shy when it comes to indie publishers, but if a publisher has been around for a decade or more, I'd feel safer. My two novellas are out with The Wild Rose Press—they just celebrated their tenth birthday and I don't think they are going anywhere. Knock on wood!!) Wherever my book ends up, it's a new page in my writing career, and I'm going to make the most of it.

Postscript (2016): Since you're holding this book in your hands (or reading it on your tablet), you know that I did indeed "make the most of it" and got my essays out into the world...

INSPIRATION

~ May 28, 2016 ~

I WROTE THE ESSAY BELOW for a "Writing Challenge." It was a fun exercise and a window into my creative process, so I decided to include it in this book. During the months of April through August I participated in more than one writing challenge, but not all of the entries fit this book, so they didn't make the cut. This one about inspiration (and a few more) did. Please forgive any overlaps:

The first thing I say to people about my novel, *Goddess of Suburbia*, is that it's not autobiographical—after all, I didn't have a sex tape that went viral. Many readers still assume that Max Green, the heroine of *Goddess of Suburbia*, is me. She's not, but parts of my life *did* inspire her (not a sex tape, though!). She and I are both always behind on laundry and we both love Target. On a more serious note, we also have in common the feeling that we don't quite always measure up or belong. Like everyone else has some secret key to keeping their lives running smoothly and their houses neat and their laundry under control. Max's worry about what other people think of her is probably my way of working out that very same flaw. It was interesting exploring the dichotomy between how others see Max and how she sees herself.

The inspiration for Max came to me while I sat in my minivan every other afternoon, while my three year old napped in the back seat, tuckered out from a few hours of preschool (that three year old is now in sixth grade!). I envisioned a story about a regular mom suddenly becoming famous for something both entirely out of her control and humiliating. I hadn't read any stories about tired moms like myself –I wanted to write a story about someone with whom I'd like to spend time. The greatest compliment to me is when a reader says that Max feels like a friend.

Ben, Max's ex who shows up twenty years after he broke her heart, was probably less inspired by my exes and more by my husband, Jeff—if we had dated in college, rather than a few years after. The first time I met Jeff was at a battle of the bands in college – just like Max and Ben—and I did have a bit of a crush on him before that. We didn't start dating until I was twenty-five—unlike Max and Ben. But once we were dating, I spent A LOT of time watching him play the drums in a band—just like Max and Ben (though Ben is a guitarist). Jeff would point his drum stick at me and once even tossed me a broken stick—just like Ben tosses Max his guitar pick. It was actually a lot of fun remembering all those shows and basement parties. There are, of course, bits and pieces of other guys I've known in Ben—because what better way to create a memorable, swoon-worthy character, than to take the best bits of different people and mush them together? Take Andi—she is a mash-up of all of my girlfriends who have my back and are there when I need an ear or a shoulder.

When I was studying writing, my teacher asked—do you write about things you know or things you imagine? My answer: write about what you know, but change all the names. My first novella, *A New Life*, fit into this. And it's still one of my favorites, because it captured a moment in time—right after my son was born—that was so special and so fraught with possible emotional landmines. It was a struggle at times and more rewarding than any other time in my life. Grace and Zach are characters inspired by real life, and I love them. Full disclosure: the confrontations in the book are exaggerated, especially with parents and in-laws, and I had to "sex it up" to get a contract.

Whether a character is sprung from real life or sprung purely from my imagination, they all have likely lived in my head for quite a while, begging to be written. Kate, the protagonist in my current WIP, *Feel No Evil*, certainly has. But, her inspiration is deep and complicated and not one I can possibly explore in a short essay. Kate; along with Tess (the main character in my novel after *Feel No Evil*— working title, *Everything to Come*); Charlotte (from *Next Stop* and *The*

Kitchen Sink, short stories I wrote years ago and melded together into a novella last year); and Alex, from my novella, *You & Me* each have a unique inspiration and each took me (or in the case of Kate, and more so Tess, will take me) on a journey I didn't expect...

PARALYZED

~ June 3, 2016 ~

IT WAS LIKE THE MORNING AFTER A TERRIBLE BREAK-UP—
that punch in the gut feeling of waking up and realizing that the
empty space in the bed next to you will stay empty. Only, it wasn't a
break-up. Instead, it was waking up and realizing that what had
transpired the night before wasn't all a bad dream—that my book,
Goddess of Suburbia, was really gone. Poof—it just disappeared into
the ether of Internet-past, where things that are no longer relevant
reside. It's floating around with EarthLink email accounts; offensive
celebrity tweets that were deleted when the poster came to his or her
senses (or a publicist intervened); photos of exes in happier times
deleted from Instagram through tears and anger. It's just gone. But
unlike a broken relationship, it is entirely in my power to resurrect it
and get it back out into the world better than ever…

But, I'm paralyzed. Completely and utterly paralyzed. There are
so many options for publishing books now—almost too many. I'm
afraid I'm going to choose the wrong one. I decided to start my own
imprint, Gold Coast Press, and I want to make sure that whatever
publishing service I use will publish it under that imprint. I would do
everything myself, but it's extremely time consuming, not to mention
difficult, to convert a Word document to an ebook and a paperback.

I have the ebook and paperback files from my former publisher,
Booktrope, but I need to take out all of the references to Booktrope. I
couldn't edit those files—only the final Word one. And I really don't
have the funds right now to hire someone to do it, not when I'm
about to plunk down $295 to purchase ten ISBNs—the "identifier
number" that's unique to every edition of every book—and will be

shelling out thousands more when our first college tuition bill arrives next month). Without an ISBN, it's impossible to market and sell a book. Publishing services offer them for free, but then they become the publisher of record—and now that I've decided to take control of my career, I want to be the publisher of record.

Despite my anxiety, it is liberating knowing that I never have to worry about another rejection, which is actually part of what made Booktrope so seductive. They published books across all genres and accepted the author, more than just the work. Everything about the company encouraged authors to submit a new project: from their author-centric business model to the constant reminders that "your readers are waiting" to the super easy submission method on the website to the lightning-speed response to a submitted manuscript. This was why I finally worked up the courage to submit an essay book, *Boys, Dogs and Chaos*, I had been working on for years. It was accepted and almost ready to go to layout when production shut down. That hurt even more than my current book disappearing.

Boys, Dogs and Chaos, the book you're holding in your hands, is my heart book—so important to me and the one work that truly represents my soul. It has to—it's all true. It opens with an essay about the aftermath of fainting in the hospital when my youngest son was one day old and dropping him on the cold, unforgiving floor and closes with an open letter to young mothers, penned just after leaving my oldest son at college, exhorting them to relish the craziness, the noise, the fullness—in short, the beautiful chaos—of life with small children, before their houses are quiet.

I didn't know who else would take on an essay book, especially a book about all of the small and big moments of parenting, plus other essays covering a range of topics, from hockey to parenting a child with mental illness. I firmly believe there's something for everyone—if you're a parent; a hockey fan; have a family member with mental illness (or you have mental illness); if your life has been affected by an eating disorder; if you love dogs… Despite all of that, I've been told by previous agents and editors that no publishing company would be interested in an essay book, unless the author has a huge platform. But, Booktrope was interested. The book was accepted immediately. So, it's my job now to get it out into the world. (An aside: since you are reading it, you know that I accomplished that.)

My awesome proofreader, J.C. Wing, has insisted on finishing up the proofreading job. J.C. was the editor for *Goddess of Suburbia*, so I know she's good. This book got the green-light to skip editing, because the essays were deemed "very strong" and "clean" and some had already appeared in magazines. That was just another vote of confidence in me—the kind of thing that makes an author fall hard for a publisher. But just like an awful break-up, no matter how hard you had fallen for your ex, eventually you have to admit to yourself that it's over, pick yourself up and keep going. Keep the good times stored in a little compartment in your heart and kick the bad stuff to the curb. There's no point in wasting any more psychic energy over something that's over and is completely out of your control. Sometimes the end really is the end. And it's okay to be paralyzed by that. Just do something after the hurt eases a bit to shake yourself out of it.

Unfortunately, the stuff I used way back when to shake myself out of the post-breakup doldrums—Little Debbie Snack Cakes and margaritas out with the girls just won't work now. (I haven't had a drop of alcohol since I was twenty-eight years old and I don't eat sugar-loaded crap anymore either, aside from the occasional Reese's Peanut Butter cup.) No, the only thing that will ease the hurt and disappointment now is to just take a chance. Just buy the ten ISBNs sitting in my Bowker cart. Just click on the open Draft2Digital window, upload my Word document and hope for the best. I'm seeing lots of posts from former Booktrope authors who did this already and I don't know why I haven't. I don't know what's stopping me. Perhaps getting this all down will allow me to grieve and move on, because writing is the greatest salve I know. That was the other thing I used to get through a bad break-up—my journal. I wrote pages and pages and pages.

At first it was about how devastated I was and little by little, it morphed into how excited I was for what the future could bring— how excited I was to get to know myself. By the time I ran out of space in that pretty, harvest gold book, graced with red and black blooms, I was equally excited to embark on a relationship with a new guy I met—one who would eventually become my husband. And I know I'll be equally excited to embark on this journey, as well.

It's pretty heady being in charge of yourself and not having to answer to anyone. (Of course, I still have two novellas with another publisher and I love them, but moving forward, it's all on me, because they don't publish non-fiction and my next novel doesn't fit their submission requirements at all.)

I have often mused that the path to getting *Goddess of Suburbia* published was A LOT like dating. You meet someone (an agent or editor) at a pitch session or even on Twitter, and it's so new and exciting—it seems like anything is possible. You give them your heart (your work) and agonizingly wait for a message or even better a phone call, which sometimes never even comes. And then…then you meet someone who sweeps you off your feet, who promises to love you for who you are and not make you change. That was Booktrope for me—*Goddess of Suburbia* went to press how I submitted it, with only very minor changes. But just like great loves don't always work out, neither do great publishing relationships. It's over and I need to move on. I need to become unstuck.

Postscript: It took me two days to write this essay, with well over twenty-five revisions listed. During that time, my other open windows included the three I needed to get started down the publishing path—Bowker, Draft2Digital and Amazon Kindle Direct Publishing. Right after I published the essay on my blog, I purchased the ISBNs on Bowker and published *Goddess of Suburbia* through Draft2Digital and Amazon Kindle Direct Publishing. As always, pouring my soul out into words helped me get unstuck and in doing so has proven to me that no matter what happens, I'm on the right path—one that will enable me to keep putting my words out in the world. As an added bonus, I added over twelve thousand words to this book. Though it originally ended with the essay about my son getting his driver's license, I felt that the essays I wrote after that (like this one) fit perfectly, as well. I look at that as the silver lining to my publisher going under—this book is better and more complete than it would have been if they hadn't shuttered and it came out six months earlier, as planned.

ENOUGH

~ June 20, 2016 ~

HEARTBREAK, THEN ANGER. That was the progression of my emotions after learning of the massacre at Pulse nightclub in Orlando. Oh I'm still heartbroken, but anger is the overriding emotion now—anger that a person on the terrorist watch list was able to legally buy an assault rifle, a weapon that has no place in civilian hands; anger that the Republican party is still doing everything they can to block common-sense gun legislation. Chris Murphy (D-Conn.) and Dianne Feinstein (D-Calif.) both introduced legislation that will save countless lives (increased background checks and preventing people on the terrorism watch-list and other suspected terrorists from buying guns, respectively). That is, if the Republicans don't block it, which according to most pundits, they will—if they haven't already. The vote is today.

Honestly, I don't know how anyone can possibly think that blocking suspected terrorists from purchasing guns is a bad idea. The counter measure proposed by the Republicans provides merely a seventy-two hour waiting period and puts the onus on the government to prove that the purchase should be blocked. Prosecutors would have to go to court during those seventy-two hours to show probable cause to block the sale permanently. What if the prosecutors can't prove it on time? The blood of any mass shootings would be on the hands of lawmakers refusing to see that the world is an increasingly terrifying place when it comes to gun violence and that something needs to be done about it.

I'm fairly certain that when our Founding Fathers inscribed the right to keep and bear arms in the Constitution, they did not envision that it would translate to the right to bust into a crowded nightclub and gun down forty-nine innocent souls just out for an evening of fun. Nor did they imagine that this constitutional right would allow a crazed madman to slaughter twenty-six beautiful, innocent children and heroic teachers. And I'm guessing that office workers eating cake in a conference room are absolutely not whom the Founding Fathers had in mind when imagining the need to bear arms against an enemy. By allowing assault weapons—weapons that only the military and police officers would ever need—to remain easy to obtain legally (and therefore illegally, as well), our country is failing to protect its own citizens.

Gun rights advocates piss and moan that they have a constitutional right to own whatever damn gun they wish. "You can pry it from my cold, dead hands," they cry. Yes, the second amendment states that one has the right to own a gun, but it was written long before assault weapons, long before terrorist watch lists, long before our country has cried rivers of tears for the murdered. PrayFor... hashtags have become so common-place, that it rings hollow now. Prayers are wonderful, prayers help ease the pain crushing our souls, but we need more than prayers—we need change. We need the Republican party to haul themselves out of the cozy bed they've made with the NRA and do something, finally. We *need* Republican lawmakers to vote for an assault weapons ban and agree to the simple measures that would make it difficult, if not impossible, for the evil among us to get their hands on weapons created to kill many efficiently.

Republican lawmakers, make the right decision. You have a racist, misogynistic, xenophobic, hateful rhetoric-spouting asshole who looks like a constipated pumpkin as the presumptive public face of your party. Do something to enhance your reputation here and around the world. Come together in a bi-partisan fashion to make our country safer. We—or at least any sane person with half a heart—beg you. Make a difference.

I'm not talking about taking away handguns, though I do believe it should be much, MUCH harder to purchase one. And I do believe there should be stricter laws governing how a gun can be kept—way too many children are killed accidentally; way too many spurned lovers are able to carry out revenge; way too many disgruntled employees can settle a score with a bullet and even way too many suicides are thanks to the pull of a trigger. I could go on and on, even though I know there are many who will say, "Guns don't kill people...People kill people." It makes it a hell of a lot easier, though. But, I get it—there are responsible gun owners out there. My boyfriend in college owned a gun and took me target shooting. It was actually fun. He never used it to kill anyone, though. The ONLY use for an assault weapon is to kill the maximum amount of people in the minimum amount of time. You don't take an assault weapon to a field and shoot at some empty Coke cans on a fence. No, the owner of an assault weapon takes it to a gay bar; a movie theater; an office building; a shopping mall simply to commit mass murder.

I'm terrified to send my children out into the world after an atrocity like the Pulse shooting, because I don't know around what corner a mad gunman may lurk. My parents worried I'd date the wrong boy; get into a car with a drunk driver; walk down a dark alley by myself late at night. Parents today need to worry about all of those things, plus if their children will be in the wrong place at the wrong time, simply doing something mundane—enjoying a movie, a night out at a club, shopping at the mall or even just going to school. They need to worry about any public place without a swat team present to immediately take out an assault weapon toting lunatic. I'm also terrified for the LGBT community—and those in it with whom I'm close. It shouldn't be like this. It's ENOUGH.

PUPPY LOVE

~ July 22, 2016 ~

THIS WAS A FUN "WRITING CHALLENGE" POST—I had to write about my First Love (I did ask my husband if it would bother him at all before I agreed to write this. His answer: "I don't care about your first love, as long as I'm your last love."):

When I muse about my first love, it kind of boggles my mind that I was two years younger than my oldest son. Yet, I felt so grown up having a boyfriend. I was sixteen, going into eleventh grade and my boyfriend, Seth, was seventeen, going into twelfth grade. We started dating right before school ended in June. I'm pretty sure that the sweetest first love is summer love. Summer nights are made for hand in hand romantic walks and kissing in the warm rain, not a care about getting wet. Languorous days on the beach, with the ocean lapping at our toes; what could be better for two teenagers? Only—I couldn't do any of those things (except maybe the kissing in the rain). I spent the summer (and into the fall) with a toes to thigh cast on my leg, having broken my ankle in six places, dislocated and dislodged it and tore all the ligaments and tendons my third day at sleep away camp.

In a way, it brought me and Seth much closer than we would have been, because I came home three and a half weeks early from camp, after a short hospital stay. Seth would visit me every day, bearing a fresh bouquet of beautiful red roses. Every single day. My room looked like a florist—so wonderful to wake up to each morning, when I was in pain and depressed about not being able to do much, except sit on the recliner with my leg propped on pillows. Kindness and compassion are two of the best attributes a person can have and not all teenage boys possess both or even one (though, I'm thankful my teenage boys do). Seth's abundance of both taught me at a young age that it's important to be treated well by your boyfriend and I'm grateful for that.

After that summer, we dated for over three more years. The summers that followed were filled with all the stuff I missed that first summer—days at the beach and nights spent hanging out with friends. As late summer afternoons slid into dusk we'd gather in a parking lot to decide what to do that night—in the days before cell phones that's how plans were made, in person. A group text can't match that. We went to concerts, including Bruce Springsteen's Born to Run tour—still one of my favorite concerts ever. One night we gathered with Seth's friends at the beach. We got lost on the way there and by the time we arrived, we were so tired, we fell asleep right away to the sound of the ocean waves crashing on the sand—only to be woken up at 5:30 am by an arriving fisherman. All of our friends had left and I found out later that my mom called the Jones Beach state police, asking them to look for us. I was livid then, but now that I'm a mom, I completely understand. I hate that my kids are so attached to their phones, but I have to admit; it was harder for our parents without a way to reach us when we were late.

As hard as it must have been for our parents before cell phones, I think first love was way better for those of us who came of age in the eighties. We didn't get to know each other through SnapChat messages or Instagram posts. We had to talk. We spent hours on the phone and wrote letters on actual paper when we were apart. There were few things more exciting than opening the mailbox to find a love letter. I often feel bad for teenagers today, even though they have no idea what they're missing and would no doubt find a hand-penned note archaic at best and completely ridiculous at worst. There's a reason John Hughes' eighties teen movies are beloved classics. It was an innocent time and I think the perfect time to be a teenager (especially a teenager in love), though I'm sure my kids would disagree. I'm lucky—my first love is still a very good friend, almost twenty-nine years after we broke up right before my sophomore year of college. And I'm especially lucky, because while kindness and compassion make for a great first boyfriend, they make for an even better lifelong friend.

DID YOU KNOW?

~ *July 23, 2016* ~

THIS WAS A PARTICULARLY FUN—and yes more than a bit challenging—"Writing Challenge." The topic: Ten Interesting Facts About Me. I worried that my interesting facts wouldn't be interesting enough. But, this ended up being the most popular post of my whole "Writing Challenge" experience… I decided to include it because…well, I love reading these lists about other people, so hopefully you'll enjoy reading mine and find it interesting:

I was jotting down this list for this in my ever present notebook while I was waiting at the pediatrician with my son. I asked him if there's anything interesting about me. Right away he offered, "You have books out and you know a lot about hockey." Since my readers obviously know I have books out, I started with hockey. Did you know…

#1. My son is right, I know A LOT about hockey. I don't mean to sound arrogant, but I know enough to have been a linesman in college for men's intramural ice hockey. I know enough that I bore most people, except for the most ardent fan, when I get started talking about my beloved New York Rangers. I have been a rabid New York Rangers fan since I was four years old. In seventh grade I cut the newspaper photo out of from every game article, pasted it in a binder and wrote my own take on the game—which brings me to number two…

#2. I really wanted to be a sportswriter from the time I was thirteen years old. I even applied for a job at *Sports Illustrated Kids* right out of college, but they weren't hiring at the time. I did get to act like a sportswriter in 1996 when I featured the NHL All Star weekend festivities in Boston in my column. My press badge allowed me to cut to the front of the line to pose with the Stanley Cup. Best use of a press badge ever. Being a sportswriter is still my dream job, though that dream is likely unattainable at this point. At least I can tweet about hockey and satisfy a tiny bit of that desire...

#3. Last hockey fact: Former New York Rangers player and current Arizona Coyotes general manager, Don Maloney, ran over my foot when I was fourteen years old and waiting for his autograph after an open practice. When I finally got his attention, I simply said, "I love you." What can I say? He was my first real crush.

#4. Another Don, Don Henley of the Eagles, wrote me the kindest letter and enclosed a crisp $100 bill in 1994. A radio station was having a "Dirty Laundry" contest to protest the Eagles high ticket prices. I wrote a letter to the Eagles (this was before email, of course) stating that I thought their concert was worth every penny, even though I spent my food money on a ticket. Don Henley told me that they had another, smaller, contest for "Sweetest Person" and I won that. That letter was hanging in a frame on my wall for years. I tried to thank him in person at the next concert I went to that he was playing—the Newport Rhythm & Blues Festival—but, I couldn't get close enough. It was right then and there that I decided to become an arts reporter / music journalist, so I could get my hands on a press badge, which brings me to my next item...

#5. I was an arts reporter and music journalist in the mid to late 1990s and got to meet some of my idols. I interviewed Mike Peters of The Alarm—I still feel horrible that I never found a home for the article I wrote about him. If I can ever find it, I will publish it on my blog. I also met my teenage idol, Howard Jones, who invited me onto his tour bus where I promptly turned into a fourteen year old, even though I was twenty-eight years old. All I could say was, "You've always inspired me so much," or something like that. He was kind and charming. I met some other very cool musicians, writers, artists and other amazingly talented creative folks. I even had cover stories for a newspaper and music magazine.

#6. I have a rescue page on Facebook called "Lucky Dogs (and Cats)" and love to play matchmaker, sending friends to the shelter when I've found the perfect dog for them. I have rescued three dogs, one of whom is three-legged. (If I had room, I'd rescue all the animals in the shelter, even the feral cats no one wants.) My first rescue, Sadie, was from the town animal shelter. My next rescue, Coco is a Sato—a feral Puerto Rican street dog, who's a big mush now. I adopted Scruffy, another Sato, two weeks after my beloved Sadie lost her two year battle with cancer. He arrived missing a leg, with his tail cut off and his ear sliced in half. We don't know what he endured before he arrived, but we know it was horrific. Please remember, adopt, don't shop! (Had to get that in…)

#7. I was a photographer for my college newspaper and had a photo on the front page. Photography has always been a passion of mine—I even majored in photography and creative writing junior year in college. But, it was a "Bachelors in Individual Concentration" and I didn't have enough time to earn the credits I needed to graduate with that major, so I switched back to English.

#8. I had big hair in the 1980s and 1990s—very big hair—and not a day goes by that I don't wish it would come back in style. My life would be so much easier. Though, I *am* a curly girl all summer. And it can get pretty big. Only rarely will I attempt to smooth out my tresses during the humid months. People would tell me all the time that I looked like Susannah Hoffs of the Bangles and make me sing *Walk Like an Egyptian*. And on my honeymoon in Antigua I was mistaken for Mariah Carey…

#9. I'm addicted to lip gloss and have been since my very first strawberry flavored roll-on gloss. My favorite now is C.O. Bigelow Mentha Lip Shine and C.O. Bigelow Mentha Shimmer Lip Tint from Bath & Bodyworks. I always have three tubes in my handbag and mix the colors (usually Bare Mint, Violet Mint and the clear Lip Shine). I'm also addicted to Doublemint peppermint gum. I guess there are worse addictions…

#10. I'm very short—4′11 3/4″—yet I never wear heels. Or at least I rarely wear heels. If you read my essay about my first love, you know why (hint—if you break your ankle in six places, heels aren't your best choice, even thirty two years later). As an aside, I was one of the tallest girls in my grade up until about fifth grade when everyone started catching up and then passed me. In fact, I haven't grown since I was thirteen (or maybe twelve)…

And there you have it. Now you know a little more about me…

CONVERSATIONS WITH THE PAST

~ *August 14, 2016* ~

THIS WAS THE MOST DIFFICULT "WRITING CHALLENGE." The topic was "Things I'd Say to an Ex." To be honest, I left most of the challenges in which I participated out of this book, but the ones I included are in it for a reason. If I included a challenge topic, it's because it either illuminates something about me (my creative process, little known facts about me, etc.) or delves a bit deeper into a subject I touched on earlier in the book. In this case, this delves a bit deeper into the eating disorder I spoke about in *Hungry*:

This is a tough one... To be honest, I've pretty much said everything I've wanted to say to my exes already. I have no need for closure. I've stayed friendly with all of them, and I'm Facebook friends with all of them. There are absolutely no lingering hard feelings. We were all very young (I started dating my husband at twenty-five, so these relationships dissolved decades ago) and we all ended up where we should have. But, I do want to tackle this topic. So, I'll write about what I did get to say to one of my exes not that long ago. In my earlier essay, *Hungry*, I spoke about how watching my son starve himself has been the worst possible karma, because I put my family and my boyfriend through the same thing when I was in my early twenties.

Back then, I couldn't see how my actions hurt others. I didn't understand that watching someone you love starve themselves into a skeletal existence is absolute hell. I was far from home, living on my own and I weighed an alarmingly low weight. My boyfriend tried to get me to eat. It wasn't easy for me, and it certainly wasn't easy for him. We fell apart—I'm sure we would have anyway, but the situation hastened the blow. But—and this is the important part—we both put our lives back together with new pieces and went on to have the futures we were meant to have, building our own families just the way they were meant to be.

I gained some weight after we broke up and gained even more when I was preparing to try to get pregnant five years later. There were some bumps in the road... I fainted while waiting for a restaurant table with my husband when we were newlyweds, after not eating much all day (just a yogurt and an apple for lunch hours earlier), thanks to stress and an inner ear infection that left me with little appetite. I knew I had to do something to ensure that I was healthy, so I could get pregnant and have a healthy pregnancy. It took something bigger than myself and thinking about someone other than myself—my future child—to finally change my ways for good. I saw a nutritionist, followed her program meticulously and gained five pounds (fifteen pounds over my lowest weight). I was finally a healthy weight (just a pound less than I weigh now) when I got pregnant. I put my food struggles behind me and moved on.

Then my middle son battled the same exact issues and the anguish of watching him fade away before my eyes made me realize how difficult it was for my family and my boyfriend so many years earlier. I also starting blogging about this difficult situation and connected with so many people who thanked me for letting them know they weren't alone. Since *Hungry* mentioned how bad I felt about what I put my ex-boyfriend through and I linked back to it in a new essay, I gave him a heads-up, just in case he read it. I also told him that I was sorry for what I put him through knowing now how awful it is watching my son. My ex was, of course, very kind. I probably should have said that I was sorry two decades earlier. But, I was glad that I finally said it a few months ago. And now, there's nothing left that I need to say to any of my exes about our relationships, except perhaps that I hope they are all always happy in the lives they have built...

A DREAM COME TRUE

~ August 20, 2016 ~

THIS IS THE LAST "WRITING CHALLENGE" featured in this book. This one was about my proudest moment:

I have so many proud moments when it comes to my kids... Watching my oldest son receive scholarships and graduate from high school with honors; watching my middle son skate onto the ice to play hockey for the first time after battling an eating disorder; chatting with my youngest son about politics and realizing that he's way smarter than most adults. But...

I feel that this challenge is about the writer's life (though, of course, I may not be entirely correct), so I'm going to share my proudest writer moment—my dream come true... Standing on a podium at the front of an amazing book store, Book Revue in Huntington, NY, with a packed house watching me as I read from my first novel, *Goddess of Suburbia*, was my proudest moment. Okay, maybe signing books just a short time later while a line of people snaked around the store waiting for their turn may have been my proudest moment. I had imagined that moment so many times. (You already may have read about this in an earlier essay: *Inspired by Real Life or Not*.)

When I first emailed Book Revue about hosting my book launch party and book signing, I was asked what made me think that I could bring in a crowd as a local author. I was informed that Book Revue hosted luminaries such as Hillary Clinton and J.K. Rowling, which I already knew...that's why it was my dream. Speakers at Book Revue have run the gamut from best-selling authors to famous athletes to musicians and comedians. It is *the* stop on Long Island for anyone with a book to hawk and I was determined to make it my first book signing, as well. I posted on Facebook asking if people would be interested in attending. Between a mom's group I'm a part of, my writer page and my personal profile, I had well over the fifty people I needed to promise in order for the store to have the faith that I could pull in a decent crowd. I believe it was between seventy and eighty. I set up an event page and handed out glossy postcards and did everything I could to get the word out. Still, I was told that it's commonplace with book launch parties and signings that at least a third of the people expected wouldn't show.

But that evening, August 25, 2015, at least eighty-five people showed up. Every chair was filled, besides the front few that were left open for my family. And as I mentioned, the line waiting for me to sign books snaked around the store. It was a truly amazing moment looking at all the faces in front of me as I spoke about *Goddess of Suburbia* and read an excerpt. It was a dream come true and truly my proudest moment (that didn't revolve around my kids)...

In the dark days that have sometimes enveloped me since my publisher shuttered and the fate of both *Goddess of Suburbia* and the book you hold in your hands hung in the balance, I revisited that moment in my mind many times. It's the dream of getting back up there behind that podium that is a driving force for me to pick myself back up and dust myself off. It is what keeps me striving to get my words out into the world, even though at times it seems nearly impossible to do it myself. It would be really easy to give up and say, "Well, I lived my dream. I spoke and signed at Book Revue and that's enough for me." But, I won't. After my book signing, I was told that I brought in such a great crowd; I'd be welcomed back to the store to sign my next release. I promised that I would be back, and I intend to fulfill that promise...

LETTING GO PART TWO

~ August 29, 2016 ~

I HAVE FELT LIKE I'M ON A RUNAWAY TRAIN with no breaks skidding toward my oldest son, Drew's, inevitable departure for college since last fall. Sure we had visited schools before then and talked about college A LOT, but the night I stayed up until 2:30 am helping him get his early action applications submitted was the moment it became real for me. In the time since then, everything in my mind has been framed with that looming event. Our vacation to Myrtle Beach in the spring; our rare family days and almost as rare dinners together (since he's always running out with friends); the first day of school; the last day of school; his last high school sports game; the last awards night—during each one of these times and many more of the mundane moments in the life of a mom, I thought... *This is the last time it will be just like this before everything changes.*

I know that everything will change. I was a different person after I went away to college. And while I thought of the house I grew up in as home until I married at twenty-eight years old, I only actually lived there for one year after I graduated. As soon as I found a job in Boston, I moved away from Long Island to be with my boyfriend. And even though we broke up a few months after I moved, I didn't return to my hometown to stay for nine long years. I got married while living in Boston and had a kid. I was pregnant with my second child, before I returned. I know that kids now move home for the long haul far more often after college, thanks to the economy, but I don't know if Drew will be one of them. He's much like I was when I moved away for the first time—fiercely independent and eager to strike out on my own. That's exactly how I want him to be... It's just a bit hard.

It's also been more than a bit hard writing this essay. I started a week ago and got down almost thirteen hundred words (more than half of which I just deleted). Something didn't feel right, though and I kept reading and rereading it, not ready to post. I opened with a hook, "I had the flu—a knock-down, drag-out bout of it, over 102 fever, chills, cough... I couldn't move out of bed, so my parents drove five hours to take care of my eighteen-month-old, from whom I had caught the nasty bug..." I went on to talk about how I dragged myself out of bed when my son wanted only me, even though my mom desperately wanted to help. I was the only one who could make things right back then—he knew it and I knew it. I mentioned that I've thought about that night as I help Drew pack up for school. I won't be there if he needs me to make things right. But, to be honest, it's been a very, very long time since he has needed that, which of course is the jackpot of parenting. I'm grateful that at eighteen years old, my son never needs me to swoop in and rescue him like he did at eighteen months old. That doesn't make it any easier knowing that I can't, though.

Tossing Tylenol and cough drops into a cart at the drug store, I realized that if Drew comes down with a cold or cough, I won't be there to take care of him. I won't be able to make him my special concoction of tea with orange juice and honey. My kids used to call it "Mommy Magic Juice." I know it's easy enough for him to make it— I've packed him a mug and bags of tea. He's got a microwave and can easily grab packets of honey and a carton of orange juice from the Dining Commons. It's not that he can't take care of himself—he absolutely can and is more than happy to do so. It's that I can't take care of him. And that's a new feeling for me. My kids never wanted to go away to sleep away camp. The only times Drew has been away for more than one night were a ski trip with friends and prom weekend on the Jersey Shore. I was nervous both times. I have to find a way to not be a "Nervous Nellie" when he's away. And anyone who knows me well knows that isn't an easy task.

It's not just the worrisome things on my mind...it's all the happy times, as well. I won't be there to watch Drew play volleyball, if he makes the club team (which I'm pretty sure he will). I won't meet the girls he dates—at least not at first. I won't get to know his friends. I won't hear him in the basement playing the keyboards; the ukulele; the drums; the guitar...a constant soundtrack to our days and nights when he's home. I think I might miss that the most of all. At least I can look forward to his breaks—the music will be all the sweeter.

I recently read a line that I wrote right before college graduation. It said, "Soon we'll be looking back on this, instead of into it." For as long as I can remember, I've thought about looking back on something while it's still happening. The night before I got married, I stared into the mirror in my parents' bathroom and thought—*Soon I'll be gazing at a married woman.* Right before giving birth for the last time, I thought... *Soon I won't be pregnant anymore; I likely won't be pregnant ever again. Everything will change.* Walking hand and hand with my youngest son into the nursery school all of my children attended, I thought... *This is the last time I'll ever do this. Soon walking my children into nursery school will just be a memory.*

Of course, getting married; having a baby; that baby graduating preschool are all wonderful, exciting milestones, but change is always a bit daunting, even if it's positive. Sending your child off to college is a wonderful, exciting milestone, as well. But, it can be scary and at times even a bit heartbreaking. I want Drew to go off into the world and do amazing things. And I'm pretty lucky, because he's attending my alma mater—the University of Massachusetts, Amherst. As much as I'll miss him and as hard as it is for me, where he's going feels like home to me. Walking around the campus each time we've visited, I've been flooded with warm memories. I couldn't be happier with his choice. It will be surreal and pretty amazing moving him into the same dorm area I lived in at UMass. If I have to let him go, I'm thrilled this is the place he's going to—one of my favorite places in the world. I know he'll be just fine (I on the other hand might need a few tissues)...

DEAR YOUNG MOM...

~ September 29, 2016 ~

DEAR YOUNG MOM,

Right now it probably seems like not a moment goes by without a tug on your sleeve; a nose that needs to be wiped; a fight that needs to be broken up; or a constant chorus of "Look, Mom." There are also probably those moments when you want to lock yourself in the bathroom, turn on the faucet and the fan (to add a cushion of noise) and just scream at the top of your lungs. Or maybe you want to let loose a tirade of expletives. You just want to release the frustration and exhaustion that can overwhelm you. I know. I've been there too...

One of the sagest observations I ever heard about parenting is that the "days are long, but the years are short."* It's so true—but I don't know if I ever fully appreciated that fact when my kids were young, when I was in the trenches, in the middle of it all and so worn down that a quiet house seemed like a miracle, rather than a depressing reality...

Motherhood is a job no one in her right mind would ever apply for, if it was a classified ad (or a LinkedIn post—I'm showing my age)... Long hours (sometimes all night, if there's a case of croup or an ear infection). No vacation. No training before you're thrown right into the job. You'll be expected to fulfill such disparate duties as chef; chauffeur; laundress; therapist; nurse; referee; baker; cleaning lady; the list goes on and on... Your heart will break a million times over big and small things. In fact, if you do your job well, heartbreak is guaranteed—when you say goodbye to your child and send him or her off into the world. Imagine a job where your most important task is to train your best employees to leave and be successful elsewhere. That's parenting. Those little babies who tugged on your sleeve and wiped their drippy noses on your shirt; jumped on the furniture after being told a gazillion times not to do it; colored on the walls (in non-washable crayons); left sticky fingerprints everywhere will leave the nest in the blink of an eye to meet the future that stretches out before them. And it should be that way, but that doesn't make it any easier.

When they do go out into that big, brave world, they might seem very far away. They might not need you anymore and then...well then you'll be left wishing—just wishing—that you could have that commotion back for one more day. You'll miss that whirl of small children playing way too rough, messing up the couch cushions, tugging on your sleeve... You'll wish that you could hear that chorus of, "Look, Mom!" just a few more times. You'll swear that instead of getting frustrated because you have work or laundry or dinner to prepare—if you could have that moment back again, you'd kneel down and look, really look, at that scribbled masterpiece; the tower of blocks; the cool looking rock that must be a piece of the moon that somehow found its way to your backyard. But, as a young mom you don't have to wish for that—it's right there. You're still feeling the tug on your sleeve, the endless loop of, "Look, Mom!" You still have the chance to kneel down and give your full attention to your small child. Do it.

All too soon, that little child will grow up and stop asking you to look. In fact, if your teen catches you glancing over a shoulder, he or she will immediately snatch her phone out of view or snap his laptop closed. Instead of details about school and friends, you'll hear, "Can I take the car?" You won't be the center of his or her world anymore and you'll be relegated to further and further outside orbits, until he or she goes away to college and your house is quiet. (Even if you have younger kids, one leaving changes the dynamics—and believe me, it's quieter.) And one day, you may send a text asking when you can call to catch up for a few minutes and get back, "I'm busy. I'll call you when I can." And then...your phone will stay silent.

So, mothers of young children—especially loud, rambunctious boys who leave your living room looking like a tornado hit it or a

Toys 'R' Us exploded; who play ball in the house and jump on the sofa; who tug on your sleeve and say, "Look, Mom!" more times than you thought possible—relish it. Revel in the noise, the beautiful chaos—the fullness of it—because it is ephemeral. Blink, and it's oh so quiet...

Much Love,
Stephanie

*Gretchen Rubin

ADDITIONAL TITLES BY STEPHANIE KEPKE

Goddess of Suburbia (Gold Coast Press)
A New Life (Wild Rose Press)
You & Me (Wild Rose Press)
Girls' Night Out (Gold Coast Press)

Visit www.stephaniekepke.com for more information.

65902694R00156

Made in the USA
Lexington, KY
28 July 2017